Heliconia adeleana.

MARGARET MEE

In Search of
Flowers of the Amazon Forests

Diaries of an English Artist
reveal the beauty of the vanishing rainforest

Galeandra dives.

Edited by Tony Morrison

Foreword by H.R.H. The Duke of Edinburgh, K.G., K.T.

Appreciations from:
Professor Ghillean T. Prance, Director Royal Botanic Gardens, Kew.
Professor Richard Evans Schultes, Director Emeritus, Botanical Museum of Harvard University.
Roberto Burle Marx, Rio de Janeiro, Brazil.

Nonesuch Expeditions

ISBN 1 869901 08 8

British Library Cataloguing-in-Publication Data

Mee, Margaret
    Margaret Mee — in search of flowers of the Amazon forests.
    1. South America. Amazon River Basin. Tropical rain forests.
    Flowering plants. Biographies
    I. Title   II. Morrison, Tony
    582′.13′09811

Published by Nonesuch Expeditions Ltd.
48 Station Road, Woodbridge, Suffolk, England

All illustrations are copyright. Illustrations are by Margaret Mee except for: p. 64,
Michael Andrews. pp. 18 (centre left, bottom left), 19 (right), 20, 21, 22 (top right),
courtesy John Brown. p. 23 (bottom), Furness Withy Group. p. 258, Sue Loram. All
maps, Greville Mee. pp. 49, 53, Harald Schultz, National Geographic Society. pp. 100,
104 (top), 107, 109, 111 (top), 112, 116, Otis Imboden, National Geographic Society.
pp. 242, 243, 246 (top, bottom right), 276, 277 (top), Rita de Pagter. p. 22 (bottom),
John Pasmore. pp. 18 (top), 22 (top left), Dora Prower. p. 11, Ghillean T. Prance. pp. 7,
16, 18 (bottom right), 19 (left), 31 (bottom), 32, 39, 42, 76 (bottom), 78, 99, 100 (top),
137 (top), 248, 250 (top), 254 (bottom), 255 (top), 284, 285, 286, 287, 290, 292, 294, 295,
296, 297, Tony and Marion Morrison/South American Pictures. p. 241, Shelley Swigert.
p. 12, World Wide Fund for Nature, U.S.A.

Colour separations by Chroma Graphics, Singapore.
Printed in England by the Antique Collectors' Club Ltd., Woodbridge, Suffolk

Contents

Contents Continued

Memora schomburgkii.

6

Author's Note

My special gratitude to my husband Greville for his constant help and constructive criticism which has proved invaluable to my work; for his patience when I overstayed my time limit in the Amazon; his understanding and affectionate assistance without which this publication would not have been possible.

I am also indebted to: Dr. Roberto Burle Marx whose unquenchable love and enthusiasm for plants and nature inspired me over the years that I have known him as a wonderful friend.

Professor Richard Evans Schultes who has given me tremendous help and support in the scientific and academic field, which, combined with his great love and knowledge of the Amazon, has been a constant inspiration.

Ghillean Prance who, during my early journeys, was an almost legendary figure, for I heard of him in the remotest parts of the Amazon. His knowledge of the Amazon and its vegetation is impressive, as was his courage in penetrating the most difficult regions. He has been a constant inspiration to me.

Tony Morrison for his untiring efforts and sympathy in editing my diaries so carefully and with such insight, and for organising a journey to Rio Negro for the concluding journey, which was a great success due to his dedication and kindness.

Margaret L. Mee

Margaret Mee
Rio de Janeiro, Brazil
August 1988

Greville Mee

Margaret Mee
June, 1985

Mormodes amazonicum
Amazonas

Mormodes amazonicum.

The bare statistics about the destruction of the tropical rain forests are simple statements of fact, they cannot hope to convey the full scope of what is rapidly becoming a major global tragedy. Hurricane 'Gilbert', the floods in Bangladesh and the famines in East and Central Africa were major human disasters, but in terms of damage to the natural environment, their combined effects cannot compare with the annual destruction of the Amazon rain forest. In 1987 nearly 80,000 square miles, five times the area of Switzerland, went up in smoke during the August-October burning season.

It needs the eyes and the talents of an artist to make that scale of destruction comprehensible to the human mind. Margaret Mee's brilliant illustrations of the flowers and plants of the Amazon, together with her acute observations over many years, so well recorded in her diaries, contrasts vividly the beauties of a particularly rich natural environment with the horrors of indiscriminate human interference.

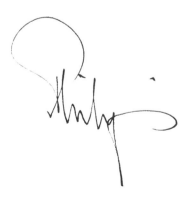

1988

Gustavia pulchra
Amazonas

Margaret Mee 1964

An intrepid, gifted and sensitive artist...

Gustavia pulchra painted by Margaret Mee: symbol of the majestic, vulnerable region called Amazonia; a symbol of an intrepid, gifted and sensitive artist.

The large white flowers, tinged with yellow or pink, release their scent into the hot, still air. The tree that bears them stands in dark, flooded forest, the black water reflecting back every detail as in a glass darkly.

The Rio Negro region of Amazonia has called to the artist in Margaret Mee, with a call insistent and persistent. The ephemeral beauty, the light and shadow, the reflectance of the water, the magic of an opening flower bud have summoned her to ignore the frailities of body, and to face repeatedly the rigors and dangers of river journeys of Sprucean extension.

Many people have travelled Amazonian waters, many people have painted Amazonian plants, but Margaret Mee outranks those other travellers and artists simply because she with her watercolours, went, saw, and conquered the region. Margaret has been able to imbue her subjects with the reality of their own environments. She has seen, smelled and touched; she has travelled, itched, ached, perspired, been delayed, disappointed and remained; and then, she has painted. No wonder, that for us all her work bears authenticity as well as beauty. *Gustavia pulchra*, Gustavia the beautiful, a representative of forest beauty and an artist's dedicated skill.

Professor Ghillean T. Prance, Director
Royal Botanic Gardens, Kew

Gustavia pulchra.

Artist, botanist and lover of nature...

Artist, botanist and lover of nature, Margaret Mee has shared her matchless skills with countless folk not fortunate enough to have enjoyed personally the floral wealth of the Amazon rain forest. A woman of extreme modesty, she herself undoubtedly does not realise the impact that her talents have spread abroad. Nor does she understand, I am sure, the great heritage that she has created for the future of natural history.

Of very special interest to me — a botanist who for the past half century has studied the flora of the northwest Amazon — is her dedication to the forests of the Rio Negro area. She loves this region. Here she executed many of her most magnificent paintings.

It was here also that one of the greatest but one of the least appreciated explorers of all time, the Yorkshire botanist Richard Spruce, spent five productive years more than a century ago. In a very real way, Margaret has honoured Spruce's extraordinary contribution. For the two have much in common: she is shy and self-effacing as was he; and both, without actually realising the extent, have enriched our knowledge of the richest part of the Amazonian flora. And their very different material contributions — her life-like paintings, his dried herbarium material of hundreds of species new to science — have given a powerful impetus to the growing outcry against the uncontrolled devastation of the largest rain forest left on the globe. In more than one respect, Margaret, the quiet and unostentatious voice of the wilderness can be credited with one of the loudest voices for conservation.

She knows these species-rich woodlands well. She travelled miles in a dugout canoe with an Indian boy paddler. When she spied a flowering plant or a spot of colour in the all-pervading greenness, she stopped, set up her easel and painted. Mud, heat, insects weaned her not a whit from that fortunate plant and her brush.

It is not easy for me to choose any one of Margaret's paintings as my favourite — they defy such classification. Yet perhaps a painting like her *Aechmea Rodriguesiana* strikes me strongly because it illustrates her appreciation of the interdependence of many of the plants in such an ecologically complex environment. This beautiful epiphyte is not portrayed as an isolated organism but as part of a vegetational whole. While this painting is but one in which the floral background of the principal subject is accurately and artistically depicted, the portrait of such a magistral bromel has always seemed to me to speak out its thanks to Margaret for appreciating its beauty and its life-style as part of a rich and in many respects a mysterious community of nature.

Richard Evans Schultes

Receiving the World Wildlife Fund Gold Medal for Conservation, 1984.

Professor Richard Evans Schultes, Director Emeritus, Botanical Museum of Harvard University

Aechmea rodriguesiana.

Margaret Mee
July 1977

Aechmea rodriguesiana
Rio Marié, Amazonas

A specialist in scientific illustration...

I remember an excursion I made not far from Rio to collect rare plants hitherto not cultivated. Margaret Mee, with her gift of keen observation, surprised us by always finding the rarest species. She has the desire to identify her discoveries and the joy of sharing them with plant lovers. It is this which takes her into the forests as an explorer, braving many dangers, illness and more, in order to arrive at the supreme moment of flowering, the moment when Nature seems to reveal herself in all her beauty, mystery and luxuriance. The artist takes advantage of this magic moment to discover and portray an infinite series of secrets and revelations, rich in colour and form.

As a specialist in scientific illustration Margaret Mee is the most efficient I have ever known. Her work achieves perfection without becoming stereotyped. Her organisation of design on the page is always well conceived. Minute details are so intelligently portrayed that they do not destroy the artistic conception of the whole; they are drawn with the greatest care and observation in order to analyse the complexity of structure and to reveal the beauty of the plants in their living manifestation. In fact Margaret Mee takes the plant form in its obscurity and shows its colour, rhythm, texture and form without ever becoming pretentious in so doing.

When I speak of the Brazilian flora there comes to my mind the numerous journeys I have made through the most diverse regions, each with its own character, where one always feels a new emotion, a sense of mystery about this extraordinary world, this world of plants. Once when I was in Amazonia, in those flooded forests where the water sometimes rises forty-five feet in a season, it was as though we were in a forested sea. Around the trunks lianas wound and clung like writhing serpents in a convulsive effort to reach the top. In this struggle for life and quest for light appear the most varied forms of life.

In hollows near the rivers the heliconias develop a theme of extraordinary richness and variety. Some of the pendant flowers have a dusty bloom on the bracts and leaves which combine vivid colours and unusual textures. To me their harmony is almost music. At other times I see them as sculpture, as forms projected in space, shapes enriched by the tension between flowers and leaves. Or I think of them as paintings of capricious shapes; I see them in sunshine and in rain when streams of light make them appear like precious stones. They are bird-like, as in *Heliconia imbricata*, at times parrot-like, as in *Heliconia rostrata*; or scorpion-like, as in *Heliconia mariae* where the jointed bracts resemble the segments of a centipede. At other times they have the delicacy of

Heliconia chartacea.

Margaret Mee

Heliconia chartacea Lane ex Barreiros
cult: Rio de Janeiro,
Sitio Burle Marx
Proc: Venezuela (Amazonas)
1975

humming-birds, as in *Heliconia augustifolia*, or they appear like a flight of green birds, as in *Heliconia sampaiona*. *Heliconia 'amazonica'* has the charm of an Impressionist painting; it hangs swinging in the breeze and, on a cinnamon-red stem, displays curving bracts of rose, purple, green and white, merging into unbelievable shades. The picture is completed by the leaves which seem to be intentionally split, giving the appearance of windswept hair. There are heliconias whose bracts are of extreme delicacy, taking the form of a chalice to protect the flowers. Sometimes they are red-orange merging into dark green with light, almost white, tips. Within the urn, cadmium yellow stands out in contrast with the ultimate blue of the fruits.

Brazil has been and continues to be the land of enchantment for the botanist. One can understand how these regions have fascinated and inspired Margaret Mee. This vast country has more than 650 species of bromeliads; some, like *Aechmea polyantha*, are known to us only from Margaret Mee's paintings. To seek out a plant, bring it from its obscurity and reveal it to those who are inspired by Nature, is a true discovery. Each plant is a mystery whose laws challenge us; whose reason for life, whose preferences, dislikes and interrelationships, teach us a lesson which should give us a better understanding of the world in which we live. I admire and respect Margaret Mee, who seeks to portray the intricate beauty of the many plants which have so far passed unnoticed in a world where greed and ambition ruthlessly destroy our wonderful heritage, the gift of life.

Roberto Burle Marx, Rio de Janeiro.

Roberto Burle Marx with Margaret Mee, 1988.

Editor's Note

As her diaries, books, and paintings reveal there is much about Margaret Mee which is remarkable. Perhaps it is no more than coincidence, but Margaret was born at a critical time in the history of the Amazon. Eighty years ago when the final act of the infamous 'rubber boom' was being played in the financial institutions of London and New York, desperation and relief were felt alternately by tens of thousands of people along the banks of the river. Some were left bankrupt while others, overjoyed, were released from a cruel system of debt bondage. The sudden prosperity of the Amazon economy evaporated overnight and by the time Margaret with her sisters and brother were listening to their grandfather John Henry's travel stories the 'boom' was over.

John Henry had been adventurous but he could never have dreamed of the challenging path his granddaughter would choose. Far from popular myth most of the Amazon region, or Amazonia, has been explored and some of it minutely examined. The 'rubber boom' provided just one impetus, and for different reasons the contributors at the beginning of this book have between them totalled more than a hundred years of Amazon experience. But Margaret Mee's exceptional travels have led her to understand the Amazon intimately. More than any artist she has discovered the beauty of the forest and by her talents conveys a message of its value with infectious enthusiasm. Over the thirty-four years spanned by her descriptions, the forests have changed more than ever before. A fresh cycle of 'boom fever' clearly emerges as page follows page of her diaries. Thus, with her unparalleled stance, Margaret Mee raises a serious warning for the future of 'the Amazon' which nobody should fail to heed.

The book is arranged in 'journeys' compiled from Margaret's carefully typewritten manuscript. Each of her finished paintings began with accurate life-size sketches made from the living flower and coloured in the forest. Their size has been reduced to fit the pages. The flowers are identified by their botanical names, and non-specialists will be pleased to know that even the experts have been hard put to give a name to some of the plants Margaret has found. Where possible the science has been brought up to date, and I would like to thank Dr. Simon Mayo, Royal Botanic Gardens, Kew, for his cautious guidance. All the flower pictures and many photographs are from originals often blemished during storage in a tropical climate. None has been retouched and luckily this unique collection is now in the care of 'The Margaret Mee Amazon Trust', to be safeguarded for posterity.

Many individuals have helped with the presentation of this unique record of Amazonia, and I wish to join with Margaret in giving special thanks to them. It is also a great pleasure to include the natural history paintings and travel sketches of Alexandre Rodrigues Ferreira, born in Bahia, known today as Salvador, in Brazil, and who at the end of the eighteenth century travelled to many places since visited by Margaret. Our gratitude for the use of his work must go to the National Library in Rio de Janeiro.

But above all my thanks are to Margaret herself, who courageously challenged and conquered the Amazon. Her work and energy are an inspiration.

October 1988   Tony Morrison, Woodbridge

Before the Amazon...

Margaret Ursula Mee was born in May 1909 near Chesham, thirty miles west of London. She now lives in Brazil with her husband Greville and, from the age of forty-seven, has travelled the Amazon more extensively than any other woman. Her fifteen long journeys place her among the greatest of all women travellers.

As an artist, Margaret Mee has created the world's finest collection of Amazon paintings and sketches. When some were seen at a prestigious exhibition of her work in London in 1968, art critic and historian Wilfrid Blunt said 'They could stand without shame in the high company of such masters of the past as Georg Dionysius Ehret and Redouté'. Now, more than twenty years later, some of the paintings and sketchbooks have an exceptional, often distressing, value, depicting as they do species which have vanished with the advance of civilisation. Over the past thirty years Margaret Mee has seen irreversible changes occurring in the Amazon and modestly, without drama, she has the proof in her hands. She began her Amazon diaries in 1956, although it was not until she was over seventy years old that she started to write this book.

Rural Chesham in Buckinghamshire, with its history of being one of the most wooded parts of Britain at the time of the Norman Conquest, was Margaret's first home. Her father, George John Hendersen Brown, was linked on his mother's side with a Swedish seafaring family. Her mother, Isabella, or Lizbelle, was the eldest daughter of John Henry Churchman of the famous East Anglian family whose connections reach back to the sixteenth century.

As a young girl, Margaret, or Peggy, Brown grew up among the leafy byways of the Chiltern Hills. Life was never dull with her two sisters, Catherine and Dora, and a younger brother, John. And although her father worked in the City, travelling daily

Margaret (right) *and her sisters, Dora and Catherine, in the garden of their family home in Buckinghamshire.*

The leafy byways of the Chiltern Hills.

Ellen Mary Churchman.

A sampler by Elizabeth Felizada Milne, Margaret's great-grandmother and mother of John Henry Churchman.

18

Above: *Margaret Mee in the Amazon, 1988.*

Right: *One of Margaret's earliest paintings, in a fairy tale book she wrote when she was nine years old.*

to the Alliance Assurance Company near the Bank of England, Margaret's home life was modest. The Browns never owned a horse and trap like many neighbours and the nearest school was three miles away at the industrial end of the town. So it was to everyone's delight that education for the children was left in the hands of Lizbelle's sister, Ellen Mary Churchman, an artist who illustrated children's books. Ellen, or Aunt Nell, and Lizbelle had studied together at the school in north London founded by the pioneering feminist Frances Mary Buss. That had been a time when 'Girls simply did not do such things' and Margaret remembers her admiration for her aunt.

Ellen, who had been partly deaf since she was fifteen, remained with the family on and off for years, even during the Great War when the events and upheavals of the times disturbed the Browns as much as any family in the land. George, who had fought with the City Imperial Volunteers during the Boer War, was officially too old to enlist, but he found a way into the army, and although never posted abroad he was far away from home. His dogged insistence to serve the country, though not creating a family rift at the time, led Lizbelle to close the Chesham house and move the children to Brighton.

Margaret, her sisters and brother were settled temporarily in nearby Hove at a small school run on solidly Victorian principles by a formidable headmistress, Miss Beatrice Cobbold. They remained there until after the war. Miss Cobbold's report in December 1922 when Margaret was thirteen said: 'Botany: Good progress made' — Margaret was sixth in the class. And for 'Drawing' Miss Cobbold wrote in unbending copperplate script: 'Steadily progressing' — Margaret had come top. 'I also joined the local library', says Margaret, 'and instead of reading traditional schoolgirl classics I found my travel spirit from such books as Kingsley's *Westward Ho!* which even mentions the Amazon'.

During holidays the children visited their maternal grandfather John Henry, who sat them on his knee to tell travel stories. According to Margaret's brother John 'He was a tremendous character, even if somewhat feckless'. John Henry had married his first cousin Ellen White, but only after she had made him wait for seven years. She

had doubts about the marriage on religious grounds, so John Henry decided to travel the world while he waited. ' "A little pinch of salt and I'm going to tell you some stories", he used to say and we were entranced', Margaret remembers. 'My mother didn't fully approve as grandfather told us how he was attacked by footpads or some colourful tales of his adventures in San Francisco or New Zealand. "Don't stuff the children with all that nonsense", she would call. He never had a profession — rather he was the black sheep of the family. But we loved his stories and all of us went on to travel'.

With their father's return from the war and a renewed hope for a settled future, the family moved back to Chesham, this time to a smaller house. While George travelled daily to London, Margaret was sent to Dr. Challoner's Grammar School in the nearby market town of Amersham. Her art master, 'Bengy' Buckingham, set weekend tasks and Margaret still retains a clear memory of how she collected flowers and sketched. 'It was my first, rather childish attempt. I soon moved on to other subjects including drama and languages'. But the peaceful countryside and crystal clear watercress beds of those days left a profound mark on her character. Her appreciation of the beauties of the natural world has solid foundations.

Margaret's father was a good amateur naturalist who knew many wild plants by name. Often he encouraged her interest and tried to keep a rein on her youthful impulsiveness. At the time, and for many years after, Margaret's closest family ally was her younger sister Catherine with whom she shared many secrets. They made friends in the town, planned travels to France and joined the local amateur drama club. On one occasion Margaret seriously considered acting as a career, but just the once, for art and outdoor sketching were usually uppermost in her mind. By 1926, when she was seventeen, she was travelling daily with Catherine and Dora by the Metroland railway through the new suburbs of London. With one change on the way they could reach Watford where they had enrolled together at the School of Art, Science and Commerce.

Dora completed a three-year course and has become an established painter in London. But Margaret and Catherine left the college, preferring to move on to work in London. The years they had spent at Watford came at a time when the social and political life in Europe was changing sharply. It was the time of the Depression, while in Germany Adolf Hitler was gaining support and thoughts of another war were day-to-day student talk, especially in the extremely political circles in which Margaret found friends.

While she painted she became absorbed by the affairs of Europe. Her art school training had led to a teaching post in Liverpool, but it was short lived when she decided she wanted to travel and see for herself what Hitler was about. In 1932 Margaret moved to Germany to stay with an exchange-student, Bruno, who had earlier been with the Browns in Chesham. Her brother John and sister Dora also travelled to Germany, John staying with Bruno's family some time later. But Germany was no place for the inquisitive, for anyone with left-wing thoughts or for those with Jewish friends. Margaret had all these characteristics, and more, which led to several narrow escapes from Hitler's police. In Berlin one close student friend thrust his camera into her hand so she could get away with his evidence while he was being arrested and beaten in the street. She ran to the subway closely followed by plain-clothes police and dodged on and then off a train: 'As the doors closed I rushed off

20

On a visit to England in 1932 a German friend, Hans, took this picture of Margaret beside one of the many farms near her home.

In the 1930s Margaret (above) travelled in Germany, staying with an exchange-student friend, Bruno (below).

leaving the police behind. I returned to my friend's house safely and told his mother he had been arrested. We hid the camera and waited. After a while he returned. He had been released but was given thirty days to get out of the country'.

Looking back to those days Margaret Mee is quietly amused by her audacity. 'But the scenes were dreadful. I was horrified'. Nevertheless she decided to stay and look for a job. 'They were intensely exciting and important times. I had all sorts of peculiar offers including one in "Red" Wedding, a part of Berlin where Hitler's communist opposition gathered. The Nazi police came and rounded up all the sympathisers — the "Weddingites". I watched the Reichstag burn in February 1933 soon after Hitler had become Chancellor, I saw Jewish Boycott Day as people were led away in chains...all frighteningly close'. She was so absorbed by the enormity of the events that she sketched only once. It was a classic portrait of a doctor who had offered her a job. She gave the sketch to him before he, too, decided to leave with his family.

Back in London in the mid-1930s Margaret's student-bred political career took shape. She married Reg Bartlett who was already prominent in trade union affairs, and became a member of the Sign, Glass and Ticket Writers. As a member of the union, Margaret at twenty-eight became the youngest delegate to address the Trades Union Congress when, in Norwich in 1937, she proposed a resolution on the first day. Her theme concerned youth in industry and the raising of the school leaving age. To a standing ovation she declared: 'This resolution, if put into action with energy and enthusiasm by the whole trade union movement, could change the future of the youth of this country'.

Subsequently she was offered a job with Ernest Bevin in the Labour Party but turned it down, for she was undecided about her future and the threat of war was drawing closer. In another rousing speech to the T.U.C. she raised the question of protection of the 'teeming millions in the industrial towns' against incendiary bombs, shells and gas attacks. At the time she was so passionately concerned with the plight of the unemployed that her love for painting was put aside. 'All I did in those years were some large placard-type cut-outs of the tragic faces of the Hungry 'Thirties which were paraded around Whitestone Pond in Hampstead'.

Her marriage was never happy and her father's death gave her the chance to join her mother in France on a trip that was meant to be a holiday. However, when the time came to return, Margaret announced she would stay behind. Lizbelle was astonished but could not persuade Margaret to change her mind. For a while she worked in a café, then as an *au pair* until finally, as the army began to march the streets, the local consul insisted she left. Protesting she wanted to stay, she was helped

Pre-war days in a village near London.

Margaret returned to painting soon after the Second World War when she was living in Codicote.

to a secret channel crossing fifteen days after war was declared. 'It was a close thing. One official couldn't understand why I had so many maps and assumed I was a spy. I burst into tears, and he remarked: ''Well perhaps you're not'', and let me go'.

Britain was preparing for war and Margaret joined the war effort, first as a machinist in a factory and then alongside her brother and his fiancée, Nancy, at the De Havilland aircraft factory in Hatfield, just north of London. Margaret's skill shone in the drawing office where she worked around the clock, hardly ever seeing daylight.

During this time she lived seven miles from the factory in the village of Codicote. Her mother, and brother John and Nancy when they married, shared the cottage in typically war-time cramped conditions, and for three years Margaret cycled to work in all weathers. As John recalls, 'Our cottage was somewhere near the end of the flying bomb run and when the engines cut out above us we had to duck for cover'.

Then, at last the war in Europe was over, and on the tumultuous night of V.E. Day in 1945 Margaret joined the singing crowds in Downing Street. Like the thousands of people crushing around her she wondered how she could cope with the future and what she would do next. 'De Havilland offered me a permanent job in the drawing office but I turned it down. I couldn't face it. I decided to work in a studio and at evening classes'.

Her first thoughts were to find the breadth of her talent and learn new techniques, and to this end she attended night and weekend classes at St. Martin's School of Art in central London. It was here that she met Greville Mee, a commercial artist who had arrived in London from Leicester in the 1930s. Greville, like countless other artists at the time, found the streets of the capital anything but paved with gold and survived by moving from one studio to another.

St. Martin's opened another horizon for Margaret. One evening the resident model failed to arrive and the tutor turned to Margaret asking her to pose. 'I told him that my stockings were muddy from cycling in the rain but he said ''Don't worry, be natural, just sit there...'', and I did. That was it!...'

St. Martin's gave her the chance to assemble a portfolio which she took to the Camberwell School of Art where she was immediately accepted as a full-time student. Her work was seen by Victor Pasmore, then one of Britain's leading painters, who recommended Margaret should receive a grant for her studies. She started at Camberwell in 1947.

'Victor Pasmore was a wonderful teacher. He would say ''Look at the shapes —

Victor Pasmore, R.A., one of the founders of the Euston Road School.

A figure drawing in pencil from Margaret's Camberwell School of Art days.

Margaret and Greville Mee in London soon after the war.

fit the shapes between the spaces...'' Then he'd go and you wouldn't see him again that day. And of course we found the spaces are just as important as the shapes. He was a hard teacher. Some of the girls would be in tears from his criticisms'. It was Pasmore's style and attention that has given so much to Margaret's own highly personal approach to the composition of her Amazon flower paintings. Victor Pasmore was a co-founder, with William Coldstream and Claude Rogers, of the Euston Road Group. Before the war they had opened a teaching studio in Fitzroy Street, and were united in their revolt against abstractism. Augustus John, John Nash and Vanessa Bell were also associated with the group. Victor Pasmore frequently used large masses of subdued colour, perhaps reflecting the grimy atmosphere of that part of London. Later the studio became the Euston Road School with a prospectus stating: 'In teaching, particular emphasis will be laid on training in observation since this is the faculty most open to training'. It is not a coincidence that the hallmarks of Margaret's flower paintings are her observation and detail.

At Camberwell she excelled at figure drawing: 'Handling proportions and depth are essential for good figure work. It is marvellous training'. Margaret recalls the discipline of the three years at the School from which she received her diploma. Greville had attended Camberwell evening and Saturday morning classes whilst continuing to build his career in the commercial art field.

The Highland Princess, *one of the cargo-passenger vessels on a regular run between Britain and Brazil, on which Greville sailed to South America.*

The chance to travel again came in 1952 when Margaret heard that Catherine was seriously unwell in Brazil. Catherine had married and spent much of the war near the Roman spa city of Bath. Later she left Britain with her husband to live in Sao Paulo, which at that time was a small city. Margaret and the family knew of Catherine's new life as Lizbelle once made a nine month visit to Brazil and returned brimful of excitement and stories. Thus, when Margaret received an air ticket to take her out to help her sister she left Greville to pack up their flat in Blackheath near Greenwich. 'It was a wonderful part of London', Greville remembers nostalgically, 'but I followed a couple of months later by sea with the luggage. We thought we would stay for three or four years', he jokes, 'but it has grown into a lifetime. Though absolutely fascinating'.

Once in Brazil, Margaret began teaching art at St. Paul's, the British School in Sao Paulo, and Greville was soon established as a busy commercial artist. He can well claim to have introduced the airbrush technique to Brazil. 'It was in its infancy then, and I had to improvise the equipment using pressured gases. In those days, Sao Paulo was a growing commercial centre and I soon had a business'.

Margaret and Greville settled into the life of Sao Paulo and made many good friends. At weekends their home was a magnet for anyone who appreciated art and good food — Greville is an imaginative cook. He also designed and built sailing boats which he used on the enormous artificial lakes near the city. Margaret was soon entranced by the luxuriant flowers and beautiful birds surrounding their home. But the city was expanding and rapidly becoming South America's fastest growing urban area. Concrete quickly spread upwards and outwards until the Mee's tiny house was totally absorbed.

To escape from the crowds and enjoy a cooler climate, Margaret and Greville hiked frequently to hills and forests outside the city and enjoyed the parks and open spaces. It was when they were walking once through rough unkempt land beside an old tramway line that Margaret spotted a castor oil plant with, to her eye, curious fruits and leaves. 'It had such wonderful shapes — I sketched it immediately'. As Greville says, 'From that time on Margaret put aside all other ideas and began sketching and painting flowers'.

Brazil's southern coastal mountains, or Serra do Mar, became their favourite area for painting excursions and collecting plants to sketch, and from these early days Margaret began to build her collection and reputation as a flower painter. She painted seriously in every spare moment, choosing as a medium gouache, an opaque watercolour technique which she had first used at Camberwell. She also kept minutely detailed notes as she had been taught at Camberwell. Her paper was carefully chosen

A painting of Brazilian life by Margaret in her early years in Sao Paulo.

for quality — called Fabriano Raffaello, it is an excellent surface for gouache. And she began to show her work, always with the idea of painting more flowers from further afield.

Catherine returned to Britain and died soon afterwards; this was the moment for Margaret to decide on her future, and as Greville was a successful commercial artist in Brazil they decided to stay there. For Margaret, too, there was a positive new interest in her work from a Dutch friend, Rita, one of the St. Paul's

Below left: *Margaret and Rita rest during a plant collecting expedition near Sao Paulo.* Below: *An embaúba (cecropia) tree from the Serra do Mar. Margaret was fascinated by the shape of the leaves.*

Margaret (right) *and her sister Catherine in Sao Paulo.*

Rita and Margaret collecting on the sandy Atlantic coast.

teachers. Rita enjoyed long hikes, often accompanying the Mees as they explored the densely forested mountain slope leading down to the Atlantic. This rich 'Atlantic Forest' is filled with flowers, giant ferns and marvellous humming-birds. More than once they hiked to the sea and followed the broad sandy coastline for miles. Each new excursion meant more plants and a growing collection of paintings. It did not take much persuasion for Rita to agree to join Margaret for her first assault on the Amazon.

In almost five centuries since its discovery the Amazon, or Amazonia, the region embraced by the river, has attracted dozens of explorers, many of them naturalists. One reason being that of all places in the world Amazonia is unrivalled for its immense diversity of animals and plants. And far from popular myth it is a region of many faces. It can be as dry as the most inhospitable desert in one part, or flooded, and often permanently swampy, in others. Sometimes the interior of a forest impresses with a sepulchral sombreness as trees rise a hundred and fifty feet or more. Elsewhere, the ground is simply covered with low thorny scrub.

In most places away from civilisation a modern traveller faces much the same problems as anyone in the past. Richard Spruce was a Yorkshireman who, in the middle of the last century, spent seventeen years along the Amazon. His book *Notes of a Botanist on the Amazon and Andes* is a classic. One experience sums up the crude, often rough life of the settlers there. He was visiting a small village of palm-thatched huts in the tropical forest: 'You will credit me when I say to the sight Esmeralda is a paradise — in reality it is an Inferno, scarcely habitable by man'.

Spruce was one of the most reliable of the nineteenth century botanists who, treading new ground, produced remarkable accounts of their journeys. Their stories were often spaced with descriptions of newly discovered species, though surprisingly few of their illustrations were accurate and many were simply exaggerated — their readers expected the unusual. Even fewer of the illustrations were coloured. Von Martius, a Bavarian who explored in the upper Amazon and Brazil in 1817, employed artists in Germany, one of whom, Joseph Pohl, produced some of the best nineteenth century work, but Pohl used dried specimens and Von Martius' descriptions.

None of this early work equals the personal style of accuracy and depth which Margaret was achieving by 1956. She worked only from living plants, usually sketched in the forest. Even before she attempted painting the flora of the Amazon her work was skilful, exquisitely composed and perfectly colour matched. The question for her

Left: *Margaret and Rita on a collecting expedition in the Serra do Mar.* Above: *A tibouchina from the Serra do Mar, one of Margaret's first flower paintings.*

was where to start. Which of the many thousands of 'Esmeraldas' should she choose as a base? And every map she saw gave the rivers different names. It was a hugely confusing new world.

The Amazon is without doubt the greatest river on earth. Unravelled, its tributaries would twice circle the equator. Put its source in Moscow, and the mouth would be south of the Sahara. Even more startling is the fact that Amazonia equals the size of the continental United States. Faced with such dimensions and the constraints of teachers' salaries, Margaret and Rita could think of looking at merely a fraction. But Margaret Mee was well prepared for her first expedition by a long background of challenges. Then forty-seven, she packed her artist's kit into a canvas rucksack and padded it with spare clothes. She also took a revolver.

Outside it was drizzling, low cloud surrounded the city. A typical misty day enveloped Sao Paulo. Greville had decided it was not his kind of trip, and in any case he couldn't leave his work. He drove Margaret and Rita to the airport and waved a reluctant goodbye. Margaret, without realising it at the time, was setting out on a journey which would launch her into history and the world of art.

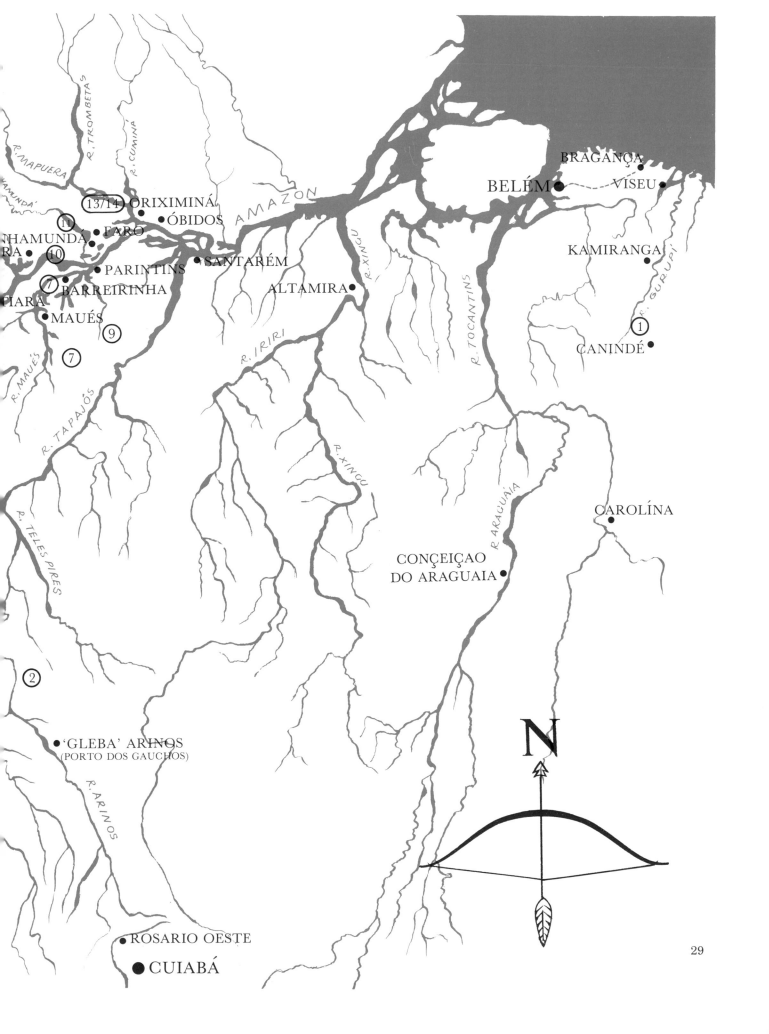

R. MAPUERA

R.TROMBETAS

R. CUMINÁ

R. NHAMUNDÁ

13/14 ORIXIMINÁ

⑪ FARO

⑩ ÓBIDOS

NHAMUNDÁ RA

⑦ BARREIRINHA

PARINTINS

SANTARÉM

AMAZON

ALTAMIRA

R. XINGU

R. IRIRI

R. XINGU

R. TOCANTINS

R. ARAGUAIA

BRAGANÇA

BELÉM VISEU

KAMIRANGA

R. GURUPI

CANINDÉ ①

CAROLÍNA

CONÇEIÇAO DO ARAGUAIA

TIARA

MAUÉS

⑨

R. MAUÉS

⑦

R. TAPAJÓS

R. TELES PIRES

②

•'GLEBA' ARINOS
(PORTO DOS GAUCHOS)

R. ARINOS

N

•ROSARIO OESTE

● CUIABÁ

JOURNEY ONE: 1956

To the River Gurupi

Margaret and Rita agreed to spend their long January school holiday on a journey to the Amazonia. They looked carefully at the cost of air fares and chose a flight to Belém, a city near the mouth of the river over two thousand miles from Sao Paulo. Other destinations were too expensive and even the Belém flight had to be with R.E.A.L., a small cargo passenger service using ageing Second World War aircraft.

Belém, the capital of the state of Pará, stands beside a broad channel flowing south of Marajó island. As a port it has been the gateway to the Amazon for over three centuries and the water's edge is crammed with a motley choice of river boats. These craft are used like buses with routes ranging along the river for up to one thousand miles. Also in Belém, and of great interest to Margaret in 1956, was the local Goeldi Museum. Named after a Swiss naturalist, it was the best source of all Amazon information.

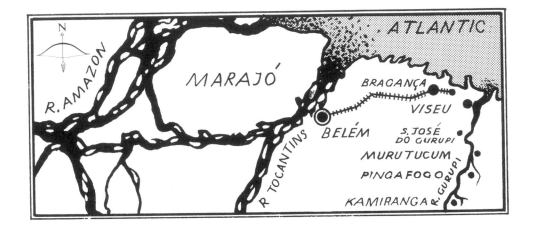

January 1956

The propellers of the small passenger-cargo plane droned noisily as we climbed from Congonhas Airport on the outskirts of Sao Paulo bound for Belém. Rita had secured a good seat with a view from a window; she was lucky as most were obscured by cargo. Our excitement was intense, for this was our first journey to the Amazon. We were both dressed for the jungle, or at least, with our complete lack of experience, we thought we were: blue jeans, long sleeved shirts, straw hats and boots. We carried very little more. Our strained purses did not allow for excess weight charges on our luggage, and my rucksack was already heavy with tubes of paint and sketch books.

We sat spellbound watching the softly contoured landscape slip by, and with each stop at small towns in the middle of Brazil our excitement grew. They had been just names on a map before. First came Uberaba, after about two hours, for fuel and more cargo; then steadily the flight continued due north until late afternoon when we reached Carolina on the River Tocantins, an Amazon tributary. Afterwards we were over forest, threaded by meandering silver rivers. The pilot flew low keeping clear of cloud, so that it seemed the canopies of the trees were above us and we could see the clear river water flowing over its rocky bed.

Eventually we reached the impressive mouth of the Amazon in time to see the sunset spreading burning gold across sky and water. So vast was the expanse of the river that

we seemed to be flying over an ocean. Large cargo ships were moored in the river and as the plane banked in the turn towards landing I strained to see the Atlantic. But it was too distant and we were already far too low.

Our first taste of tropical heat came as we stepped out of the plane on to the tarmac at the tiny Belém airport. Rita's smile changed to a laugh as she watched the perspiration pour over my face. Already her shirt was drenched. Thankfully we did not have to carry our bags to the row of waiting taxis, one of which took us quickly to the centre of the city. In the busy main street we soon found a simple hotel, the Central, where we changed into cooler clothes after a shower. The water from the cold tap was as warm as the room but it was refreshing — at least for a few minutes. When we went outside again to find a place to eat supper, the pavements were still warm from the heat of the sky.

We grew to like Belém but, even under the shade of the massive mango trees with which the town abounded, the heat was intense. We stayed for a few days, exploring the little town, strolling through the fascinating port and market, and when exhausted with wandering in the heat, sat at the café tables outside our hotel drinking the delicious refreshing fruit juice of the region made from the soft mushy *graviola* (custard apple) and *maracujá* (passion fruit). Another fruit new to me, *cupuaçu,* is related to cacau.

But most interesting were our visits to the Goeldi Museum, where we hoped to get suggestions for journeys into the forests of the interior. We were not disappointed, for the Director, Dr. Walter Egler was most sympathetic, and gave us helpful introductions. He even allowed me to work in the museum, and sent a *mateiro* (woodsman) to cut flowers from a towering Cannonball tree, *Couroupita guianensis,* for me to paint. Whilst I was sketching, Rita explored the gardens and made friends with various animals resident at the museum, including a group of Spider monkeys. One of them decided to claim her as his property in the traditional manner whilst she was innocently holding him by the hand. His well aimed drenching made both of us laugh.

The Goeldi Museum in a rich tropical garden.

We saw the first Giant anteater, *Tamandua bandeira,* acquired by the Goeldi Museum. The strange animal with impressive nails had so injured his keeper when he was trying to introduce a new diet of eggs to substitute the animal's natural food of termites, that he appeared swathed in bandages.

In his enthusiasm for the animals, Dr. Egler, who had an ability to tame any animal, showed us round the wooded garden. He called to a young *onça* (jaguar) who came meekly to have her head stroked. Then he coaxed a jealous *Porco do mato* (Peccary or Wild boar) to the fence of its corral. This animal, using its sharp teeth, had just

Above left: *Tukuna Indian necklace of carved seeds.* Above right: *A flute decorated with macaw feathers.*

cut the tendons of another keeper's legs as he fled to escape its rage. We moved on to the snakes — closer than I had ever been to one in the Serra do Mar, and Dr. Egler picked giant blood-swollen *carrapotos* (ticks) from an enormous *jibóia* (boa) lying coiled in the foliage of a clump of bamboo. My fascination quickly overcame my revulsion. The poor animal's head was covered with ticks.

The museum's anthropologist, Dr. Hilbert, showed with pride some of the pick of Indian artefacts in the collection: bows, arrows, baskets, necklaces made from seeds, and many feather adornments. According to Dr. Hilbert much of the collection came from tribes of forest dwellers who were still untouched by civilisation.

We had begun to think that we might journey from Belém to the River Gurupi where we could expect to find some people of the Tembé and Urubú tribes. Our decision to go to the Gurupi was finally made when we were introduced to Dr. Froes, a botanist of the Regional Agricultural Office. We had spent some time in the Herbarium with him looking at the dried plants of the region, and I must admit I felt very flattered when he asked me to look for a Strychnos vine, reputed to grow in the forests of the Gurupi. He said that some forest Indians use an extract of this plant when they make curare, the poison for their darts and arrows.

'Anthropologist Max Boudin from the Goeldi Museum has just offered us the use of a thatched hut (of a type widely found in Amazonia) at Murutucum, a poor town on the Gurupi, and given us an introduction to a Sr. Raschid, who he describes as 'a retired gentleman farmer of Lebanese descent'. We leave tomorrow.'

A small clay figure by the Karajá Indians.

A small wood-burning vintage engine was pulling the train between Belém and Bragança, a little coastal town not too distant from Viseu at the mouth of the Gurupi. The journey turned out to be painfully slow and there were interminable stops at every station where the *camponeses* (country people) were selling home-made food. Brightly coloured sparks from the burning fuel poured through the open windows as we clattered along. To my amazement, Rita suddenly sprang to her feet and banged me over the head, for my hair was about to catch fire from a large chunk of burning charcoal. When I arrived in Bragança, my white and green cotton slacks were pitted with black holes.

In the village, a small port forgotten by the outside world, we aroused curiosity and even hostility amongst the local people, for women preparing to visit the forest, especially those wearing straw hats and boots, were an unwelcome novelty there.

In the main street we found the Hotel dos Viagantes, a very unassuming travellers' hotel which had been recommended to us as being cheap and clean. Our tiny room, with two partition walls, certainly lacked comfort. The only furniture was a broken piece of mirror hung above a rickety table, and four hammock hooks. The cubicle showers were shared by all the guests, which as we soon found, were exclusively

Left and above: *Tembé Indians on the Gurupi.*

commercial travellers. Much to my embarrassment, one of the travellers was selling 'religious' prints, and wanted my opinion of them. I had seen them out of the corner of my eye — pathetic designs, debased sentiment, horrible colour and production, and at the sight of them I fled. But Rita came to me with a private message from the salesman. Would I look at them closely and give my opinion? Fortunately, fate intervened, and I never underwent this ordeal.

In spite of the irritation caused by the men noisily spitting in the adjoining room and the general inconvenience, we enjoyed the first days of our adventure; but as the days passed without news of the boat destined to take us to Viseu, our spirits sank and boredom set in. I could find few things to sketch, for if we ventured any distance we became the centre of too much attention. So there was little to do but wander around disconsolately. On one occasion we met the only other two travellers in the town, two French lads who had made their way on foot from nearby French Guiana. The story of their journey fascinated us, so they invited us to the only bar to have a coffee and a chat. But we could not dally there, for all the men were staring at us; one even had the audacity to enquire of the Frenchmen, who flushed scarlet, how much we cost!

After what seemed an eternity, but was in fact only five days, the boat bound for Viseu arrived. It was a rough little river boat built of wood, with a closed cabin packed with at least twenty passengers, all from the locality and with a number of children. Conditions were far from ideal, and when we arrived in the choppy waters of the open sea, children began crying and fretting as some of the women became hysterical. With the pitching and tossing of the boat, one mulatta of strongly African descent was in such a state that I offered her brandy from my precious hip-flask, which she drank too long and too eagerly. I was to regret this offer, for during the rest of the voyage she was constantly worrying me for more.

Rita and I hung our hammocks side by side, mine against the cabin wall as I fancied it was a secluded spot. But I suffered for this choice when we pitched and tossed in the strong currents off the rugged coast at night, and in the morning saw that I was bruised black and blue. Furthermore, the kerosene hurricane lamp, which hung over the foot of my hammock, jumped from its hook during the stormy passage, falling on my feet, but fortunately extinguishing itself as it fell. After this disturbed night, I saw one of the loveliest sights by the morning light, as flights of *guará* (Scarlet ibis) rose against dark green forests like a shower of geranium petals.

At Viseu, Sr. Raschid, Max Boudin's friend, proved most kindly and helpful, and soon had our journey to Murutucum organised for us. Whilst in Viseu we were introduced to Joao Carvalho, the amiable chief of S.P.I. (Indian Protection Service), whose headquarters were in Canindé. This was the name of a *maloca* (a large Indian house for several families) at the headwaters of the Gurupi. The area was inhabited by Tembé Indians, whilst the Urubú tribe's territory was on the lower reaches of the river. We were told they were famous for their music and feather work used for adornments and this intrigued me. Joao's son was sick with hepatitis and he was taking him to Belém for hospital treatment; nevertheless, in spite of his worries, he invited us to stay at his house until our boat arrived to take us upriver to Murutucum.

A sketch by Margaret in Bragança.

Rich forest along the banks of the Gurupi.

We were already settled elsewhere so we declined his kind offer but took the opportunity to talk to him about the journey ahead. We were to travel by a trader's small boat which would be leaving Viseu at three in the morning the following day. So we packed that night in readiness for an early departure and moved to Sr. Raschid's house near the jetty. Some Urubú boys employed by him helped us with our rucksacks which we later found in some disorder — the boys had looked through their contents, their curiosity being greater than their shyness. I was fascinated by their soft voices speaking a strange language, their copper skin and blue-black hair.

We hung our hammocks in a small loft where not a sound could be heard. I fell into a deep sleep, awaking with a start to see by the dim light of the kerosene lamp that it was almost three. I called Rita frantically, but she lay dead to the world and I had to pinch her to arouse her. We dressed hastily and descended the precarious steps to call Sr. Raschid as he had requested. A tall, sleepy figure in pyjamas, carrying a hurricane lamp, he led us to the jetty, accompanied by two Urubú boys. Dozens of narrow wooden steps led down to the river where we could see the dim light of the boat. At Sr. Raschid's command, the Urubús took our hands and led us down the shadowy precipice. A thick mist hung over the river, and once enveloped in the humid pall my teeth began to chatter. The boat glided from her mooring and the Archimedes outboard motor began to splutter. We were on our way up the River Gurupi!

We searched our baggage for some protection against the chillingly cold pre-dawn air, pulled out plastic sheets intended for use against rain, and wrapped ourselves up like chrysalises until the sun rose and dispersed the mist.

Callandario, the trader who owned the boat, was a kindly middle-aged Portuguese, who sailed up and down the river, supplying the riberine population with everything from buttons to hammocks and, of course, rice, beans and sugar. Malaki, a dusky young black Brazilian with a wonderful smile and character, was the senior member of the crew. A young half-Urubú boy helped him with the cooking. When the motor failed (as it did frequently), or was too weak to pass a turbulent rapid, Malaki would stamp and dance, shouting, *'Vai, motor, vai!'* (Go, motor, go!). At times he jumped lithely into the foaming river, roping the tilting craft to a rock, and then he and the boy would haul it through the rapids to calmer waters. This was the pattern of our voyage.

On the first night we hung our hammocks from the trees beside an enchanted lake. I could not sleep for listening to the magic sounds of the forest. Only the trees were silent, while the lake was alive with sparkling, splashing fishes, and the frogs' chorus mingled with the plaintive cries of night birds.

One of our first calls was at the village of Sao José do Gurupi, a cluster of palm-thatched wooden huts where the people were most hospitable and spared no effort to entertain the two 'foreign ladies' with exaggerated tales of their encounters with savage animals, all this washed down with the juice pressed from the fruit of two palms, the *assaí,* which was purple, and the clearer *bacaba.* Thus we meandered up the river, bathing in the warm water, talking with other traders and stopping at huts and settlements until we reached its most dangerous and challenging *cachoeiras* (rapids). There Malaki called an old, greying, black Brazilian, who had lived beside the torrent for most of his life, to pole us. For a moment I thought of days punting on the Thames. The gaunt old man stood in the prow like a giant *caranca* (beautifully carved figurehead) used on another Brazilian river to ward away evil spirits. Swinging his bamboo pole from side to side, his dark face and body streaming with sweat from

Margaret and Rita — the two 'foreign ladies'.

34

'We were greeted with generous hospitality in the settlements along the river'.

exertion, the old man edged the boat through the rapids the way he had learnt by heart. The ordeal over, Malaki and the old man departed, leaving us with Callandario and the boy to proceed upriver to Murutucum.

Frances Huxley, the anthropologist son of Julian Huxley, had travelled through this region only three years before, and the memories of the young author were still fresh in the minds of the villagers, who recounted stories of him and his generosity for leaving his *rancho* (supplies) to them. He journeyed far up the river and his book *Affable Savages* resulted from this trip among the Urubú and Tembé tribes.

With our lack of experience our *rancho* were minimal, but before Callandario left us alone in the forest around Murutucum — which he did with much hesitation — he gave us a large bunch of plantains, banana-like fruit but not sweet, and a good quantity of rice. The latter was invaluable during our last days in Murutucum, but the plantains proved a great disappointment as they never ripened, and uncooked were quite inedible. We had no means of cooking except on the open fire of the neighbouring hut, where we were allowed to boil water and rice, but it was always in use. This hut belonged to Zico and Benedita, a man and his wife who were the *caseiro* (caretakers) for Max Boudin. As Zico was somewhat hostile and Benedita very demanding, even of our modest store of food and medicines, we avoided too much contact with them. Their 'housemaid' was a girl of four years old, who had the worst case of chicken-pox we had ever seen, and always carried a broom in her hands, sweeping and drudging the whole day long at the harsh orders of Benedita. She dragged herself around, more dead than alive, and even seemed too ill at times to heed the constant scolding.

Our hut was tiny, primitive and open to the sky above the wooden door. The roof was of *sapé* (coarse broad-leaved grass) and at night scores of spiders invaded the ceiling. We watched them fascinated from the depths of our hammocks, though at first with some apprehension. Could they be venomous? Luckily we never found out, but we soon noticed that their only interest was in trapping insects, which they seemed to attract by tapping with their bony front legs on the straw ceiling. Everything was strange and mysterious by the flickering light of the kerosene flame which cast billowing shadows across the earthen floor and wattled-mud walls.

Daily, and sometimes by night, we made a pilgrimage down to the narrow *igarapé* (channel) which flowed into the river, to fill our canvas bucket with water. By day we were able to bathe in the river and never a soul came near. From our hut it was some distance to the *igarapé,* and on one occasion when we were on our way to bathe we heard an outboard motor approaching up the river. Wildly excited we hurried down the track, quite certain it was Joao Carvalho who had arranged in Viseu to take us

Embaúba trees flourished in cleared places.

35

'We washed in the cool igarapé, *a little channel, near the hut'.*

further up the river to Canindé. On our way, to our chagrin and their horror, there appeared on the path a procession of *macumbeiras* (priestesses of a spiritist cult derived from a religion of West Africa which had come to Brazil in the slaving days). A wizened old man led the way beating a drum, followed by men, women and children, obviously dressed in their best, ribbons fluttering, and one woman carrying an image of a saint on a red velvet cushion.

Rita and I mastered our astonishment at this unexpected sight, politely greeting them with *'Bom dia!'* (Good morning!). There was no reply and the old man, with his head bent and gaze averted, followed by the others who stared at us fearfully, passed on. When we reached the river the boat was disappearing upstream. We bathed rapidly and returned to our hut. From the attitude of these *macumbeiras* it was clear that we had been mistaken for devils or evil spirits. In reality, it was an encounter of two different worlds.

There was excitement in Zico's hut — loud talking and laughter. Benedita came to us, animated and dressed in her best, to invite us to the 'ceremony' of killing a cockerel. It is well-known in parts of Brazil where the African *Candomblé* cult is strong. Hiding our horror, we explained that our religion would not permit us to participate, but we gave her a small contribution to the fête which she clearly expected and took eagerly. The ritual of drum beating accompanied by chanting went on late into the night.

We spent our days in the forest, enjoying the beauty of the shady trees and the

'Our collecting was hard work, sometimes we walked many miles to find new flowers'.

creatures which lived under their protection. A Bird-eating spider, brown and furry, crouched on a tree trunk against which I was leaning; a *papovento* (small lizard) with its throat extended to an orange ball, struggled to swallow a leaf-insect as large and as green as itself; a pair of curious *tucanos* (toucans), with their large ungainly bills, followed our antics with interested amusement from the branches above as we struggled to reach a white flowered orchid, a sobralia. The gorgeous plant had been dislodged by the previous night's heavy rain and dangled on a liana among a sodden tangle of branches. There were flowers to paint in plenty: the pink and white blooms of *Gustavia augusta*, the purple-red ones of the delicate orchid *Rodriguezia secunda*, those of the delicately perfumed *Epidendrum fragrans*. Everywhere we looked in the humid forest we found bromeliads, mostly growing on trees or branches as if stuck there by magic.

Gustavia augusta *(Lecythidaceae)*.

During the frequent storms at night, I lay in my hammock listening to branches crashing through the forest, and in the morning collected any fallen plants. On one such search, I encountered a grey snake, stretched right across the track in front of me and no amount of tapping with my stick would move her. She merely gazed at me insolently, daring me to step over her. I decided not to chance my luck and returned later to find she had gone.

Our store of food was near an end. Rita was ill with a fever, lying in her hammock. I began to worry — would Joao Carvalho ever arrive? On the third day of a boiled rice diet (and little of that), we were so weak with hunger that we decided somehow we had to leave Murutucum at any cost. If we could get a boat to take us upriver to Pingafogo, the name of the *sitio* (piece of land and house) of Antonio Carvalho, Joao's father, we could wait there until Joao fetched us.

Zico was still away in the forest, where he had been for some days, but was due to return. His dog had already found his way back. The poor beast's ears were cut and pouring with blood and he had a high fever. He came to our hut and drank pints of water which we gave him, and lay there as though in need of our protection. We were horrified at his condition and asked Benedita what could have happened to him. Very casually, almost contemptuously, she replied that Zico had cut off his ears because he refused to hunt. We were appalled by this cruelty and decided that we would leave as soon as Zico returned. Unhappily, there was no alternative but to go with him, for he was the only owner of a canoe, and we were completely isolated in Murutucum.

Zico returned, his dark face more sullen than ever. We heard Benedita's gibes — 'Even your dog will not look at you nor obey you!' It was true, the dog resolutely ignored him, and no amount of threats or shouting would even make him turn his head. The animal was so aloof and contemptuous that Zico became obviously fearful of the huge beast, possibly thinking that the dog was possessed of a spirit who would avenge his cruelty.

I spoke to Zico, asking him to take us by canoe to Pingafogo, but he blankly refused. Then I told him that we should die of hunger if we remained in Murutucum, and that he would be responsible. This seemed to perturb him, but he began to make excuses until I showed him money (it was all I possessed) and explained we would pay him for the journey. He wavered but eventually agréed to leave by canoe in the morning. It would take six hours to get there. Joyfully we packed our belongings, though we were so weak from lack of food that the effort nearly killed us.

Zico had a solid dug-out canoe moored near his hut. It was full of a stinking liquid, the poison squeezed from wild manioc, a root which, when grated and dried, is used like flour, the village girls using a *tipiti* (supple basket-work press) to express the juice. Before we got in, we persuaded Zico to clean out the canoe. Then we pushed out from the bank, the overloaded canoe well down in the water.

The river was glorious in the sunlight, and our spirits rose as the paddle dipped through the water, bringing us nearer to our destination. About half-way there, the sky lowered and inky clouds spread across the trees darkening the river. All the bird and insect sounds were unusually quiet. We were in mid-stream when a sudden stormy wind spun the canoe round and round with incredible force. I held my breath, praying that Zico's muscular arms would get us to the safety of the bank. Straining his muscles he managed to reach the shore where the three of us hung frantically to low branches until the storm passed. We were drenched, as were all our belongings bar my sketch books, which I had carefully covered in plastic wrappings.

Banana leaves at Pingafogo.

'Small igarapés were shady and filled with a rich flora'.

Shivering in our wet clothes we eventually reached Pingafogo to be welcomed warmly by Antonio Carvalho, a dear old man. He led us to an airy room where we could hang our hammocks, and prepared us a meal, which was eaten wolfishly. He was, in fact, kindness itself.

Antonio Carvalho was the sage of the river. The peasants living up and down the river came to him to have their letters read or written or to hear news from the papers which he received from time to time from Viseu. His *sitio* was flourishing for he cultivated wisely. Instead of cutting and burning the forest around his hut, as others did, he cleared some of the undergrowth from under the massive forest trees and planted young fruit trees, using the leaf mould which the natural cycle continually renewed. His citrus, mango and native fruit trees and coffee bushes thrived under their forest protection. Possessing such a flourishing orchard had its drawbacks as well as advantages, for the envious neighbours, seeing his fruit-laden trees, began to worry him. Although he repeatedly told them how to plant their own he was driven to refusing to help the lazy ones. He was known best for curing sick people with the medicinal plants in which the Amazon abounds, for he had an amazing knowledge of their properties. I asked him about the Strychnos vine which Dr. Froes at Belém had asked me to look out for. Antonio knew the plant but said it grew some way from the *sitio*.

Whilst we were at Pingafogo we witnessed the recovery of Antonio's old dog whom he had cured of wounds made by lead pellets from a shotgun. When we arrived the animal was lying behind a screen in a semi-coma, but after treatment with a herbal mixture, only known to Antonio, she recovered, and the day of our departure got up, wagging her tail.

But in spite of this scientific knowledge, the sage of the Gurupi was superstitious, as were most of the *caboclos* (people of mixed Indian-Portuguese descent) and to him the 'evil eye' was very real. Among the stories which he told us was one about a young woman who had visited him and his Indian wife, Mocinha, and sat in the shade of a beautiful lemon tree. The next day, the tree was brown and withered and eventually died. The young woman came again, sat under another lemon tree, and curiously the results were the same. After that visit she was forbidden to come to the *sitio*.

Rita listened to this conversation on the 'evil eye' with some concern, for she has one blue eye and one brown, and feared it would bring her under suspicion there. Afterwards we were alert to the reaction of the *caboclos* and noticed how many would not look straight at Rita.

Besides Antonio and Mocinha, two *caboclos* — a young girl and boy — who fished, hunted and generally helped out, lived at Pingafogo. One evening they went to fish in a distant *igarapé*. As time passed we noticed how Antonio was worrying about the lateness of the hour and fretting that they had not returned. At last they appeared. As darkness fell, they had been surprised by an *onça*, and in her terror the girl looked like a spectre, while the boy's short hair literally stood on end. This made dear Antonio very nervous about me and Rita collecting in the forest alone, where we were lured further and further afield by the wonderful plants.

Peccaries, pig-like mammals, root for grubs and tubers.

Pingafogo was wonderful for collecting and I had already found the brilliant red spikes of the rare *Heliconia glauca* of the banana family, the white bells of the lily-like *Eucharis amazonica,* and the silvery leaves of a climber, *Philodendron melinonii.* My greatest find was the beautiful orchid *Gongora maculata,* with a perfume like a hundred lilies. On one occasion we had completely forgotten the passage of time when a shot rang through the forest, followed by loud shouts from Antonio. As he drew nearer we saw that he was clearly distressed and angry, fearing that some harm had befallen us. But he soon forgave us, and on the return walk took us to a settlement where the black descendants of African slaves who had escaped over a hundred years ago lived in isolation, never mixing with other races. They were handsome people and seemed very independent in spirit. Antonio told us that many such communities exist in the jungles of Pará.

The flowers of the tree Bombax spectabile. *'I was painting in the quiet of my room, when I heard a rustling behind me. For a moment I thought someone was there, then I realised that the flowers I had left on a table were opening'*

A paca, *one of the many forest rodents.*

40

Gongora maculata *(Orchidaceae).*

Margaret Mee

Gongora maculata var. bufonia
Rio Gurupí, Pará
February 1959

Downstream

A boat was due to leave for Viseu from Kamiranga, the most important village some distance up river from Pingafogo and, so we could be sure to get space, Antonio offered to take us there by canoe. We left Mocinha and the beautiful *sitio* with regret, yet eager to return to Sao Paulo, for we were long overdue at school. We bid a sad farewell to Antonio who had literally saved us from starvation and proved a wonderful friend.

The wooden passenger-cum-cargo river boat tied up at the bank in Kamiranga was crowded with *caboclos* and loaded to capacity with high inflammable *marva* (fibre similar to jute). We could scarcely find a place to hang our hammocks between the tightly wedged cargo, and when more passengers and still more cargo piled in we gave up in despair and decided to sleep on the *marva,* where we had as much leeway as rats in a hole.

Mangroves along the river bank.

Among the passengers were a couple of young *caboclos,* a boy and his wife, cigarette smoking like chimneys and with faces as yellow as golden guineas. It took no time for the boy to show us a suppurating gash below his rib-cage, inflicted by a 'friend', he said, who had been high on *maconha* (marijuana) during a quarrel. His wife had bravely rushed to his defence and had been badly cut about the face and arms. The flesh had healed, but the skin had puckered and her face was disfigured. They were both bound for a hospital in Belém. The woman threw lighted cigarette ends around, which kept us from sound sleep all night on our highly combustible *marva* mattresses. As it was we slept, packed like sardines, though I was aware of the hot soles of a man's feet in my back, heavy feet that I could not push away.

The 'comandante' of the boat was fond of the bottle, and by our third night had had more than enough to drink. In this condition he insisted, against the advice of the crew, on sailing through the night. The river was pitch black and the sky starless. Soon after midnight a horrible jarring crash followed by screaming and shouting announced we had hit a rock. The boat ground forward with the current and shudderingly landed on top of the rock with the hull tilted steeply. Rita and I, feeling like rats caught in a trap and tense with claustrophobia, struggled out of the layers of *marva,* rapidly put on our shoes, dragged out our rucksacks from the mêlée and prepared for the worst. Happily there was no 'worst', and the craft settled down, though with a considerable list. The 'comandante', sobered by shock, called for calm, promising to right the boat by daylight. So we snatched a little sleep, only waking just before dawn when we heard the men working feverishly to get the boat off the rocks. This they eventually managed to do, helped by the river which was tidal and brackish at that point.

All that day we headed through low-lying land with the sea not far away. It was a strange dream-like area of grey-green forest and black mud, where there were very few different species of trees, and all those we saw had mangrove roots through which ran little crabs who lived in the mud below. The heat was stifling, with a burning sun above and, since we were at sea level, the torrid air was not stirred by a breath of wind. During the day the crew told us the drinking water had run out but that there was a settlement somewhere across the mangrove forest at that point. At this stage the boat stopped so one of the crew could lower himself into the gluey mud and struggle to firmer land in search of supplies. Meanwhile the small boys on board climbed down and caught crabs, coming up covered from head to foot in black mud. They passed the muddy crabs, which were still alive, to an old woman with frizzy hair and a bony black face, who threw them into a pot like a witch over a cauldron. She almost forced us to eat one, telling us afterwards that she suffered permanently from dysentery, and we were thankful for the distraction when the crewman returned without having reached the imaginary settlement. We continued on our way until nightfall, when we moored by the trees to rest.

At dawn there were loud shouts of dismay from the crew. Our hull was stuck in the mud of the riverbed and was impossible to move. With long faces they told us that the tide had gone out during the night and would not be deep enough to lift the boat for at least twelve hours. 'Perhaps much longer', some of us murmured, for the tides were getting lower. The only alternative to remaining there for some days was to chain haul the boat to where the water might be deep enough to float her again. All the men and a few women, including Rita and myself, started hauling. It was back-breaking work, but after a long struggle we reached deeper water and loud cheers went up as the boat came afloat.

When we eventually arrived in Viseu, we did not have to wait long for transport to Bragança. By now we were getting used to the boats, and once more the cargo stowed aboard must have outweighed the passengers — twenty-four of the passengers were pigs, lean and hungry, which resembled *Porco do mato* more than fat, domesticated pigs. A squealing, sorry band, they were driven into the hold with shouts, blows and a waving of sticks and, as the hold was open to the deck, the pigs and their smell remained close for the whole of the voyage. Worse still were the ticks which deserted the dried-up creatures for us.

During the voyage one unfortunate pig got his hind leg trapped by a floorboard and uttered such unearthly screams that the passengers protested, and a man went down to release the suffering beast. But he was so brutal that the pig screamed in agony and sprang through a cabin window into the river, swimming swiftly for the shore. Immediately two of the crew lowered a canoe and, armed with bush knives, paddled madly in the pig's wake, but the animal swam like a fish, and when it reached the shore dashed through the dense vegetation bordering the river. The crewmen tried to hack their way through this jungle, but retired defeated, much to my delight, for I was horrified by the sight and the pig's anguished cries. The animal was lost forever. Would he be a prey for the *onça* with his lack of jungle experience? No, he would become the leader of the herd, we were told, and the most savage when attacking man. Not without justification we felt.

When we reached Belém by train, Sao Paulo and smart summer dresses were only twelve hours away, though now Amazonia was in my blood. Murutucum, that haven of green peace, seemed to be the other side of the planet but I knew I would return.

Margaret returned to work at St. Paul's, and during every spare moment she perfected her flower painting technique. Accuracy was as important to her as composition. Her sketches from the forest included botanical details and precise colour matching. This information was just what the experts at the Sao Paulo Botanic Institute needed to identify the plants she had found and they encouraged her work. The Institute arranged a small exhibition of her painting in Sao Paulo and this led, in 1958, to Margaret's first important exhibition. Held in Rio de Janeiro, the capital of Brazil at the time, seventy-six paintings were on display. In 1960, following a small exhibition of her work in the Royal Horticultural Society's Halls, London, she was awarded the Grenfell Medal for her paintings.

The Rio exhibition brought her into contact with Roberto Burle Marx, the Brazilian landscape artist whose international reputation was already firmly established. Burle Marx found common ground in Margaret's talent and adventurous spirit and he helped her on her path to success. Their friendship has lasted throughout her career.

Tillandsia paraensis
(Bromeliaceae).

JOURNEY TWO: 1962

To 'the Denser Forest'
The Mato Grosso

Margaret and Greville had been settled in Sao Paulo for almost ten years. Following her very successful exhibitions, Margaret was offered a commission to work with the Sao Paulo Botanic Institute and Dr. Lyman Smith of the Smithsonian Institution, Washington. For almost fifteen years Lyman Smith had been studying bromeliads, a fascinating plant family well represented in Brazil. The job with the Institute, which was Margaret's schooling in serious botany, took her to many parts of the country north and south of Rio. But it was demanding work and she decided she would have to leave St. Paul's.

Very quickly Margaret became an experienced backwoods traveller, and Harald Schultz, a Brazilian ethnographer and photographer, invited her to join his expedition to the Mato Grosso. This romantic name, meaning literally the 'denser mato' *(scrubland and forest), stems from the past when central Brazil was literally an unexplored natural fortress of forested tablelands. When describing their gold-seeking adventures, the first explorers of the region simply waved their hands in the direction of the* mato, *about twice the size of France, and let their imaginations run. Some of these explorers searched the* mato *for mythical lost cities and in 1925 one, the legendary Colonel Fawcett, disappeared without trace. In another incident, less than a year before Margaret's visit, a young British geographer following a well-worn track was ambushed and killed by Indians.*

Harald Schultz, who worked for the Paulista Museum in Sao Paulo and for the National Geographic Magazine, *was well versed in Amazon ways, and he and his wife Vilma were studying the Erigpactsá (or Aripaktsá) tribe for the museum. Harald was already at a camp at Aripuana in an Indian house on the Alto (upper) Juruena river, over a thousand miles from Sao Paulo, when Vilma and Margaret set out to join up with him.*

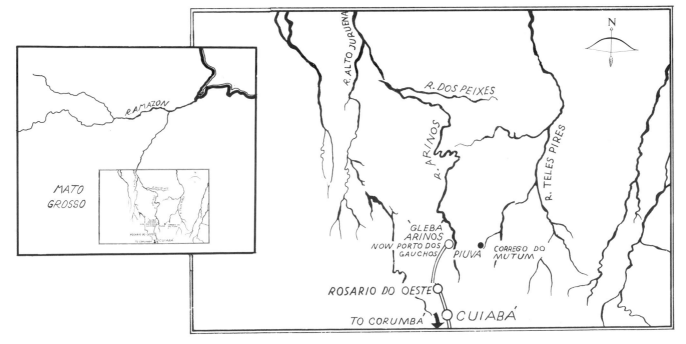

A jaguar (onça), *the largest South American carnivore.*

1st July, 1962

Vilma and I left Congonhas Airport, Sao Paulo, in a Curtis plane which had seen better days. The flight was not direct and first we headed westwards to Corumbá, a river port on the far side of Brazil. After refuelling we took off and climbed through leaden rain clouds towards our destination, Cuiabá, the capital of the state of Mato Grosso, another two hours away. Between Corumbá and Cuiabá the primeval landscape of lakes and waterways of the Pantanal stretched to the horizon; the only solid land to be seen were small hills, either isolated by the flood water or linked by necks of land. Nearing Cuiabá, the landscape changed to table-topped mountains, extensive lakes, and dense forest clothing plains and mountain slopes.

Cuiabá is a small town, the outskirts recently built and dull, but the centre is old and charming with a church dating back over two hundred years which overlooks the village square and a row of tall, graceful palms. But we had no intention of staying there, for we had to go another 350 miles north to Harald's camp. We had planned to continue our journey by flying to 'Gleba' Arinos, a new ranching centre, on a plane owned by a local firm known rather grandly as the Gleba Travel Agency.

After much running to and fro we found Gleba Travel and immediately cancelled our reservations in view of the weather which threatened storms. We had also heard that the little five-seater plane on which we were to travel had suffered forced landings and near disasters on at least eight occasions, and now it was long delayed somewhere in the interior of the Mato Grosso with no news of its whereabouts. We had to wait two days in Cuiabá until the next bus left in the direction of 'Gleba'. The 'bus' turned out to be a battered station wagon, its doors hanging loosely on bits of wire.

On Tuesday afternoon, Manoel the driver beckoned us to clamber into the wagon which was already so full of passengers that our luggage was restricted to hammocks, rugs and food for the journey. The light was low as we bumped along the half-made road out of Cuiabá towards the small, dusty town of Rosario do Oeste where we stopped to drop passengers and pick up even more. Once back on the road we entered a *cerrado* (forest of stunted, twisted trees surrounded by high grass) which closed around us. The road for what it was worth soon deteriorated into a narrow sandy track along which we bounced and swayed. By now it was dark, the track had become rougher, and we had to get out and push the vehicle out of deep sandy ruts. We grew accustomed to this work as the track progressively worsened. A cool wind was blowing. We passed no houses, no people. It was the loneliest place imaginable.

On our way, wild animals appeared from time to time, dazzled by the headlights. Two beautiful foxes, silver-grey with ears tipped with black, ran across the track, four *jaguatiricas* (ocelots) vanished into the night, and whilst helping to push the station wagon out of the sand I saw the imprints of *onça* pads. Large birds rose like spectres from the ground, gliding silently into oblivion. Two *macucos* (solitary tinamous), partridge-like birds, narrowly escaped a trigger-happy fellow passenger who, fingering his gun, hung out of the cab window.

Manoel manoeuvred skilfully over ditches, holes and crude, gaping bridges consisting of loose logs. Eventually, close to midnight, we reached the banks of the Arinos river where we pulled up at the solitary hut of some *seringueiros* (rubber tappers) who were friends of Manoel. A fire gleamed in the kitchen shining on the simple tiles in the roof, the wattled mud walls and earthen floor. It reminded me of houses I had seen on the Gurupi. I hung my hammock from the rafters and Vilma slept in rugs on the floor.

We left before dawn and by daybreak had reached a wonderful *cerrado* where I found the first bromeliad of this journey. Many areas we passed were densely covered with trees and bushes, where the trunks formed fantastic arabesques, growing almost horizontally at times amongst the flowers; then, where there was a transition to 'gallery' forest which borders streams and rivers, the trees were flowering. The purple ipé, a bignonia and golden vochysias glowed on the canopies.

Manoel did not have time to stop, for we had another rough eighty miles to cover to the outpost where he expected to spend the night. With the closing darkness our headlights transformed the forest into ghostly shapes. The jungle towered around us and I could see the trunks of silk cotton trees of enormous proportions, ribbed like gothic columns. Between them, the solid forms of miconias, trees of the Melastomataceae family, were draped with wonderful clusias, or strangler plants, which grew in profusion.

We passed the night in a grand house belonging to a *Baiana* (lady of African slave descent from Bahia on the coast). She appeared to be well known and quite a character. Her family had carved out a *fazenda* (ranch) from the forest. Vilma and I had the luxury of a room to ourselves. A sunny morning greeted us after the cold night, and from the treetops I could hear the calls of parrots and *araras* (macaws). That day we drove through virgin forest, the territory of an Indian tribe known here as the Beiço de Pau, due to the large wooden discs worn by the men in their lower lips.

> ' Their village was some hours away and Manoel tells us that we may not
> see them. Recent fires have thinned some forest beside the track and there
> in the light hung vines of a scarlet *maracujá*. '

On arrival in the small settlement of 'Gleba' Arinos we were led to the house of Willi Meyer, a cattle rancher and breeder from the south of Brazil, who had been in 'Gleba' Arinos for some years. Here we were assigned to a room with a shower, the greatest luxury after the dirt and dust of the journey. Later we dined with the family, which included a four year old Indian boy of the Erigpactsá tribe, who was being brought up by Mr. Meyer and his wife. When the wild deer venison appeared on the dining table the boy refused to eat, for it was forbidden by his tribe. Our angry host immediately ordered him to leave the table, which he did with all the dignity of a *tushaua* (chief). After the meal we were shown photos of the boy's tribe, a fine looking people. Of course, we were told stories of those who visited the tribe and never returned...

> ' Harald's camp is set in their territory, so we will soon learn whether the
> tales are true or not.
> We are waiting for our baggage to arrive by jeep with supplies for
> Harald's camp. I pass the time by venturing into the forest where today
> I collected a delicate bromeliad — by its long narrow mottled leaves it

The rubber gatherers' boat.

Araeococcus
flagellifolius.

appears to be an *Araeococcus flagellifolius.* In the midst of collecting we were startled by a heavy animal crashing through the bushes — possibly an *anta* (tapir), of which there are many in this region.

Mrs. M keeps birds: two *jacutingas* (black-fronted piping guans) related to pheasants, three *araras* and a parrot, as well as a fierce *tucano* which is cruelly isolated in a cage too small for him. My heart bleeds for the poor creature. There are two *emas* (rheas) — like small ostriches — who feed from the hand. But the birds of the forests flying free are wonderful — *japims* (oriole-like yellow-rumped caciques) flocking in bands, hundreds of the beautifully coloured *curicas* (orange-cheeked parrots), as well as other parrots and *araras.* But there is a strange lack of epiphytes clinging to other plants here. Maybe they were sprayed with D.D.T. used on these farms. '

In the afternoon we went down to the 'port'. Such a name for a few logs by the river bank from which we could step into the boat. The Arinos river, a tributary of the Juruena, flows strongly and is about as wide as the Thames at Marlow. It was hard to imagine we were over 1,500 miles from Belém. Our small wooden boat, the *Santa Rosa* was simply the roughest I had travelled on, but our pilot Candido, a Munduruku Indian and very handsome, was courteous and helped me with my baggage. At night we slept aboard, the boat moored beside the hut of two rough *seringueiros,* and a miserable hut it was. Soon after dawn we moved on up the river which grew more and more beautiful, broken up by rocky islands with white sandy beaches; scrubby forest crowns them. All along this part of the river are groups of stones of huge dimensions on whose submerged surfaces grow rose-pink aquatic plants — podostemons, with only their flowers on the surface. Two cormorants dived smartly into the river at the sight of the boat, their black heads with yellow beaks appearing just above the water.

The country was flat and forested as far as I could see with small hills occasionally rising behind the forests where beautiful *assaí* and dark-leaved *buriti* palms are numerous. Without warning the river widened, flowing swiftly around islets and groups of rocks and leaving only a narrow navigable channel. Locally this dangerous spot is known as Cinco Bocas (five mouths). Suddenly the tow rope broke and two of the five canoes we were towing tilted away between the savage rocks and began to fill with water, threatening the precious supplies we had loaded for rubber gatherers downstream. Candido leapt into the water, scrambled across a bare rock on which there was absolutely no toehold, gathered the rope from the rushing water and secured the craft. All in a day's work for a Munduruku. The day over, we moored outside the very smelly hut of a *seringueiro* near the mouth of the Rio dos Peixes (River of Fish), aptly named as the men had caught two enormous fish, a *bacud* (catfish with long

A common opossum
(gamba).

whisker-like barbels) and weighing over forty pounds, and a *pirarucu* (arapaima) almost the size of the fishermen, who told me they could be even larger and weigh up to two hundred pounds.

We departed early the next morning before the mists had lifted from the river and a short way downstream moored to a giant fallen tree whilst the men prepared to pass another great rapid. The *pium* (tiny, very irritating biting simulid fly), which leaves swellings which turn black, were more numerous there and I had to wear a netting veil, but I braved the hordes to swim and wash away the day's sweat in the cool, refreshing river.

The river was getting broader and soon another larger river came in through the forest on the left. This was the Alto Juruena. Ipé trees, their slender white trunks bearing branches and branches filled with panicles of yellow flowers, lined the banks all the way to Seringal, a small settlement with a trading connection with 'Gleba' Arinos. There I met Geraldo, 'chief' of the *seringueiros,* who was supervising the loading of the rubber gatherers' boat on its way upriver. He explained how the boat came by several times every year to collect the large balls of natural rubber made by the *seringueiros* from the latex of the rubber tree.

Our next stop downstream was Altimira, a small rather rough village built by settlers. Soon afterwards we stopped again at a lonely hut on the margin of the river. The crew laughingly told me that it was known as the 'house of the beautiful wife'. Poor woman, she was anything but beautiful, but very happy to have visitors. She stood in the dark doorway of her ramshackle hut, a strange figure, her dusky face looking from beneath a once white headcover, her tatty long dress hanging sloppily over her trousers. She smiled happily, showing large gaps between her teeth. Perhaps she had once been attractive and the hard life in a primitive hut had destroyed her looks.

We continued easily with the current, passing one of the biggest and most difficult rapids at sundown. We rushed through without any difficulty. The river here is magnificent, tremendously wide with scattered islands and groups of smooth stones, white above the waterline and black below. At nightfall we arrived at the hut of an unusual *seringueiro,* Jeronomus, known to everybody as the 'Baiano'. He seems to be a rare type, for he says that he does not smoke... or drink... or hunt... or fish, and lives in a very clean well-ordered hut. He is a dark mulatto of about forty years. He gave us pints of condensed milk to drink and we supped there too. On my return the 'Baiano' promised he would have many *parasitas* (epiphyte plants) for me to sketch.

Tillandsia paraensis
(Bromeliaceae).

'Today has proved quite eventful. We called at four or five huts down the river where the *seringueiro,* who were out working, had left notes of the supplies they needed, so I did my collecting whilst the rice and *farinha* (dried manioc flour) were being weighed. Soon after midday the first Indian village on the river came into view, a village of accultured Indians, where we were invited to a meal. The children are most curious about my black veil which I am wearing against the relentless *pium.* '

Margaret and Wilma were heading downriver into the forest home of the Erigpactsá tribe where Harald had made friends with the family of Radiokubi.

We were still at the village when the sound of an outboard motor broke the silence and a large aluminium canoe came in sight from downstream. It was Harald's canoe piloted by an Urubú Indian nicknamed Pará. Candido and his boys helped to transfer all our luggage to the aluminium boat, and after thanking him for the safe journey we sped off in the direction of the camp a short distance away at Aripuana, the Indian clearing, the base from which Harald and Vilma were studying the Erigpactsá.

Harald had set up his hammock in one of the Indian *malocas* in which the roof and walls were of palm leaves carefully woven together. There was no obvious door and the only way in was by pushing the palm leaves aside; although this made the interior very dark it had its advantages for *pium* do not like the dark.

While Harald and Vilma settled themselves I was put in the care of the camp manager, a younger, tall blonde man, Roberto Neuman, from south Brazil. Roberto had established a base in a forest clearing some distance from the Indian houses and Harald suggested I should hang my hammock there under the open sky. As there was no rain during July and August this was no problem, although I could expect heavy dews. Roberto's boy helper, José, slung his hammock next to mine, while a porcupine lived in the tree's canopy overhead. Roberto and Pará hung their hammocks together some distance away, which was fortunate, for every night Pará, who had become addicted to *cachaça* (raw sugar cane spirit), was violently sick in the bushes. When the *cachaça* gave out he drank the pure alcohol we used for cleaning.

Lying in my hammock I slept little and lay listening to the strange forest sounds and looking into the trees above, wondering and thinking. Nearly all the Indian men, I was told, had left the *maloca* in quest of a special bamboo for arrows they needed to make war on a neighbouring tribe. The Erigpactsá were fine looking people and, as everyone on the river seemed to know, had eaten some of the *seringueiros* who had ill treated their womenfolk. The killing and ritual feasting had happened only a year or two before. The men wore only a small tuft of *buruti* palm fibres hanging from their waist cord in an appropriate place. They all wore numbers of heavy necklaces, monkey skin bracelets, and some wore large discs in their ear lobes. The women were beautiful, petite and, apart from their masses of necklaces, were completely naked.

The *pium* was a plague in Aripuana and made painting difficult. I tried working with a veil, but it distorted the drawing and finally I had to wrap my hands in plastic to ward off their attacks. To get some respite from the insects and the heat I decided to visit the big *maloca* which housed twenty-five people, for inside it was dark at night. The 'front garden' was decorated with a row of skulls on sticks, skulls of various animals of different shapes and sizes, which gave a rather grim impression in the shade of the dark forest. I went into the *maloca* and was led to a seat on the ash-covered floor beside the hammock of a young woman peeling yams the colour of amethyst in a ray of light. Silence reigned. She brought me sweet potatoes and *castanhas* (brazil nuts), talking softly in her own language. Later she came into the forest accompanied by another woman and two men, to be photographed by Harald, all of them with ornaments and beautifully groomed hair.

Apart from his interest in ethnology, Harald was an ardent collector of ornamental fish. One afternoon two of the Indians took us by canoe to an *igarapé* which yielded some new species, avidly collected by Harald and Vilma in plastic bags. Harald showed me a pool, left by the river's high season overflow, which was drying out and on which strange fish lay eggs in the mud after 'walking' on their fins for some considerable distance. He told me that the fish die when the mud rises but the eggs hatch when the rains return.

We were so engrossed with the fish that none of us noticed the Indians had gone and we realised that we could not find our way back to the canoe. Harald at once

A passion flower.

'Seringueiros *(rubber gatherers)* wore white cotton hoods as protection against the relentless biting pium *(simulid fly).*'

become alarmed and angry, and his words rang out: 'Here we are in the Alto Juruena with dangerous animals all round!' It was then that I noticed how the light in the forest was beginning to fail. Harald curtly ordered us to wade through another *igarapé* which he knew would eventually flow into the Alto Juruena, but Vilma refused on the grounds that it would spoil her only boots. I had no such excuse and plunged into the water which at times was well above my knees. Then I suddenly hit a submerged hummock and stumbled. Harald, carrying his plastic bags, also tripped on a hummock and fell flat on his face with a tremendous splash (he was tall and heavy), while the fish returned joyfully to their native habitat. The burst of language was colourful and unrestrained as Harald emerged covered with black mud. Drenched to the skin, we wandered through the forest calling loudly to the Indians. It was already dark when the distant voice of Pará responded, and with great relief we emerged from the forest just as the sun disappeared over the river.

The Indians

'The rubber gatherers' boat did not arrive today and my letters are still in the tree waiting collection. Yet another day has gone, a day of triumph for the *pium*. But in spite of them I have finished my painting. First I attempted to paint in a net and gloves, but the mesh is too open and the *pium* frisk in and out giving me playful bites without respite... My left eye has suffered and is badly swollen.'

The next day I left the camp early in the morning to escape the heat of the day, and returned before noon. I sat awhile in the boat near the bank watching the wonderful fish in the crystal clear water as they darted among the smooth rocks. This particular spot is the haunt of the *sucuriju* (anaconda), a huge snake about which I had heard

A giant otter (ariranha) — such animals can be almost six feet long.

many a tale some nights ago. The Indians say they have seen one here which was over twenty feet long. They also told stories about their 'king of the forest', the *onça*. Geraldo called at the camp that night with the disturbing news of an intended Indian attack on the *Posto Indigena*, the local official centre for Indian affairs. According to Geraldo it would seem that the unpopular German pastor there was largely responsible for the situation, having absurdly insisted that the Indians should work an eight hour day in his mission. Geraldo talked until dawn.

'Last night was somewhat disturbed. First a coati rushed screaming through the camp. Then there were strange noises in the river — plop! plop! and Roberto, investigating by the light of his torch, saw a *maracaja* (small wild cat), and then a ten foot long *jacaré* (caiman) hunting fish in the river. The large porcupine started exploring the canopies of the trees above us, and finally, as Harald and Vilma left the camp to go to the *maloca*, they heard a *jaguatirica* nearby.

But this afternoon we were in a state of real tension when two *seringueiros* met Roberto and Pará fishing up river, and told them that the Indians were attacking the *Posto Indigena* and that all the *seringueiros* were fleeing from the area. Of course, it may be just a rumour. Then one *seringueiro*, Paraíba 'Doido' (Crazy Paraíba), accompanied by another tapper, landed by the canoe and gave his version of the story — not that one can give credence to him. He is sick and came to have an injection which H. is giving him now. According to him the attack of the Beiço de Pau on the Araras, another tribe, is an annual affair, and they do not leave their territory. However, after his departure H. inspected his guns and ammunition and we were warned not to go into the forest alone. Does this mean goodbye to my plant hunting? Let us see.

As time passes I am beginning to feel I have made some friends with the Indians whose simple life seems enviable. The Indians visited the camp today and I talked with a pretty little woman carrying a large-stomached baby. She is loaded with necklaces and has about eight bracelets on each arm. Apart from this she wears nothing else but a palm fibre sling to carry the child — oh, and a small necklace with four *onça* teeth. She was accompanied by Tapiama, who has been watching me sketch, and his son Menmeme. It is said that Tapiama is a 'killer' and a good hunter and today he went hunting in the forest with Pará. It nearly killed Pará as Tapiama ran all the way. They had hoped to bring back *Porco do mato*

A galeandra orchid.

52

Top: *Stalking fish on the Alto Juruena.* Above: *An Indian mother and her child resting in a hammock made from fibres from the forest.* Right: *The Indian women are 'loaded with necklaces . . . with about eight bracelets on each arm.' Courtesy ©National Geographic Society. Harald Schultz took these photographs for* National Geographic Magazine *at the time of Margaret's visit to the Alto Juruena.*

Left: *Radiokubi's wife was carried in her hammock to a canoe.* Right: *Collecting plants.*

(peccary), but only succeeded in killing a poor little chestnut-bellied *jacu* (guan). I could not eat any. But later they went fishing and came back not only with fish, but also with two small monkeys, one only a baby. I took one look at them and saw with horror the baby had had its head blown off, and the eyes of the dead mother looked reproachfully from her agonised face. They tried to trick me into eating some of the corpse, but failed. '

I had a happier encounter with other animals. I awoke early one morning to hear what sounded like the barking of a dog. I jumped out of my hammock and ran down to the river from where the sound came, just in time to see six powerful *ariranhas* (giant otters) plunge into the water and swim away to a sandy island where they stopped to sun and play. There were four adults with two young. From the island they swam across to another shore which is only just visible as the river is so wide here. These beautiful animals are becoming scarce as they are hunted for their skins. That same morning we walked from a narrow, secluded *igarapé* into the middle of the forest. There, well hidden amongst the trees, was the *maloca* of *tushaua* Barari who was travelling. His brother, with the extraordinary name Radiokubi, was also living there with his wife. Her foot was painfully swollen and the leg half paralysed but she seemed unconcerned. She was very pretty, though dirty and thin. It appeared a tree or branch fell on her and injured her leg when she was walking from her forest 'garden' with her little son.

Radiokubi was quite handsome and lively. Harald somehow persuaded him to bring the woman and child to the camp so that his wife's foot could be treated. She was carried in her hammock to the canoe, and we all eventually reached the camp where a horde of people, mainly children, were waiting for remedies, mainly for dysentery and malaria. Harald was concerned about giving medicines in case the people did not get better — or worse, for if they should die they would suspect us of witchcraft. Their reaction could be to kill us, he said.

After the 'surgery' Radiokubi stayed to talk and that evening he told us, mostly in

One of the Indians making fire in the traditional way, with a wood spindle and tinder.

Radiokubi and his son.

'*A pretty little woman carrying a large-stomached baby.*'

sign language, of the many deaths amongst tribes caused by white men's diseases and even poison. The story I heard from Radiokubi confirmed rumours I had heard of the way the ranchers take Indian land by giving the tribe gifts of sugar and rice poisoned with arsenic. Radiokubi spoke dramatically of the revenge his people had taken on some *seringueiros* who had introduced illness by poisoning: quite gruesome details of the cutting off of heads and limbs, and of eating eyes, cheeks and tongues. His tribe had five human heads in the *maloca*. The teeth were made into necklaces.

That night the first signs of trouble came when the night monkeys in the silk cotton tree started to scream, their signal that some big cat was lurking nearby. It was not long before I heard growling near the head of my hammock; I lay cold with fear. It seemed as though the animal had passed underneath me. I heard Radiokubi calling frantically to Roberto that there was an *onça* around, then a shot from Roberto's rifle, and a loud crashing through the undergrowth as the beast fled into the forest.

Later I heard what had happened. An *onça* had attempted to seize a child of some Indian visitors camping in the open nearby and the father had thrown burning logs at the animal, but to no effect. The creature merely retreated a little further into the shadows, waiting for an opportunity to return. In desperation, Radiokubi, unarmed, called Roberto who reacted quickly with the rifle. I was restless for the remainder of the night, listening with one ear to the noise of the men building up the fires, and the other cocked to the myriad sounds of the forest.

With the dawn, Pará returned from a hunt. He had been far away in the jungle for three days and nights, and had shot two *antas*, though at some cost. His back was covered with blood-engorged *carrapatos* as large as my thumbnail. Vilma and I had the greatest difficulty in removing them, and after trying spirits, lighted cigarettes, etc., we had to do it manually. The Indian men went off to fetch the poor *antas* by canoe. I only saw them when they had been cut into pieces. Tapiama left carrying an enormous bloody leg.

'Roberto tells me that two thousand *antas* have been killed in 'Gleba' and even here at Aripuana the numbers must be high. I wonder how long it will be before these beasts are extinct?

José, an Indian boy of seven years, has replaced the other José as

Night monkey.

Roberto's helper. He is a lovely boy, extremely quick and intelligent. He comes from a tribe of accultured Indians in one of the villages at which we stopped on the Alto Juruena river. He climbs with the ease and confidence of a marmoset, and consequently I now have some lovely plants, including a perfect bromeliad — *Aechmea sprucei.*'

The Indian guests and Radiokubi and his family had built themselves a small hut of fresh green palm leaves. Radiokubi made himself a fire on which he roasted *anta,* having received his share from Pará, as is customary between Indians. They were story telling and talking about Paraíba 'Doido' who, after a drunken brawl, had recently murdered his *seringueiro* companion with an axe whilst he was sleeping in his hammock.

Aechmea tocantina.

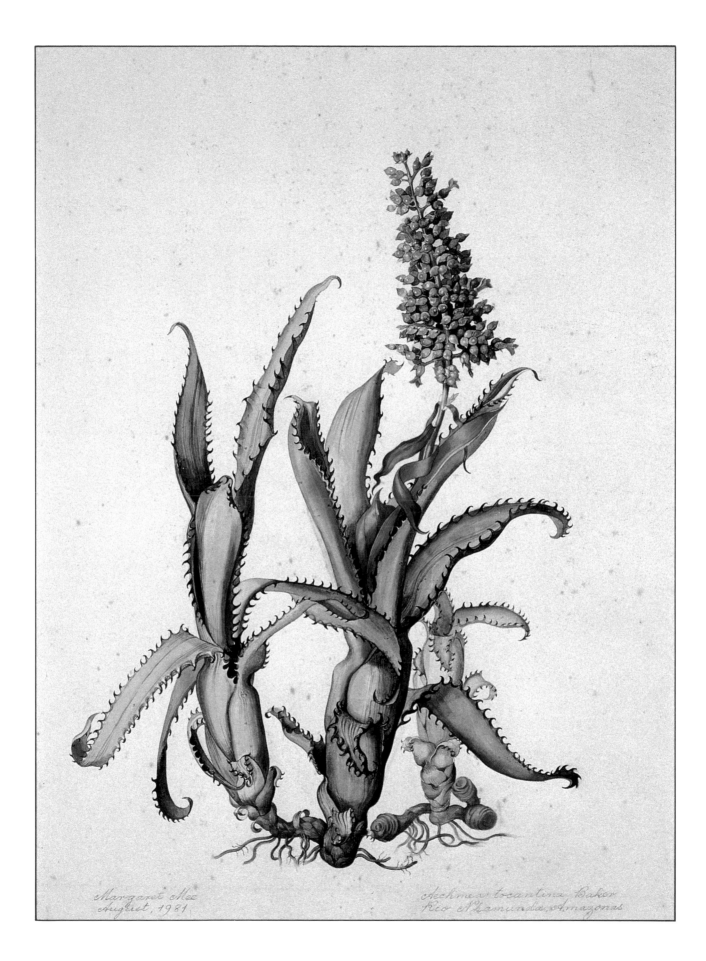

Margaret Mee
August, 1981

Aechmea tocantina Baker
Rio Nhamundá, Amazonas

The next day began with more bad news. Harald had an attack of malaria. But in spite of this he still had enough strength to fly into a rage when he heard we had been into the forests collecting plants without leaving a message. And to make matters worse, that night a gang of men from the *seringal* (rubber tree forests) of Bacarao, several days away upriver, arrived for medicines and stayed until next morning. They made sleep difficult, for they had their radio playing at full blast until I asked for less noise as Harald was unwell. My head was raging too and I could only hope that it was not a symptom of malaria. But that was just the beginning of my troubles. Soon we had two more invalids, Roberto who had pains and sickness, and Paraíba 'Doido' who fell ill as a result of drinking a litre of kerosene!

Another night and everyone seemed to have fever. *Tushaua* Barari and his wife Talaao and child Tcherite arrived out of the forest and came to our camp. Vilma spent some time with them learning their vocabulary as they pointed to different things. Harald was not around and Vilma said she was worried that he could have kidney trouble. By the next day he was worse and Vilma decided she and Harald must leave. The men loaded the aluminium canoe and helped Harald, his face like greenish parchment, down the bank to the river. He could scarcely stagger between two men and was laid flat in the boat. As he was so tall and bulky there was only room beside him for Vilma and Pará to work the motor. There was no space for me or the sacks of plants I had collected. I bade them farewell but as I turned away back to our camp I could not restrain my tears. The Indians, who had been watching our leave-taking closely, came to me and gently stroked my hair in sympathy. I felt I had friends. They rehung my hammock between the trees and sat down around me. As I pondered my next move I realised I still had a canoe and a paddle, though against the rapids and current 'Gleba' Arinos was days if not weeks away. As Roberto was also still unwell, for the first time I was alone and cut off from the world.

Our food supplies had been getting low before Harald and Vilma left, and gallantly, considering he was so ill, Roberto went fishing with José, but they returned empty handed. That night they tried again as food was getting very scarce. To make matters worse, a *gamba* (common opossum) raided our supplies and Roberto shot it. Poor creature! It looked so harmless and pretty in death.

> ' I have been left a rifle but the ammunition is in a place unknown to me. There is silence and darkness around so I am building up a good fire to drive away the shadows, as I feel very nervous and strained by the loneliness. I have been calling Roberto but he is out of earshot. At last they have returned and Roberto is covered with terrible red weals. It looks like urticaria.
>
> Directly the lights dimmed the night monkeys were around us, quarrelling fiercely, and a loud-voiced *coruja* (screech owl) sat in a tree above us, calling incessantly. Roberto, already in a nervous state with his stings, jumped from his hammock, swearing and cursing the owl, took his gun and shot the poor creature. The noise awakened the Indians who came out to see what the trouble was. I was furious with Roberto and near to tears at this savagery. To placate me (so he imagined) he asked the Indians to make a collar of the feathers for me. Strange, that I, who hate all this killing, should be the recipient of the spoils. But I dare not refuse the collar for that would give great offence to the Indians. '

One day a horde of *caboclos* descended on the camp and cleared off the remains of our food like a swarm of locusts, then formed groups around, killing time. There was no point in objecting — for they were a rough, poor crowd of settlers with nothing. There were lots of small children who tore up all the paper they could find. The camp looked like the day after Carnival in Sao Paulo. As Roberto had left with two *caboclos,* paddling over to an island to fetch a canoe, and would not return before nightfall, I supposed that I had to suffer these hordes until then — in fact the crowd stayed all night. I could not sleep for there was shouting, crying of babies, coming and going and eating all night long. Then during a moment of dozing oblivion, a *gamba* crunching loudly in a tree awakened me. It occurred to me that he was devouring the last of our fish, and I jumped out of my hammock and, torch in hand, ran to the trees from whence the sound came. I flashed the light on him, hoping to scare him, but he ignored my efforts and, bold as brass, crunched all the louder. The last remnants of our fish littered the ground.

> ' Roberto definitely has malaria. He returned in bad shape from fetching the canoe, but perhaps he is exaggerating his ills to get out of routine work. Anyway, he is a bad invalid, and I pray for the arrival of the rubber gatherers' launch to get me out of here. I am marooned in the camp, and unable to do my work, collect or paint. Fed up. Hopeless and abandoned.
>
> José developed malaria today, and is lying in his hammock with high fever. The fever I had seems to have gone. Maybe I'm lucky. I keep taking my tablets. It seems that the island is the source of the trouble, for it was after a journey there that Roberto developed it. And we have hardly any remedies left. I walked over to the *maloca* this afternoon, only to find that Tapiama has malaria too: not so very serious, as I suppose he has a certain immunity being an Indian of the region.
>
> Inside the *maloca* it was dark and peaceful. I sat on the floor with the beautiful Indian girl, Sheba, and her baby, eating sweet potatoes which Sheba was peeling. She put them in a *pilao* (wooden mortar) and mashed them, then she put them into a pot with water and added fish tripe. The soup should be sustaining, though I prefer the wild honey which Tapiama got from a tree last night — it is delicious. '

As a sequel to the urticaria which Roberto was suffering, was the cure effected by Radiokubi, who had knowledge of herbal remedies. He came from the forest with rolled leaves under his arm — I could not identify them — which he then roasted over the fire until the sap flowed. This he dabbed on the affected parts of Roberto's skin. In a short time the weals had all disappeared. But Roberto succumbed to malaria and fell into his hammock where he spent most of the day in pain and delirium. I felt desperate, and asked Radiokubi and José to paddle upstream for help, perhaps even to José's parents.

Another night and without my various preoccupations I could have enjoyed the marvellous stillness. The wide river was before me backed by a star-filled sky, with only the strangely melodious cries of nocturnal birds and the droning of insects to break the silence. Along the river bank hundreds of little phosphorescent eyes looked at me. I thought that one pair might be those of the coral shark. I saw him close one day — three feet long, black white, black red, yellow bands — sliding along the river bed. Then I decided to sleep, put on my pyjamas, got into my hammock with my revolver at my side.

I had just settled my mosquito net when I heard a splashing of paddles as José and Radiokubi returned with Raimundo, a trusty *seringueiro.* Raimundo took things in hand immediately, and by the fitful light of a kerosene burner and the help of my torch to see the syringe, he gave Roberto two injections. He also made an offer to move us, lock, stock and barrel, to his hut, and I would have gratefully accepted, but Roberto

A necklace of seeds from a forest tree, one of the many of the Leguminosae family.

Aechmea fernandae.

was insistent on keeping the camp near the *maloca*. Anyway, he argued, we had to keep the Indians here in case Harald returned. But I had a strong suspicion that the Indians were already preparing to go away to another *maloca*; in any case they were fed up with the mosquitoes and the lack of fresh food. All they have been getting is rice, *farinha*, a few fish and some nuts given them by Tapiama's family.

By morning I was proved correct, for José came to me and said that the Indians were leaving. Then I spoke with *tushaua* Barari who confirmed this story, explaining that the *pium* were insupportable here. In his region there were none. He was going back to plant maize, sweet potato and bananas and to live well, he said. Of course I agreed, as it was the only reasonable thing to do. He said that he would wait until the rubber launch arrived. Tapiama's *maloca* was not affected by malaria and the families would stay.

Raimundo was a fine character, kind-hearted and truly concerned about our difficult situation, and he spoke from experience, warning that without help we could die. Apparently he once had malaria and was alone for eight days without food before another *seringueiro* found him and took him to 'Gleba'.

At noon Raimundo came and gave Roberto another injection. The more I saw of this *seringueiro*, the more I admired him for his for his calm stoicism and courtesy. In appearance he reminded me of a renaissance sculpture of John the Baptist. He renewed his offer to take us upstream to his house.

That night and early next day things reached a climax. Roberto cracked up both in health and spirit — a total collapse. The fever raged and he vomited, cried for home and sent me running to get water and a hundred things. I was desperate and vowed that at the first opportunity we would accept Raimundo's hospitality. And the moment soon arrived when he and another *seringueiro* and his companion turned up. They were so kind that I forgave their frequent spitting on the floor and the way they left the camp littered with dirty cups and plates. Must I confess that I cried for the first time more with relief than with tension? Raimundo and his friends had to leave next day and insisted we should not remain.

I agreed but Roberto was adamant that we stay. I then took charge, firmly saying that come what may we were going to Raimundo's hut even if I had to paddle there myself. Raimundo had to leave early and I promised to follow with Roberto and José in our canoe. Roberto's fever had lessened slightly but his complaining rent the air. Radiokubi was off

Catasetum fimbriatum.

Margaret Mee

Catasetum fimbriatum
Morren Lindl.

in the forest hunting monkeys and the other Indians were totally absorbed in a ceremony in the clearing outside the *maloca* — I never discovered what it was about, preoccupied as I was with Roberto's illness and the problem of moving. Roberto refused to leave, and I did not have the strength to paddle him. So I decided to leave without him and to rely on help from José.

Just after midday we set out in our heavily overloaded small canoe — 'one and a half paddles!' — me at the back with stronger arms and young José, who knew the river, at the front. Aripuana had not been a happy experience though I was sad to leave Radiokubi and Tapiama. I wore my leather collecting gloves and we paddled hard against the current for four hours or more, stopping only once at Paraíba 'Doido's' hut. There we accepted a coffee with some misgivings in view of his reputation for violence. But despite everything I had heard, he was kind and offered us a better canoe, ours being so unbalanced that a sneeze would have tipped it over. Had there been no urgency, the journey would have been a pleasure, for the woods, plants and birds were enchanting. We passed groups of perfectly smooth stones enclosing lakes and forested islands. Several times we edged through rapids by keeping to the wider, slower channels, and twice José got confused and we struck rock. But somehow we were lucky and managed to keep an even keel. Then suddenly the child, completely exhausted, began to cry, declaring that he would go no further.

The river was as broad as a moving lake and darkness would soon overtake us. Inevitably we would be lost, so I tried to cheer José, my one hope, telling him to take courage. He responded with spirit and, repeating 'courage, courage', paddled with all his might. The sun was touching the forest when we sighted Raimundo's distant hut at the tip of a long, narrow island dividing the river into two arms. Rapids seethed towards us on both sides. It was with supreme courage and concentration that the little Indian boy followed the channel, which his father had once shown him, through the turbulent waters. For what seemed an age we paddled furiously, urging the canoe forward until finally we reached calm water. We fell exhausted on the white sandy beach just as the sun went down behind the forests. Raimundo had seen our progress and come down river to meet us, expressing amazement at our feat. He got into our canoe and paddled, towing his canoe by a short rope.

Night had already closed around us when we started our journey towards Raimundo's hut. There was half a moon and a star-filled sky, a heavenly night. Only strange bird cries and the beating of our paddles broke the silence, We had covered half the distance when we struck a rock and water came rushing into the canoe. I baled until my arms ached, but to no avail. Then Raimundo, José and I all baled together, and though we managed to clear some of the water it was very late and Raimundo suggested we should stop and camp. We were on the point of sinking by the time we reached the bank. Raimundo hung his hammock for the night, and I went off and had a bath by moonlight.

Early next morning we loaded two canoes with my plants and other baggage, leaving some heavy cases belonging to Harald hidden in an abandoned hut. Then, after an exhausting journey in the heat of the morning sun, we reached Raimundo's hut. On the way I was thrilled to see an *onça* sunning herself on one of the islets.

'The hut is typical of this region, lightly built and covered with *babaçu* palm leaves. It is spotlessly clean, and the pans hanging in the kitchen shine like silver. But there are some *caboclo* guests, and not very welcome, I feel, who litter the place — two men and two women with three children. They engage in orgies of eating *tracaja* (river turtle) and the sight and smell are quite revolting. They simply eat and eat.

I have told Raimundo that I prefer to sleep in the open, as I feel too crowded with the women and children inside the hut. So again I am under the trees. And my plants have been well looked after, for Raimundo made a rack down in the forest, where I hope they will be safe from the attacks of the *saúva* (leaf-cutting ants) which are a menace here. Every time I go to visit the plants an enormous lizard bounds across the path. '

The next day, Raimundo took me downriver again, and I found Roberto, sicker than ever. We loaded the camp goods and once more set out for Raimundo's hut where we waited for the arrival of the rubber gatherers' boat which would take us up to 'Gleba' Arinos. Harald's equipment was collected by Raimundo and two men and packed under Raimundo's careful eye. Later the same day the sound of a distant outboard motor gave rise to much speculation as to who could be coming. At last a river boat, piloted by Candido, the handsome Munduruku Indian, came into view. Our greetings were enthusiastic; better still was the arrival of the rubber collectors' launch which tied up at the crude array of logs and mud which served as a 'port' outside Raimundo's hut.

A crowd gathered, taking packages on and off the boat. There was a much delayed letter from Greville and some cartons of malaria medicine. Voices in English greeted me for the first time in two months. There were two students studying Indian languages, a Swiss, and Geraldo with the crew of the rubber boat. The students set up camp and the night became a party. A tall *seringueiro,* Joto from Ceará in the north east of Brazil, came to visit us and spun unbelievable stories of the forests. Others appeared from the river, including Paraíba 'Doido', and we had quite a feast which I helped to prepare.

The next day the crowd left with the rubber boat for the *Posto Indigena*, to return in a day or two before going to 'Gleba'. So, in the meantime, I went collecting by canoe with Raimundo. It was gloriously peaceful paddling along the river to a rocky little island where I found some remarkable catasetums, or orchids, with huge seed pods. Beside them some wasps had made tiny nests of a substance like paper mâché, each a beautiful little pot with a lid which opened neatly. On the bank as we returned I collected a delicate yellow orchid, absolutely wonderful, an *Oncidium cebolleta*, worth all the days of uncertainty.

I went down to the rack in the forest to prepare my plants for the journey to 'Gleba'. But I did not get very far before I saw an *onça's* tail waving from behind some bushes. Remembering Raimundo's warnings not to run away in panic, for the *onça* is a big cat and likes to play, I walked at a smart pace, looking behind me from time to time, until I felt the distance between us was enough. Then I took to my heels and ran like the wind. Raimundo came out, rifle in hand, but fortunately the beast had moved away and was safely hidden in the forest.

' There are rumours that Harald is returning soon. He will get a shock to find his camp dismantled, the Indians and his henchmen gone. Apparently he has not been suffering from malaria for some time. News came today that the rubber launch is returning on its way to 'Gleba'. The news arrived with the German pastor, who had left the Indian Post down river and about whom we had heard so many rumours at the time of the Indian attacks. The pastor was at the helm of his river boat, and aboard were the two linguists. They stopped here to prepare a wild boar which they had shot and to give Raimundo a portion as is the custom. The pastor is a dour, humourless German, who speaks a very poor Portuguese. The boat left with a list to portside and nearly took away two trees from the river bank. '

Rapids on the River Alto Juruena.

Before my departure Raimundo took me for a last collecting trip on which I found some *Tillandsia paraensis,* a tiny bromeliad with cyclamen coloured flowers. And not far away I collected some catasetum bulbs. We heard the rubber collectors' launch as it neared the house and returned. The plants were all ready to embark, and just as well, for Geraldo was in a hurry and did not stay long.

Out of the Juruena

I left Raimundo with many regrets. He had been so kind and generous, his hut had been so pleasant and peaceful, and the collecting trips with him so rewarding. There had been wonderful moonlit nights when Joto, the Cearense, had joined us, and we had talked far into the night under the trees. I had been able to bathe in the River

Cycnoches haagii
*(Orchidaceae) (courtesy
The Tryon Gallery).*

Alto Juruena by moonlight after the heat of the day. Now there was a difficult journey before me.

We passed two *seringals* and were approaching Joto's house when we saw the pastor's launch moored. The motor's crank had broken, so his complete crew with baggage boarded our already overladen boat. When we came to the most dangerous of the rapids we had to land five of the men to lighten the load. A great barrier of rocks and foaming water confronted us and how Candido found the channel I do not know. At times the current was so strong that we were stationary. In spite of the tension I noted a pink aquatic flower — the podostemon, growing from rocks beneath the powerful water.

Once in calmer river above the rapids, we turned to the bank to pick up the men who had to wade out waist high to embark. After the excitement it was relaxing just to watch the forest slip by; all the way along it was lit up with the golden flowers of ipés in full bloom, and silk cotton trees sprouting new leaves from recently bare branches. It must be spring here.

Seriema.

65

Before nightfall we moored off a small island and hung our hammocks in the trees. The isle was one enormous rock, full of inland pools and forested on two sides. The men loaded their guns before retiring to their hammocks, assuring me that this was a haunt of the *onça*. After supping by the light of a big fire and full moon I had a dip in the cool waters. The night thrilled with bird cries and the humming of a myriad of insects.

> ‘These river islands are paradise, I have seen scores of herons in small bushes almost submerged by water, minute purple and yellow flowers on the exposed sand, shrubs full of berries and lichens amongst which grow orchids and tillandsias, delicately leaved bromeliads. And I have found the aggressively-armed with black thorns *Aechmea tocantina,* another bromeliad. Tiny bats are about and the river current is rushing past a loose branch and slapping it gently up and down. It is a marvellous and peaceful night. ’

At Baracao I did a ridiculous thing. Stepping into the boat from a canoe (the waters are too shallow to coast there) and the canoe not being secured, I fell backwards, knocked the back of my head and was totally immersed. My first thought was for the camera and sketch books. One of the linguists rescued them, whilst Candido hauled me up, a groaning, dripping mess until I could stagger into a hut to change. My head ached the next day and I had a large lump on the back of it.

> ‘There is no room to move on the boat, as today a woman with three small children embarked. The woman, wearing the headscarf of a *seringueiro,* delicately pushes my foot aside when she needs to spit into the river. ’

The morning sun shone on an imposing barrier of rock across the wide expanse of river, the Cachóeira dos Indios. There we proceeded to unload the cargo as the water is shallow and the current furious. Fortunately it was only a short distance on foot through the forest and over the rocks to reach calmer water. From the shore we watched the lightened boat struggling to cross the rapids, but three times she failed. So the men discharged the remaining cargo of raw rubber and shifted some heavy petrol cans forward. At last the boat made the passage into calmer waters, but this was shortlived and a few hours later our pilot was struggling again, and again everyone had to disembark and wade from the foaming river to the land.

There was no end to our adventures that day, for soon after passing the mouth of the Rio dos Peixes, and entering the Arinos, we struck rock with tremendous force. The crash tilted the craft to the left. Then, as Candido tried to right the boat, the other side hit the water so fiercely that I was drenched. Cargo shot off the roof of the boat into the river. I saw with dismay my precious plant tins and sacks careering downstream with assorted boxes and a big petrol drum following. A rescue team dived after them like a pack of *lontras* (otters) fishing out the cargo. Once they had recovered all the floating objects the divers got busy salvaging torches, tin mugs and plates from the depths. It took some expert manoeuvring on Candido's part to reach the groups of men on the rocks securing the cargo. I hardly dared look at my plants, though the tins had floated beautifully. I think most of the food went down, including my last precious packets of soup.

The next day proved eventful too. We saw seven *antas* on our way up the Arinos, two of them young, lovely creatures. The men shot at them, but missed every time, happily. So they decided to disembark and hunt the next *anta* they saw. Soon a large animal came in sight, bathing in the river. The men took their guns, and one of the linguists his camera to photograph the kill. But the wily *anta,* facing a row of rifles, charged into the midst of them, scattering the 'brave hunters' on the forest floor, and knocking the cameraman and his equipment flying. I laughed with delight when they returned empty handed and dishevelled with glum faces.

We took two more passengers aboard, this time a very interesting couple. François Alves, a *garimpeiro* (gold and gem washer), quite different from the usual type, and his beautiful wife, a Munduruku Indian and the sister of our pilot Candido. François gave me a beautiful oncidium with a long pendant inflorescence from his forest garden. He had travelled widely and knew many Indian tribes of Pará and Amazonia.

We slept in the forest that night, hanging our hammocks after dark. That was a mistake as I could not see what trees I tied my rope to, but a sweet smell seemed to come from the bark. In the morning I saw my shoes and the surrounding ground were black with ants and I had to call for help before getting out of my hammock. Fortunately my mosquito net had a fine mesh and not one ant had entered.

The last rapids of the voyage were the spectacular Cinco Bocas, and one of the most difficult to pass at that time of year when the water was low. But Candido managed superbly, and we got through the treacherous channels without a hitch. It was like heading for a winning post. We were almost home and as the boat was so overcrowded and the children fretful, I was thankful to come in sight of 'Gleba' Arinos. Geraldo put my plants and baggage in his waiting truck and, through clouds of red earth dust, drove me to the 'hotel' where Harald and Vilma were staying. When I reached the doorway of this large hut on stilts, I ran straight into them. Had they seen a ghost they couldn't have paled more nor looked more incredulous. Apparently they were convinced I had died of malaria. At the time I was thoroughly upset that they had not sent anyone to the rescue, and was embarrassed by the lame excuses they gave: shortage of petrol, ill pilot, etc., etc., so I chose to ignore the event, though it will never leave my memory.

By the time I came to leave 'Gleba' I had recovered my calm and on the journey south by truck I was rewarded by the unforgettable sight of the superb tree *Qualea ingens.* There, in the gallery forest of the distant headwaters of the River Cedro, gleamed a blazing blue canopy, the colour of gentians. The colour was spectacular. I saw the qualea again bordering a little stream, the Corrego do Rio Mutum, and again in Piuva where the riverside swamp was covered with blue petals. One day I would have to go and paint them, but later; first I had to tell Greville I was safe.

Margaret returned to Sao Paulo and within days developed severe malaria. For some weeks she was critically ill and the symptoms lingered several months. Her plants survived the journey and were transferred to hot-houses in the Botanic Institute where expert examination revealed she had found two new species.

JOURNEY THREE: 1964
To 'the Far North'

The northern edge of Amazonia presents a fascinating blend of the mysterious with the familiar, and so when friends at the Sao Paulo Botanic Institute suggested this distant region could be a plant collector's paradise, Margaret needed little persuasion to go and find out. Thus the 1,300 mile long, tea-coloured River Negro became the pivot for her next, and many subsequent, explorations. The upper reaches of this exceptional river extend well beyond Brazil's borders, via a maze of channels, to another great river, the Orinoco, flowing in an entirely different direction. Here, between mist-shrouded mountains lies a wilderness which has attracted seekers of a golden El Dorado — they called it 'Manoa' in Sir Walter Ralegh's time.

The Negro and Orinoco were paths for nineteenth century naturalists. The Prussian explorer von Humboldt was there in 1800, as was Richard Spruce, a Yorkshireman, fifty-one years later. But 1,300 miles is a long way from anywhere, especially when the starting point is already 1,000 miles up the Amazon, so even in the early 1960s much of the upper Negro and its tributaries was untouched. The only settlements of note were either small villages or the church missions devoted to the well being of scattered forest tribes. Connections with the regional capital Manaus downriver were by boat or vintage amphibious Catalina aircraft, and from Sao Paulo the entire area was as remote as the other side of the planet.

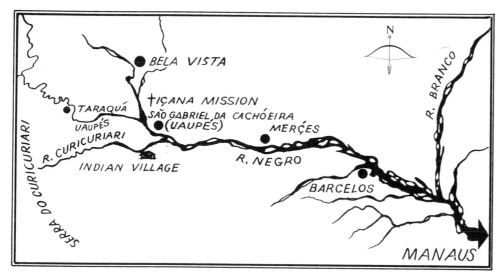

3rd November, 1964

The Brazilian Airforce plane left Congonhas Airport on a cold, grey day with a chill wind. The interior was spartan — wooden benches and no comforts of any kind, but the crew were pleasant and friendly. I was particularly happy as the flight had been offered free of charge by an Airforce General, a friend of Guido Pabst, second in charge of the Brazilian airline PANAIR and a devoted naturalist and orchid hunter. The Amazon was a long flight from Sao Paulo and the pilot jokingly said I would see half of Brazil on the way. Our destination was Manaus on the River Negro close to the point where it joins the Amazon.

We were just four passengers. Myself, a Uruguayan writer who was to be dropped at an Indian village where he wanted to experience tribal life and study snakes, an old,

A pitcairnia, one of a group of bromeliads named in honour of W. Pitcairn, a London doctor.

Streptocalyx poeppigii *(Bromeliaceae).*

very friendly Indian on his way to Manaus, and Claudio a young, energetic man who was going to the diamond washing *garimpo* near Jacarekanga on the Tapajós river, a major Amazon tributary flowing from the south. Our pilot landed twice for refuelling before we eventually landed for the night at Aragarças, a small village on the Araguaia river which forms the boundary between the Brazilian states of Goiás and Mato Grosso. I looked for a hostel, but the only one which existed, though very picturesque outside, was far from clean or convenient and was without washing facilities. However, it was Hobson's Choice and it had the advantage of an open air restaurant where even the stodgy food of beans was welcome after the long flight.

The *garimpeiro,* Claudio, and I dined there together, and before parting for the night, strolled to the bridge which spans the broad river. The dark forest on the Mato Grosso side revived old memories and made me wonder what was in store on the Negro.

My room in the hotel was minute, almost filled by a bed with a messy mattress which I covered carefully with my indispensable hammock. The dreary, dried blood mottled walls recorded the deaths of legions of mosquitoes, and were darkened by the shadows cast by the flickering light of the kerosene lamp. Through the thin wooden partition dividing the quarters I could hear two woman angrily discussing the dingy attributes of their room. One of them shudderingly suspected that it must be alive with Chagas' bugs — these pass on the lethal Chagas' disease which strikes the heart. So I took the hint and let my lamp burn all night to keep the creatures at bay. The thought of these aptly named 'assassin' bugs crawling around was not conducive to sleep, and added to these disturbing thoughts were the cries of a baby and constant attacks by hordes of mosquitoes. It was a relief when daylight came.

Back on the plane the next day I discovered that the baggage and cargo which had been stowed in the aircraft included the revolting and bloody carcass of an ox, the hoofs gruesomely sticking out stiffly from the torn corpse. The meat was destined for the Indians along the way and by the time we took off the meat was already high and fly ridden. We passengers crowded as far away as we could from the cargo section.

As the journey proceeded the country became more beautiful, the unbroken stretches of forest varied occasionally with *cerrado* (scrub) and escarpments of red stone, whose sheer walls had been scored deeply in prehistoric times. Glistening rivers meandered through the endless jungle, the sun gilding them each time we changed direction. The plane flew low until I could see the detail of the colossal trees of the forest where occasionally I glimpsed a pair of brilliant macaws or the yellowish leafy rosettes of bromeliads on the highest branches. For about half an hour we flew over this paradise, then landed in Xavantina, a clearing in the Mato Grosso. On the dirt air strip a group of Xavante Indians were waiting to see the plane land. Survivors of a warlike tribe, these Xavantes were handsome men, powerfully built and tall, but now converted to wearing the tatty clothes cast off by the 'civilizados'. They posed to have their photographs taken by the Uruguayan against a horrible background of ceramic lavatory bowls dumped by some hopeful developer, and then demanded payment.

We said goodbye to the Uruguayan at the next landing strip, the Reserva Villas Boas. Set up by two Brazilians, Claudio and Orlando Villas Boas, this was an enclave solely for Indian tribes. The Uruguayan told me that he would be collecting and studying there for some months. Next stop was another small clearing in the heart of the Xingu forest, near the Xingu river, another Amazon tributary. Here an Indian woman wanted my moss-agate necklace and I had to try to explain to her that my mother left it to me. We talked in gestures and about two words of Portuguese, though somehow she seemed to understand and prevented a young Indian boy from tearing it off my neck.

Xavante Indians 'now converted to wearing the tatty clothes cast off by the "civilisados".'

Our stop lasted into the afternoon and gave me time to look around the clearing. It was backed by wonderfully coloured forest, richly green broken with masses of russet flowers. Some Indians arrived from the river with an enormous fish, like a bewhiskered *pirarara* (catfish), with a white belly and orange tail and fins. Then we were off again heading for Cachimbo, a military base on a plateau dominating a wonderful vista of dense forest below.

In Jacarekanga, the last call before Manaus, Claudio the diamond washer left. The pilot did not even leave his seat on this stop and minutes later as the plane climbed I had a splendid view of the river, sprinkled with forested islands and bordered by sandy beaches. We continued almost due north to the point where the main Amazon river is joined by the Negro, and as we came low across the forest we passed over the muddy brown Solimoes — the Brazilian name for the Amazon above the mouth of the Negro. We were preparing to land when I saw the River Negro, an enormous expanse of clear dark water with shades of rich peaty brown along white sandy beaches. I peered down, filled with excitement at reaching the other side of the Amazon for the first time.

By the time we landed in Manaus I was truly weary, for it was five o'clock on the second day of the flight. Claudio had recommended a modest hotel, the Lider, in the centre of the old town and not far from the ornate Palacio Rio Negro, the State palace. Here I was able to have a refreshing shower and to lie flat on a clean bed.

The next day I moved into the student quarters of I.N.P.A. (Instituto Nacional de Pesquisas da Amazônia — National Institute of Amazon Research) from which I made various visits to the Ducke Reserve, a very beautiful area of forest named in honour of the Brazilian botanist Adolpho Ducke, who lived in the Amazon forests for long periods studying the flora throughout the seasons.

I painted enthusiastically for there was plenty of material both in the Reserve and its environs. *Heliconia acuminata,* a banana relative with pale yellow bracts, flourished in a large colony beneath the forest trees. Then I found two gorgeous bromeliads, *Streptocalyx longifolius,* whose flowers are pollinated by bats at night, and *Streptocalyx poeppigii,* with long red and purple inflorescences. These and many other wonderful plants kept me occupied while I waited for a place on the half regular flight by amphibious Catalina plane stop by stop up the Negro.

The River Negro

The flight, over densely forested archipelagos and jungle criss-crossed by sinuous rivers, was exciting and we finally landed on the river in a cloud of spray before the little settlement of Mercés, consisting of two or three wattled huts to which we were ferried by canoe. From Mercés a priest, two nuns and I embarked on the mail boat bound for Uaupés (now Sao Gabriel da Cachóeira) three days away. As the boat headed into the current we were watched by a small group of Tucáno Indians from the local missions.

Evening on the River Negro.

We had scarcely left our mooring before driving rain forced us to close all shutters along the sides, and as we chugged on Tucuma, our half-Tucáno Indian pilot, peering through a small opening, had to battle with numerous rapids. When the storm had passed the distant Serra do Curicuriari was visible on the horizon to the left, a sure sign that we were getting close to the mountainous northern limit of Amazonia. Due to its contours, the local name for this mountain range is Bela Dormicinda (Sleeping Beauty), and it dominates the landscape for many miles, forming a seductive background to the groups of granite islands in the broad expanse of the river. In one place tumultuous cataracts stormed over a rocky barrier of stone stretching from shore to shore, masking all other sounds with their roaring waters.

Some hours of travelling brought us within sight of the white tower and monastery of the Salesian Mission, which lies on the outskirts of the little town of Uaupés (Sao Gabriel) on the right bank. It was to be my base/starting point for three journeys. We coasted gently to the beach and were picked up with our baggage by a lorry and taken to the mission. There I met Sister Elza Ramos, the Director, who was very kind and treated me with great friendliness. She showed me my little room, rather bare and secluded though light enough for painting, and then gave me lemonade to quench my raging thirst.

My next move was to explore the country around the mission and to wander beside

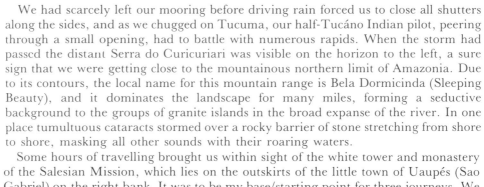

Heliconias are relatives of the banana.

A pirarara (catfish).

72

Heliconia uaupensis.

Heliconia uaupensis E.M.
Amazonas, Rio Uaupés

Margaret Mee

Sao Gabriel da Cachóeira.

the spectacular falls of Sao Gabriel, where from every angle superb vistas came to view. Down on the sandy shore hordes of pale green and yellow butterflies rose like petals in the wind and vanished. I learned that they came to suck mineral salt from the wet mud on the river verge. Only a short walk away I found a swamp teeming with flowers new to me.

Four Tucáno Indian girls from the mission borrowed a canoe and took me with them to collect plants, paddling past the rapids and landing in a *caatinga* (forest of short spindly trees). As I wandered through this strange dry forest, examining the enormous anthuriums of the arum family with big dark cushiony leaves, and small red-leafed bromeliads (neoregelias), I chanced upon a primitive shelter. Hesitantly I approached and found two Indians, a wrinkled old Maké and a young Dinian boy making curare arrow poison in an earthern pot. They were shy and obviously found it difficult to communicate but did not seem to mind me watching the intricate process. I could not help thinking it was quite remarkable that generations ago the forest people had discovered a blend of plant extracts which could kill by relaxing the muscles.

We came out of the *caatinga* into a dark jungle of giant trees where scarlet heliconias grew shoulder high and the ground was carpeted with moss and selaginellas. Then we lost our way and wandered hopelessly around until eventually we reached the river bank not far from where our canoe had been moored. The canoe was no longer there; in our absence someone had exchanged it for a smaller one which would only hold three, and I and one of the Indian girls had to make our way back through the forest on foot.

We struggled on in dense woods always careful to keep within sight and sound of the river. The petals of a blue qualea, for which I was always searching since my journey to the Mato Grosso, littered the ground around me, but I was too exhausted to investigate, and voices from the now distant canoe urged us on for the forest was darkening rapidly. At last we reached the mission, sweating and weary.

That night, at the customary hour of 'lights out', an Indian girl, Ceci, came to collect my kerosene lamp and brought the news that the priest's mission boat would be leaving for Curicuriari, a Tucáno Indian *aldeia* (village), very early next morning. She explained that I could go too, and that she would wake me at five. Aware that there would be no light at that hour I did some hasty packing and then snatched an hour or two of sleep. I was awake before the appointed hour, for the air was sultry, and a full moon in a lightly clouded sky shone through my window.

A vampire bat flew in and out of the open window and the sound of its beating wings was like the sound of muffled drums. As I arose in the semi-darkness, in a streak of moonlight I saw a large spider advancing towards me, but a light kick sent him scurrying away. I drank coffee in the mission where a few nuns in white habits flitted around silently and, being in *retiro*, uttered no words. But in handing me a box of food, one whispered sympathetically that there was nothing to eat in Curicuriari.

By the dawn light three Tucáno girls and I made our way to the port where the boats were moored. I embarked on *Pope Pius XII* where I was happy to find Tucuma, the Tucáno pilot who had brought me on the mail boat from Mercés. He greeted me warmly. Then he introduced me to another Tucáno, Joao Firma, whom he explained would take me to Curicuriari, for Tucuma had to return down the Negro to Mercés. When Tucuma told Joao that my objective was to collect plants in the Serra do Curicuriari, the Indian looked at me with obvious doubt, saying that I did not appear strong enough for a two day trek in the hills. I felt slighted by his remark and assured him quickly that I had experience walking over forested mountains. Tucuma added his assurances, but I was disconcerted at being left in the sole charge of Joao who, on

my arrival at the port, I had seen in the company of a very disreputable looking fellow well soaked in *cachaça*. Later, however, I realised that he was a highly intelligent and reliable man, and, I suspect, a descendant of a former *tushaua* of his tribe.

The River Curicuriari

As daylight broke we set off down the Negro and into the mouth of the Curicuriari coming in on the right. We passed through the rapids to the foothills of Bela Dormicinda, passing glorious vistas all the way. On the isles in the river the trees were white with orchids and the air full of their perfume. After about three hours of motoring against the current, we reached a small village. We did not land here but threw cargo ashore beside the tangled roots of an old tree, like Medusa's hair, and at the same time picked up a friendly little man whom I discovered lived opposite the village of the Tucános, our next stop.

The hut in the Indian village where we stayed that night was lent to me by Joao. It belonged to his brother, who was travelling at the time, and was a wattle construction with a thatch of *buruti* palm; though the walls were full of chinks it appeared weather proof. The doors and windows had beautifully made shutters of *assaí* palm on bamboo frames; the floor was clean-swept earth, and the furniture consisted of a rough table, a box and four wooden steps from the doorway.

'Outside the black river flows silently, copper red in the shallows. The falls can be heard softly in the distance. In this Tucáno village there are a number of huts, all fairly distant from one another and well hidden by the trees. The spacious original *maloca* is now only used for ceremonies, I am told. The only ornaments in my hut are of Tucáno feathers hanging on the walls.

Tomorrow at dawn we shall start the journey to the Serra. Just me, Joao and another Indian. It is, as they said, a two-day journey so we shall need to spend the night in the forest. Joao had just told me in detail what I shall need to carry — a hammock and as little else as possible. As for food, I may take what I like — they will eat birds. When I told him I did not want to see dead birds he laughed long and heartily.'

I was doomed to disappointment for it stormed during the night. The palms bent flat and rain pelted down — the heaviest storm I had seen. It was followed next day by an amazing glitter in the trees and a broken, stormy sky. Joao reluctantly decided that the weather was not stable enough for a long journey. However, he offered to take me by canoe to collect along the river, but there again I was to be disappointed as a trader from Manaus arrived at the riverside landing place with a cargo of *cachaça* and bullets, and everyone, including Joao, disappeared from the village and stayed away all the morning. When he returned, to pacify me he climbed a rotten tree for a catasetum orchid that I had had my eye on since arriving. To my horror, he had just reached it when the tree collapsed and he fell about twenty feet landing neatly on his feet amongst dead branches and thorns. With a wave of contempt he brushed aside my suggestion that he might be hurt, and climbing a neighbouring tree, swung across on a liana and threw down a *Catasetum barbatum* — a bearded orchid.

With evening came a group of Indians, who while they questioned me fiddled incessantly with jungle cane which fell to pieces all over the floor. I had just finished

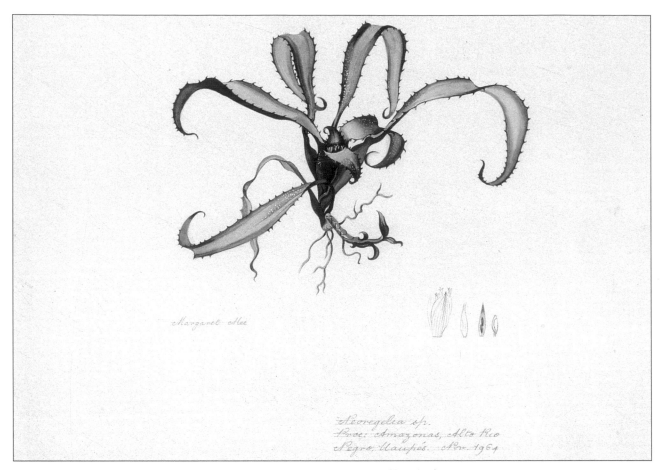

Neoregelia species (Bromeliaceae) from the Uaupés river.

Many of the forest trees have these buttress roots.

sweeping up the mess when another crowd arrived. My heart sank and I look meaningly at Amelia, Joao's wife, for the hour was late. Seeing my hopeless expression she understood, explaining tactfully to the visitors in Tucáno that I had to rise early next day for a two-day walk in the Serra.

At five in the morning Joao arrived and, though it had been raining all night, told me to my delight that he had found a companion for the journey and was on his way to fetch him. Octavio, also a Tucáno, was a strong, fine looking fellow who had not been in touch with the 'civilizados' and thus spoke not one word of Portuguese.

We paddled upstream for about an hour with no rapids to hinder us, while I kept my gaze riveted on the river banks where I was rewarded by finding the bromeliad *Aechmea chantinii* and a fine sweetly-perfumed galeandra orchid.

The *igarapé* by which we entered the forest was dry, as they all are at that time of year. The way was surrounded by many enormous trees with *sapopemas* (buttresses supporting the trunks). Then quite suddenly from the dark forest we emerged into a brilliantly green *caatinga*. The contrast was most extraordinary, for instead of being impressive, the trees were shorter — very green and festooned with epiphytes growing down their ribbed trunks, over the arched roots and down to the fern-covered ground. On leaving this remarkable green luminosity — it could have been some exotic hot house — we found ourselves again in sombre jungle, relieved only in colour by the glorious amethyst flowers of *Heterostemon ellipticus,* a legume growing high in the tree canopies. No wonder they call it the orchid tree — its flowers superficially resemble laelias and cattleyas, some of the grandest orchids in the forest.

76

Heterostemon ellipticus *(courtesy The Tryon Gallery)*.

The drizzle which had started as soon as we left the canoe continued, and the light began to fade rapidly. Joao announced that it would not be possible to reach the Serra before nightfall, for though it was only four o'clock, it was already dark in the forest.

*Yours very faithfully
Richard Spruce.*

Richard Spruce, a Yorkshireman, was a self-taught botanist. His travels and meticulous diaries fascinated Margaret.

The Indians chose a camping site beside an *igarapé* and started to build two shelters, working together in complete silence. Great *pataua* palm leaves were dragged rustling over the dead leaves for the roof, saplings were posts and *cipó* (vine) bound the joints. In five minutes it was ready and I was told I could hang my hammock in the beautiful green thatched shelter. Then they lit a fire and cooked my packet soup over the flames.

I slept fitfully for insect bites were driving me frantic, and I was only calmed by the strange noise of nocturnal birds and the chorus of frogs and *pererecas* (small frogs) which later I found in the reservoirs of rain water trapped in the whorls of the bromeliads's leaves. Dozing lightly, I saw through half-closed eyes Joao and Octavio spring out of their hammocks, cock their guns, and run towards a dark mass of trees into which they were peering cautiously. Nothing happened and I tried to rest, but in vain — the eerie forest sounds kept me ready for anything.

When I asked Joao in the morning the reason for the commotion, he told me that night monkeys, objecting to our presence, were pelting us with branches. It seemed reasonable but I was convinced that the little animals were giving warning that an *onça* was around as they had in the Mato Grosso.

We started our climb in the Serra do Curicuriari after a simple breakfast of *farinha,* boiled water, and fruit. Richard Spruce in 1852 had climbed the Serra do Gama, a similar range on the River Negro. Well over a hundred years had elapsed since his journey and the maps were still without exact courses for the rivers or even a height for the Serra. I could only guess that I faced a climb of over 1,500 feet through dense, humid forest (mapping by radar has since discovered the height to be 1,476 feet). It is doubtful if the Serra has changed at all since Spruce's days, for a century is but a moment in the life of an ancient mountain. Deeply fluted columns of granite, green with lichens, guarded the way to the summit, and we struggled through a tangle of roots, lianas and moss for some hours. But climbing over rocks and roots still rain sodden from the previous night left me no time to collect. Even more bitterly disappointing was the summit, for the view which I had hoped to see was obscured by dense foliage. We turned back, but the descent was more difficult than the ascent, for the danger of slipping was greater. Eventually, however, we reached the camp without mishap and with a few plants to treasure.

As we returned to the forested plains a brilliant orange bird with a flaming crest, the *galo da serra* (cock of the rock), followed us, watching with curiosity from on high. I was afraid that the Indians might kill him, but Joao exclaimed that he would not think of killing a *galo da serra* as it had some deep spiritual significance. But he did kill a *paca* (large rodent) and tried to kill a *jacu,* but it made off in a hurry, to my great relief.

My boots were hard and heavy, and I must admit that the last few miles had nearly killed me, so it was a welcome sight when at midday we saw the river and the canoe moored beside the banks. I climbed in and sank down wearily. How soothing the sound of dipping paddles can be!

The Indian *aldeia* of Curicuriari was deserted and silent, for the Indians had gone

Margaret's hut at Curicuriari.

to attend their *roças* (small clearings with cultivated plants — gardens in fact). They would paddle away at dawn prepared to spend the day working in their plantations until dusk. Joao and Amelia had departed taking the two children with them, but leaving Marciana, a girl of twelve to look after the house.

I was arranging my plants, naming those I had collected on the journey, when to my astonishment I heard a motor canoe coming up the river. I listened intently, wondering who could be paying a visit. The motor shut off in front of Joao's house and I hurried to the door of my hut to see who had disembarked. A crowd of rough looking fellows, led by a burly half Portuguese wearing a black sombrero, came swaggering up to my cabin. I was more than alarmed by the aspect of this man and wished that Joao would return quickly. The fellow came up to me exclaiming that he had not expected to find a woman like me in Curicuriari, and where was my husband? His familiarity was most disturbing, but I realised that above all I must show no fear, so answered that I was working in the forest and my husband was in Sao Paulo. The fellow informed me that he was a *garimpeiro,* going up the river with his team of goldwashers to look for gold and wood. Had I any whisky? No. *Cachaça?* No. Well then, alcohol? to which I replied that I had a little alcohol for my stove. What else had I for him, he enquired insolently, moving towards me aggressively as I stood in the doorway. He wanted 'to talk with me', he said, full of heavy implications, but 'that could wait' until he returned.

The gang left and with intense relief I heard the motor canoe passing on downstream. I was alone again, thank heaven! And before the gang's return, which might be in many days, I should have left Curicuriari.

But I was not alone as I discovered, for when I peeped through a crack in the wall I saw three of the *garimpeiros* circling my hut. Avoiding them catching sight of me I ran across the room to Marciana with the little money I had to be hidden in Joao's house nearby. Then I hid my camera under an old cloth, my diamond ring in a chink in the wall — it was my mother's engagement ring and my most precious possession, being full of memories. Continuing preparations for any eventuality I put some spare bullets in an old shoe, loaded my revolver and concealed it under the box I used as a seat. Then I sat and waited for what seemed an eternity.

My heart beating furiously, I heard the *garimpeiros'* canoe returning; it coasted to the bank, the motor stopped and the men moored again in front of Joao's hut. A few minutes later they were coming up the path, and their leader was at my door, swinging unsteadily and as drunk as a lord. He made no bones about entering my hut and started to come up the steps, but I was ready and faced him, revolver in hand. Taken aback, his dark face paled and he held up his hands, backing away as he did so. He thought that I could be as unpredictable as any local woman who has a gun. Suddenly I felt calm and in control of the situation and seeing the humorous side laughed aloud as I followed him down the steps into the open.

The hills of the upper River Negro.

Tucuma, Margaret's river pilot.

The burly *garimpeiro*, disconcerted by my unexpected reaction to his attempted assault, began to speak in a calming vein. Then recovering his bravado he sprang forward to disarm me but failed as I dodged. The other *garimpeiros* were watching at a safe distance, out of the range of my revolver. Little did they know that my only practice had been on tin cans in the garden in Sao Paulo. The two Indians, impatient with the delay and apprehensive of the outcome of this incident, insisted on leaving immediately with the gang, threatening to abandon the journey up river.

As they left urging the leader along, Marciana, who had been a witness from afar, ran to me and flung her arms around me weeping with relief. The tension over, I too burst into tears.

Joao and Amelia returned within half an hour, with reinforcements including a tall, powerful looking Indian. The story had already spread to the whole neighbourhood, for the ill fame of the *garimpeiros* was common knowledge both in the village as well as from the source to the mouth of the river.

This horrible incident changed the attitude of the villagers towards me. Hitherto there had been a suspicion that I was a spy — a rumour started by the trader from Manaus who had managed to convince the villagers with some imaginative story, helped along by draughts of *cachaça*. As a result they had been unwilling to trade food with me and I had gone hungry, but now, realising that I was an ally, they treated me like a queen, coming to my hut with plentiful supplies of fruit and fish.

My collecting came to a halt as I was by then in continual state of alert and did not wander far, always expecting the return of the gang. It was especially lonely in the village when the Indians left for their *roças*. However, without going too far there was plenty of wildlife to be seen around the *aldeia*. When the sun rose, a slender *teju-açu* (iguana), which attains six feet when fully grown, basked on the stone, and three small *tucános*, black and yellow billed, disputed territory with quite alarming cries.

The night before my departure I sat in the gloaming talking with Joao and Amelia outside their hut. They told me about the Serra, the animals and birds in the vicinity, the trees and plants of the forests. Then they left me to sleep whilst they paddled downstream in their canoe to visit friends. As I heard the paddle's faint splash in the

Neoregelia leviana (Bromeliaceae), known only from Margaret's collection.

Margaret Mee

Neoregelia (unclassified)
Proc. Amazonas, Rio
Uaupés   Dec. 1964
Neoregelia leviana L. B. Smith (1968)

Rounded, weathered rocks beside the river.

Beside the record makers' boat.

Robin Hanbury-Tenison and Sebastian Snow (right) *on one of the longest river journeys on record.*

river it seemed to mark the end of this journey.

Morning came, but still no Tucuma to fetch me as had been arranged, and I became rather agitated at the thought of staying another week in the village, so Joao went down to the riverside 'port' to make inquiries and returned with the news that Tucuma would arrive the next day. By way of consolation for waiting, he brought me fish and *farinha* cooked by Amelia. I left the village the following day in the mission priest's boat. The sky was magnificent with storm clouds. We dashed through rapid after rapid, stopping only once at a village to pick up a man and a boy. The boy had chicken-pox and occupied himself during the whole journey by levering the spots from his skin with the thorn of a pineapple leaf, so that my appetite left me and I kept at a safe distance from him the rest of the day.

When we landed in Uaupés, I saw to my astonishment a rubber boat with two powerful outboard motors tied at the bank among other river craft. On further examination I noted a couple of crash helmets, British and Brazilian flags and a nice Paisley scarf, so by deduction I concluded that the boat was British owned. A blond, suntanned young man came up to greet me as 'the English woman they have been telling me about'. Who was he, and where was he going? I wanted to know. His name was Robin Hanbury-Tenison and his companion was Sebastian Snow, both young travellers already experienced in exploring the Amazon. They were temporary representatives of *The Daily Telegraph,* and had come to Amazonia by way of the Orinoco from Venezuela. Next day they were heading for Manaus and then south along the Madeira river in their speed boat, reporting on and writing a book about the longest river journey on record. So that evening we supped together at the invitation of Sister Elza and talked late into the night.

Robin confided to me that they were worried about the weight of their pilot, as his bulk could slow down their journey to Manaus. So I suggested Tucuma, who had done so well for me, as the ideal pilot, being very small and light, and, by repute, the best pilot on the River Negro. I talked with Tucuma and introduced him to the two Englishmen. Then, carrying an umbrella bigger than himself, he went to the church to persuade the heavy Salvador, who was celebrating Mass before his journey, to let him take his place on the voyage to Manaus.

He returned with a smile of almost delirious delight, for Salvador had renounced the trip, and this meant Tucuma would meet his son, whom he had not seen for nearly twenty years, in Manaus. Like an Indian he was ready to leave without preparation and with only a small bag. The departure of the rubber boat and crew caused a sensation and the whole village turned out to witness the event. As she took off the unusual craft appeared to be airborne, followed by a shining trail of spray like the tail of a comet.

There had been a warning of an approaching storm that night, for white aquatic birds had been circling against a black sky streaked with red flashes of lightning. As predicted, the following morning it broke with tremendous fury. As I sat painting, I heard a voice behind me say 'Hullo!', and starting with surprise I saw Hanbury-Tenison standing there, a trifle disconsolate. I enquired why he had returned, for I believed him to be well on the way to Manaus. Then came his tale of misadventure.

Villagers return from fishing along the upper River Negro.

He, Snow and Tucuma had reached Mercés when a violent tempest broke and they had to take shelter in the forest. Not having eaten for many hours they decided that some soup might warm them up and tried to light a fire. Taking advantage of the stop they also decided to replenish the petrol in the tank from the supply they had got from the mission. It was only then they discovered that they had been given paraffin instead of petrol. They had to return to Uaupés, clean out the tank and start afresh.

The next stage of my journey was to Taraquá (giant ant), a small mission on the west bank of the river Uaupés. The journey by PANAIR Catalina was memorable. Below meandering rivers threaded their way through high forest varied with scrub land. From low lying swampy ground isolated groups of hills rose, densely forested between wisps of rain cloud. Taraquá lies on a tremendous rock on the left bank of the river Uaupés not far from the Colombian frontier, and the local people believe the footprints of the *Jurupari* (devil) are imprinted on their great stone.

The plane touched down in a cloud of spray and soon I was heading for the Salesian Mission, a long building which can be seen from afar as it is built on the crest of the hill. I was assigned to the Santa Casa where, after various introductions and handing over a letter kindly provided in Uaupés (Sao Gabriel) by the visiting Mother Superior of Barcelos, I escaped the clouds of mosquitoes by diving under my net.

I was very eager to explore my surroundings and on the first excursion to the nearby low forest I found many fascinating plants — a very beautiful white and yellow bignonia, *Distictella magnolifolia,* which was first found by Humboldt in the same area, and had only been found again by Koch in 1905. There were clusias and a variety of orchids and an extraordinary swamp plant, *Rapatea paludosa.*

Almost six weeks after leaving Sao Paulo I celebrated Greville's birthday by a trip into the forest led by Vincente, a very mercenary Indian. The *caatinga* of Taraquá was one of the most beautiful I have seen. Epiphytes clung to the trees half enveloped in richly green wet mosses, and in the middle of a lake surrounded by swamp grew a clusia tree bearing panicles of white flowers. It was gorgeous. The flowers were red at the centres and pendant between large oval leaves. It was just possible to reach by walking along a fallen tree trunk, and so Vincente was able to get me a few clusters of flowers and leaves. The whole area was a paradise of plants; I saw three species of rapatea, anthuriums and a charming orchid with feathery spikes of greenish flowers.

When I tried to move one of these plants embedded in moss, an unseen creature stung me so viciously that I cried out with the pain. As I was accustomed to finding ants in every plant, I imagined this must be a *toçandira* (large ant) which is best avoided, but the pain was so acute and persistent that I asked Vincente what it could have been. He suggested that it might be a small red scorpion, then hurried on towards the river. I had difficulty in keeping up with him, dizzy with an aching head, stumbling as I went. He increased his speed and was almost running when he reached the boat. I was in an angry mood, having already been drenched by a heavy shower in the forest, and decided there and then that I would never ask Vincente to collect with me again.

Wandering alone and tranquil through the partially cleared land behind the mission, I found a spectacular clusia tree covered with deep rose-coloured flowers and hung with fruit which looked like Chinese lanterns. This was the feminine form of *Clusia viscida.* What luck! And then not far away on the following day, I was able to

Margaret and Tucuma on the Uaupés.

Tillandsia paraensis *from the Uaupés river.*

Rapatea paludosa — *'an extraordinary swamp plant'.*

collect the masculine form of the species — white flowers with a tinge of yellow growing on a slender tree in the *campina* (open scrub forest).

Having finished my paintings, I took advantage of a rainy day to visit Father Martins, who had a fine collection of Amazonian butterflies and beetles. His collection, he told me, was to be offered to one of the museums in Brazil. He was most interested to hear about the miniature lizard less than an inch long which had fallen out of a piece of rotten wood on the roots of a bromeliad I collected. He told me that these minute creatures are extremely rare and that he had seen a blue and green one but never a mottled brown like the one I found. The lizard was still in his wood dust home when I returned from my visit, but I found a safe and suitable place outside where he could live in peace.

My stay in Taraquá came to an end too soon when the river boat *Dom Savio* arrived late at night bound for Uaupés downriver. I embarked in the morning and spent the day seated in the prow watching the banks slip by. We moved on steadily without stopping until eight o'clock that night, when we coasted for a brief moment at Ilha de Paacú and Irovao, two tiny settlements. We then continued our journey until we reached Bela Vista just before midnight, where we moored for the night (there are many Bela Vistas — this one is on the river Uaupés). I stood watching the jungle come to life after the heat of the day, hearing the splashing and sighing of the dolphins playing beside the boat, until sleep overcame me and I dived into my hammock, thankful for my net, for the mosquitoes were ravenous.

At dawn we were on our way again, with two more passengers, a woman with a

84

The upper River Negro.

Aechmea tillandsioides, *a bromeliad, on the River Curicuriari.*

small child, bound for Uaupés. By daylight I could see that Bela Vista (opposite the *serra* of that name), was a pretty group of huts among tall palm trees. The villagers came out as we left to see us off.

We passed forests filled with flowers, the most spectacular being *rabo de arara* (macaw's tail) *(Norantea amazonica),* of the Marcgraviaceae family, whose long scarlet plumes crown the tallest of trees. It is a true parasite I believe.

Beaches and sandbanks started to appear after we passed the tiny village of Na-Na. The river level falls considerably after August and by December is very low. The temperature too had dropped and it was almost cold, quite a relief for my sunburnt skin.

A fellow passenger was a great source of information about the names of the villages, trees and plants along the river and turned out to be a pleasant companion, though very ugly. By contrast, the crew of Tucanó Indians were rather handsome, besides being very attentive and friendly. For lunch they gave me an enormous plateful of rice and locally made sausages, washed down with plenty of coffee.

As we approached Uaupés we passed a series of turbulent rapids. The few isolated huts along the river were perched on rocks amidst palm trees beside eddying falls. Most of the *serras* were distant, though I learned that the nearer ones could be reached by canoe without difficulty.

Shortly after the junction of the Uaupés with the Negro, we reached Ilha das Flores (Island of Flowers), which belied its name. I had expected to find the superb bromeliad *Aechmea chantinii* there in great quantity, but instead found that most of the natural vegetation had been destroyed by temporary settlers. It was disappointingly dull. Beyond this little isle I saw a region of enchanting beauty which I believed I should have to explore one day unless, like the Ilha de Flores, the natural beauty has been senselessly destroyed by them.

The River Içana

On arrival in Uaupés I hurried to examine the plants I had left in fibre baskets slung in the palm trees of the mission garden, and found them fresh and green due to the frequent rains and the conscientious care of Ceci. When talking with Ceci, I learned something of the *garimpeiro* who confronted me in Curicuriari. He was the son of a pastor in Manaus and one of five brothers, each worse than the other. It appeared that no woman was safe when they were in the region, and anyone who dared denounce the ruffians was threatened, so no one opened their mouths and the villagers continued to be terrorised. It seemed, that because I had a revolver, I was the first woman to confront one of the villains successfully.

From Uaupés I hoped for a journey to the Içana mission on a F.A.B. (Brazilian Airforce) plane, but the supposed day of departure was one of complete chaos — packing, unpacking, rushing, journeying, returning, waiting. What happened was this: I had woken early in the morning and heard what I took to be a Mass for a departing aircrew. So, thinking that they must have arrived the previous night and would leave at dawn, I dressed and packed in record time, only to find that I was mistaken, and that the plane would not arrive until midday. I filled in the time by conversing in the little mission shop about future journeys, and learning about the River Cauaburi (a river I longed to explore) which flows into the River Negro about halfway between Uaupés and a village known as Tapurucuará. The Cauaburi was virtually unexplored according to well-known botanists — Froes and Ducke — and my friends in the shop confirmed this.

During *merenda* (snacks) I heard the drone of the F.A.B. plane overhead and everyone made a mad rush to the river beach despite the pouring rain — but no plane was visible. Then the big mission truck, with Sister Elza sitting in front, came tearing towards us. I got in and we sped towards the airstrip where the plane had already landed. It was forty-five minutes of jolting and splashing through mud and water, and at one extra rough jolt Sister Elza would have fallen out had I not clutched her flowing habit and dragged her back. The engine began steaming and we had to stop and wait impatiently whilst the dry radiator was filled with muddy water from the nearest *igarapé*. Eventually we reached the landing field, which looked more like a lake. The crew were drenched and stood disconsolately on the soggy ground. My rucksack was running with water and my shoes squishing, but my main preoccupation was for my precious sketch books packed in my dripping baggage.

Finally the plane took off with visibility nil, though, as we climbed, we entered patches of clear sky from which I could see towards the Venezuelan frontier and the magnificent indigo *serras* and peaks (some over 2,000 feet high) above a bank of cloud over the distant Içana headwaters. We had been flying for almost half an hour when I noticed an extreme tension amongst the crew who were peering down at the undercarriage, signalling to each other, running to the pilot and generally in a state of nerves. A young Salesian sister was praying beside me, pale with fear as she fingered her beads. The only other passenger, an Indian, sat silent and mystified, his eyes as big as an owl's.

We were less than half an hour's flight from Içana when our captain decided to return to Uaupés, sending us a message to keep calm, saying that he would do everything possible to make a safe landing. As if to comfort us he explained the difficulty: only one of the two wheels had retracted on take off. It was impossible for the amphibious plane to land on the narrow channel of the River Içana, for the floats would not descend if the undercarriage was faulty. In returning he tried to reassure us that landing on one wheel on land was not impossible. The scenery of endless forest suddenly seemed less exciting, but as we came over Uaupés the crew managed to get both wheels down and we landed safely. Everyone on the plane cheered with relief and triumph. And so ended my first attempt to reach Içana.

'So now I am on my way, writing against the throbbing engine of the mission boat, heading upriver to Içana with the priest from the mission. We have been travelling since the day before yesterday without stopping — even braving the dangerous and frequent rapids after dark in spite of the pilot's protests. But the

Falls and a storm on the River Uaupés.

priest insists on keeping schedule and his word is law.

Last night the sunset was unbelievably beautiful, and so it is tonight — pure gold. Tomorrow we reach Sao Felipe.'

After Sao Felipe, a simple village of a few thatched huts, we chugged onwards through the most lush and tropical region I had ever seen. Jungle seemed to merge into river, for tree trunks, lianas, roots and foliage were inseparable from their reflections; it was a picture of luxuriant vegetation, where the *igarapés* were transformed into dark, mysterious tunnels through the forest. The flowers of a creamy white lecythid, the same family as the cannonball tree, hung low over the water, perfuming the hot air, and attracting humming-birds and bees, whilst the trees hosted robust epiphytes, many in spectacular bloom. Unwillingly, I hung my hammock in the airless boat above piles of cargo, for there was little free space. Above me, in my straw hat, a little catasetum which I had found on the way was bursting into flower.

We arrived at the mission long before daybreak, and still half asleep I staggered up the slope leading to the primitive wooden mission house where the Mother Superior saw me installed in a large unoccupied room. Next door teemed with children, all curious, some with whooping cough, and adults too, hanging in hammocks and chatting. But, despite the noise I slept soundly until dawn.

Eager to explore this inviting region I waited impatiently for the promised guide to appear, but, losing patience, I set off alone. I had not gone far when I heard shouts behind me from a girl who had been sent to see that I did not lose my way; two other Indian girls joined us. They had warned me of the danger of going alone into the forest as the *Jurupari* might be lurking there to attack wanderers. They said he had the unpleasant habit of pulling off the head of his victim and devouring the brains. The only way to kill this devil with one eye and backward facing feet, they all agreed, was to stick a knife or sharp bamboo into his navel, but that would be difficult for they believed he was a giant and very agile.

It was in this awe-inspiring forest that I found a tree of *Heterostemon ellipticus,* with a wealth of amethyst flowers. I was able to collect some of these as well as some leaf sprays, for the tall heterostemon had fallen in a tempest and was lodged in some branches — luckily within easy reach. I had been longing to paint this flower ever since seeing it in Curicuriari.

The *guaribas* (howler monkeys) roared loudly in the forests that night, Christmas Eve — and with it came an invitation from Mother Superior to attend a Midnight Mass. I was curious to see how it would be celebrated by the Indians and in this isolated village. Before leaving, I locked my room as I was doubtful about some neighbours, strangers to Içana, who were drinking heavily, whistling and screaming.

The Mass was impressive, held in the half-finished church, where the lighting consisted of candles and one or two smoky oil lamps. The Tucáno women wore full

The mission at Taraquá was a landmark.

Some of the sisters on the River Uaupés.

skirts and brightly coloured dresses, as instructed by the sisters, but their heads were covered in white veils; they went barefoot, walking with the freedom that they had learned in the forest. The nuns were in spotless white and the painted Madonna wore a halo of tiny lights. More than half the service was sung and spoken in the Tucáno language, and I had time to observe the fine faces of these people so reminiscent of Gauguin's paintings of South Sea Islanders.

The celebrations over, a more appropriate and exciting invitation came from the sisters — a day's visit to the Serra da Içana with six Tucáno Indians, which I accepted eagerly. The early morning mist was hanging thickly over the river when we started the boat, but the sun soon dispersed it, and by the time we had reached the *igarapé* which flows from the Serra da Içana the heat was intense. However, on entering the shade of the trees the temperature fell by several degrees, which was fortunate, as we had to make the journey by foot, the *igarapé* being blocked by fallen trees and impassable by canoe. First we passed through a small *caatinga* and from then on were surrounded by high forest all the way. The ground was swampy and in no time my shoes were completely saturated and the sisters' white habits drenched and thick with mud at the hems. We crossed many streams, stopping eventually beside a narrow *igarapé* for lunch. It was an idyllic spot, remote and silent but for the faint trickling of the stream and melodious bird cries.

'A sudden storm brought an end to the excursion.'

A fire was kindled with amazing speed in spite of the fact that everything around was saturated, and we had lunch shared with thousands of ants and bees — bees which got into the mouth and eyes and proved very acid and bitter.

Although the forest was shadowy and dark, plants were plentiful. A beautiful scarlet bromeliad, a pitcairnia, grew on the loamy ground; there was an elegant aroid with a stem marbled like a snake skin, possibly a protective mimicry, but the outstanding find was the rare orchid *Gongora quinquenervis* — such spectacular purplish mottled flowers. Wonderful! Inspired by this collection, I decided to join the six Tucános who were gong to climb the *serra,* but they moved at such speed I had trouble keeping up with them, and after following at a distance for some time I stopped to pick a plant and found myself alone in the forest. I was reminded of the experience of being lost in the forests of Alto Juruena when the Erigpaktsá Indians had run ahead and left Harald, Vilma and me to find our way back to the camp. But on that occasion I was with two companions; here, alone, I felt utterly helpless. I walked back a little, but seeing two diverging tracks could not decide which to take, so I shouted; my voice, muffled by the trees, sounded so weak that I despaired of ever being heard. Teasingly the birds answered my calls. Then I tried to follow the stream, but in that spot it was just a trickle and I could not tell which way it was flowing. Despairing, I decided to stay put hoping the Indians would pass on their return. My hope had almost ebbed away, when in the distance I saw with tremendous relief an Indian girl from the mission coming towards me. She showed no surprise to see me in that isolated situation and, as she could speak no Portuguese, told me by signs that she had taken the sisters' lunch by mistake and was bringing it back. Her forgetfulness was my salvation and we returned together to the bank of the *igarapé.* Soon after a sudden storm brought an end to the excursion.

On the return journey down the Içana I was anxious to see a group of rocks strangely inscribed with symbols, so we landed and climbed to a little hut on the summit where we had to drive off six snarling dogs. No sooner had the surly pack been

An Indian from Uaupés before the mission was established.

My boat and Indian friends on the River Içana.

driven off when I turned to see two Indian girls from the mission run shrieking to the river pursued by a snorting pig. When they had reached the safety of the launch, the enraged animal turned, caught sight of us and charged. Like lightning another Indian girl was up a tree, and I scrambled on to a tree stump, somewhat impeded by the camera hanging round my neck. No sooner had the pig disappeared behind the hut than we dashed to the boat and boarded it just before the infuriated animal charged again. We did not see the inscribed rocks.

We reached the mission at sunset. My little catasetum was flowering, a charming creature with a fringed labellum — in fact it was a fringe of fascinating construction and quite complicated to paint. Having finished the painting I cleaned up my plants and packed them provisionally as a sister told me our old friend Salvador was leaving in a boat for Sao Felipe.

My return journey to Uaupés was to take this form: Salvador would take me there in his motorboat, stopping for a day or two on the way at his home in Sao Felipe, where he would arrange a canoe to take me into an *igapó* (flooded forest) to collect. So I left Içana with many adieus to the kind and hospitable sisters and priests.

The boat was really too small to accommodate Salvador (a heavy man), Arminda his wife, son Eduardo, daughter Maria, *tio* (uncle) and three small boys, as well as me and my plants. However, his Penta motor ran well in spite of the weight. During the early stages of the journey we were caught in a heavy rainstorm and everything was drenched, for our only protection was a half *toldo* (roof) of ageing straw. We stopped often *en route,* for it seemed that Salvador was a trader in a small way. His Baniwá Indian wife was a pleasant woman and spoke good Portuguese, though naturally she preferred to speak Baniwá whenever possible. She told me that most of the women of the region only speak Baniwá or Igaté. As a guide she was excellent, for she knew all the names and locations of rivers and *igarapes,́* as well as animals, trees and plants in the area.

Salvador's intention was to reach Sao Felipe that night, but a storm was blowing towards us, and he was afraid of using the wide and exposed channel where the Içana flows into the River Negro. We agreed to spend the night under an open-sided shelter in Vila Içana, a small village. The rain swept through. It poured and stormed until my rucksack with all its baggage was saturated, with the exception of my camera stored in a *tucum* (palm fibre) bag.

At five o'clock stirrings of life began both among our own party and the *guaribas*, who were roaring in chorus as they do at dawn of day. I packed and rolled up my wet hammock, had a miserable clean in the dark and, after drinking watery coffee, set off for the boat. It is always surprising how rapidly dawn turns into day on the Equator, and how quickly the sky becomes rosy, lighting the remnants of mist hanging over the river. Salvador stopped at one or two huts along the way, including that of *'Tia Surda'* (Deaf Aunt), as she was popularly known. The poor old woman was only half there and had become stone deaf after taking a remedy for worms. Unable to read the instructions, she had taken and swallowed at one go the entire contents of a complete de-worming package intended to be taken over a good period of time.

That morning we reached Sao Felipe, where the three boys, Armindo, Joachim and Adhemar, paddled me by canoe to collect in the *igapó*. It is all very well relying on boys to collect but they soon weary of it and want to go home, so at the first signs of a storm we paddled back, having found little of interest. At least the boys were good at climbing trees, and when Armindo was in the branches a lizard with a long neck and friendly, upturned face fell into our canoe. His expression of astonishment was amusing and he took some time to regain his equilibrium. Then he dashed over the side of the canoe and swam across the water to a little tree. Up he climbed, but Armindo came sliding down the same branch so he got another shock, jumped into the river and disappeared...

'... the canoe has nearly capsized twice, due to quarrels in the rear.'

It was more tranquil to explore the forest behind Salvador's house, and more interesting too, for ancient trees grew there, including three enormous clusias, two of which had the most glorious flowers, deep purple-bronze petals with lemon fringed centres. Petals were scattered over the ground below and the trees were so tall that the flowers in the canopy were scarcely discernible. I realised it was most unlikely that anyone would climb to get them for me, for between the roots of the strangler, which formed a basket work around the trunk of the victim, there were dark hollows which Maria said were the home of a dangerous *surucucu* (bushmaster) (*Lachesis muta*), a snake

A Colombian at Taraquá collecting bromeliads.

A Colombian family in the forest at Taraquá.

Clusia viscida
(male).

Clusia palmicida.

Clusia palmicida.

Clusia viscida
(male).

Neoregelia margaretae *(Bromeliaceae)*.

Margaret
Mee
May, 1979

Neoregelia margaretae L. B. Sm.
Col. Amazonas, Rio Içana
Cult. Sitio Burle Marx

A grey-winged trumpeter.

A troupial.

A philodendron (Araceae) from the caatinga *of the upper River Negro.*

that when adult can reach eight feet in length and with enough venom to prove fatal.

Maria's keen ears heard this snake rustling through the undergrowth below the clusias as we wandered through the forest. We fled rapidly, scrambling over and under fallen trees and branches, through scrub and underbush until we reached a lighter part of the forest. There I was fortunate to see, as we paused for breath, a group of bromeliads within easy reach. Maria climbed quickly and brought down two which I put in my bag. Although not flowering they looked interesting.

In Salvador's house I was honoured with a room to myself — what a relief it was to be alone for a little! Not quite alone, for the voices in the only other room never ceased. And in spite of a refreshing bath in the river under cover of darkness, my *mucuim* bites were driving me mad, though my eyes were closing with sleep. Salvador, Eduardo and I left for Uaupés the next day.

'This is now the third stop and it looks as though Salvador is not going to reach our destination today. He is always hanging about with his merchandise. And it is raining, cold and miserable in the boat where I am sitting shrouded in plastic but still feeling chilly, while Eduardo is spitting away for dear life! And it is the smelliest spot that we have stopped at yet — very dirty looking people. But there is a brighter side to the picture, for a fascinating bird, an *agami* (trumpeter), followed me like a dog into the woods where I have been to stretch my legs. I gave him *bejú* (sago pancake bread). He had to fight the hens and pigs but succeeded every time in seizing the *bejú* and keeping it.'

It began raining hard whilst Salvador was still away drinking *cachaça* and driving a bargain, so I rejoined the boat and ate a greasy, unappetising lunch. The rain was steady, having set in for the day. I fidgeted about, then remarked to Eduardo that his father was away far too long, and that I needed to arrive

The cock of the rock — 'a brilliant colour in the dark forest'.

Epidendrum ibaguense, an orchid collected from the forests of the River Uaupés.

in Uaupés with urgency. So very hesitantly Eduardo left the boat and soon Salvador came rushing back full of excuses.

Downriver the rapids became more and more difficult to navigate. Then the river widened and the *serra* came closer to the shore. The rain petered out. At the most tremendous *cachóeira* of all, two fishermen were stranded on the rocks, one using his

Distictella (Bignoniaceae).

white shirt as a signal. The men, poor wretches, were surrounded by swirling eddies, calling for help, their canoe half under water. One was still searching for their possessions among the raging rapids. Perturbed by this accident so far from anywhere, I asked Salvador anxiously if the men were in imminent danger of drowning. Though I was not over keen to attempt a rescue in those turbulent waters, I felt that at least we should make an attempt to save them. Salvador just waved. 'They are accustomed to this', he said callously, and sped on.

As we neared Uaupés we twice narrowly missed grounding on the rocks, but at last we arrived and moored some distance from the mission. Everyone was pleased to see

Catasetum
appendiculatum.

us back safe and sound and I was invited to stay at the mission until the PANAIR Catalina came by *en route* for Manaus. I sank into my hammock but not before I had fed a tiny caged troupial which someone left in my room.

'He loves *grillos* (grasshoppers), which the boys get in quantities. Now he goes crazy when he sees me — I do hope the sister who releases captive birds will free this little one.'

Margaret returned to Sao Paulo with her plants. Some were put in hot houses at the Botanic Institute and some went to Roberto Burle Marx's sitio near Rio. The bromeliad she found near the home of the bushmaster eventually flowered and was named as a new species — Neoregelia margaretae. She had also discovered a new philodendron. At about this time, and with her job with Lyman Smith complete, she left the Botanic Institute and decided to concentrate on painting as a freelance artist. An exhibition at the Sao Paulo Art Museum in November 1964 led to the beginnings of her first book and exhibition with The Tryon Gallery in London.

Also at the same time a portfolio of her work was shown in Washington D.C., and some paintings on view in a small shop caught the eye of Mrs. Woods-Bliss who arranged a soirée at her famous home, Dumbarton Oaks. Dr. Leonard Carmichael of the National Geographic Society was among the audience and so Margaret's next, and first major expedition was conceived.

A small armadillo, one of the forest's curious species.

JOURNEY FOUR: 1967

To 'the Mountain of Mist'

Margaret's friend Dr. Leopoldo Froes in Belém once mentioned how in the early 1950s he saw an immense mountain among clouds in the distant reaches of the River Negro.

Though it may be hard to believe that any mountain almost 10,000 feet high was still unexplored by 1953, the year Everest was conquered, Froes had not been tricked by a mirage. And no one in the upper River Negro had any doubts about the existence of a great, unchallenged Amazonian mountain. But aviation maps of the time were cautious, and captions in large blank areas warned pilots of the possibility of abrupt cliffs.

Part of the story stemmed from a letter sent a hundred years earlier to Sir William Hooker, Director of the Royal Botanic Gardens, Kew. Richard Spruce writing from the banks of the Negro said: 'I could distinctly see, though at a great distance, the serrania *called Pirá-pukú or the Long Fish'.*

Spruce never reached the mountains, and though in later years priests and prospectors travelled around them, it was left to a botanical expedition to make the first recorded ascent. In 1953 an American, Bassett Maguire, Curator of the New York Botanical Garden, fellow botanists and Venezuelan explorers approached the mountains from the north. Their expedition lasted eleven weeks, and after arduous trail cutting through soaking forest they reached a summit. Through a break in the clouds they sighted yet more peaks about ten miles away and estimated them to be higher still. A canyon over a mile deep lay between them. The explorers named the entire massif the Cerro da Neblina — Mountain of Mist.

About ten years later another expedition was sent to establish the boundary between Brazil and Venezuela. The main peak of 9,985 feet sitting astride the frontier became known in Venezuela as Pico Phelps, after one of the Venezuelans on the original expedition, and Pico da Neblina in Brazil.

Margaret, although she was already fifty-eight, needed no urging to explore the mountain and paint its flora. Moreover, she would be the first woman traveller to make the southern approach. The mountain is over six hundred miles from Manaus and Margaret's undertaking needed good support. She found it with the help of Dr. Leonard Carmichael and a scientific grant from the National Geographic Society. The Society also despatched a photographer, Otis Imboden, to cover the story.

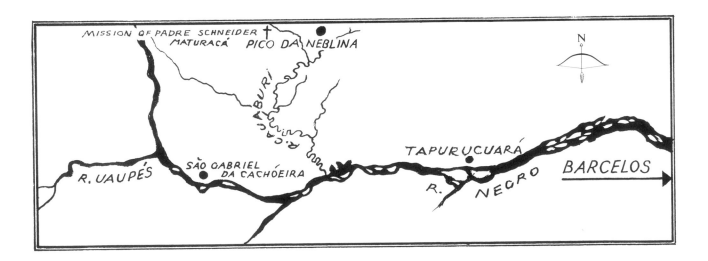

An igarapé *overlooked by wooden, shanty-town houses in Manaus.*

18th July, 1967

On my return from the River Uaupés in 1965, I had seen from the plane the distant Serra Imeri. The highest peak of this range of mountains is the Pico da Neblina and, true to its name, the elusive mountain was capped in cloud. But the sight of this beautiful and mysterious *serra* excited my imagination and I had vowed that one day I would return to explore the wonders of its forests.

I arranged to meet my travelling companions in Manaus where I had hired a boat — Otis, laden with cameras and boxes of film, from the National Geographic Society in Washington, and Paulo Cardone, a young Brazilian. My plan was to travel up the Negro visiting places I knew on the way and then follow a tributary upstream to the mountain. Altogether a wonderfully adventurous journey of between one and two months.

We left the hot and busy town by the narrow back streets, picking our way through black mud to an *igarapé* overlooked by wooden, shanty-town houses. The boat was typical of the River Negro with a small deck fore and aft and a wooden cabin of rough construction sheltering a noisy, oily inboard motor. The crew came as part and parcel of the boat and Santino an *Amazonense* (from the region) was 'comandante' in charge. With him he had Joao, a Tariana Indian, who was very deaf since doing his military service — due to gunfire, he explained. He was a pleasant, good humoured fellow who bore patiently the frequent gibes of Santino.

The food supplies were left to the crew to purchase, as they had more experience of our needs and knew what we could buy on the way. Once the luggage was stowed aboard we chugged out of the *igarapé* through a clogging, floating mat of aquatic plants and turned right, upstream, into the Negro. Towed behind we had a small canoe for the practical purpose of getting to the bank in shallow water. It would be ideal for plant collecting.

We kept close to the bank passing ocean-going cargo ships, flotillas of river boats like ours and the occasional canoe. Above the houses and shanties the gilded dome of the Teatro Amazonas — the 'rubber boom' opera house, shone brilliantly in the warm sun. We had scarcely passed Ponta Negra — a rocky point where, from a distance, the port of Manaus almost disappears from view, when Santino discovered that he had left all his possessions in a suitcase in the city. We pulled over to the bank, mooring near a hut, and Santino was lucky to find a passing truck which took him back to town. Whilst awaiting his return we bathed in the cool, dark waters of the river, and it was already nightfall when we saw the small light of a canoe approaching rapidly. It was Santino who, with some embarrassment, came aboard with his suitcase. During the night we sailed on until weariness overcame the crew and we moored in an enchanted spot beneath a great tree, which, by morning light, I recognised as a swartzia, full of white flowers.

During the night it had rained heavily. To our consternation the canoe in tow had

Margaret collected in the forest, keeping her plants in plastic bags until she returned to her boat.

filled with water and submerged the motor which, in spite of our efforts, would not show a spark of life. After these mishaps in the first twenty-four hours of the journey I began to lose confidence in the efficiency of the crew. It was not at all comforting, as we had a long way to go, but I decided to keep to my plan.

The floods were still high, nearly thirty feet above low water, and the trees stood deep, bringing me nearer to the flowers in their canopies. I could reach to massive philodendrons crowning most of the older trees; among their roots hung those of the clusias in curtains, seeking sustenance from the soil. A beautifully woven nest of a *japim* (oriole-like oropendola) hung from a low branch. Parrots and toucans were playing and feeding in the spreading boughs. Delicate violet mimosa flowers fringed the river banks and mingled with yellow aquatic blossoms floating like fields of buttercups.

After drying the motor, we moved on, heading upstream amongst a flood-sodden debris of abandoned, isolated shacks, some completely flooded, their tattered straw roofs floating among the remains of plantations of bananas and sugar cane. Such was the rise of the water that for endless miles there was no terra firma.

Soon after passing this rather depressing area the vista was spectacular: the giant trees were clustered with epiphytes and entwined with clusias (*mata-pau* or stranglers), and on the verges of the river bloomed a *Bombax munguba,* a kapok tree, with large white flowers, its fruit hanging in scarlet pods which, as they burst, loosed silken parachutes to cover the deck as they drifted in with the wind.

A band of *macaco de cheiro* (squirrel monkeys), small and yellow limbed, followed the boat, whistling with excitement as they peeped between the leaves. They were soon followed by small chestnut coloured monkeys springing from branch to branch, chattering loudly.

We made good progress up the Negro, stopping each evening beside the forested bank. On our second night the sky was beautifully clear and starry so I decided to sleep on the deck in the open. From a deep sleep I awakened with a start on hearing a commotion on board; at the same time I felt heavy drops of rain. I hurried down to the cabin but not before I had seen our predicament. The boat and canoe had broken loose from their moorings and were being carried back downstream together with a great floating island of half submerged vegetation. The crew worked frantically to

Squirrel monkey.

Cattleya violacea *(Orchidaceae).*

Margaret Mee
1981

Cattleya violacea
Rio Curni, Amazonas

Margaret sketches her plants beside the river.

release the boats but did not succeed in freeing them until daybreak. The outboard motor had been standing in the flooded canoe all night so it was hopeless trying to get any life out of it. After another long delay for the motor to dry, we were on our way upstream again. The men were accustomed to problems with the floating islands they told me, and we would have to be particularly careful near the mouth of the River Branco, the next major landmark.

Soon after midday on our fourth day we reached an enormous inland sea where the River Branco enters on the right. Before crossing this enormous expanse the experienced boatman looks at the sky and takes good note of the weather, for this passage can be dangerous for small — and even large — boats. Wind and blinding rain are the main dangers as the river is filled with difficult currents and rocks. Our pilot was skilful and we passed the mouth of the river safely and headed on towards Carvoeiro, a village on the west bank where we planned to stop. As we crossed the open river to Carvoeiro, the gigantic trees we had been passing became dwarfed by distance, yet still stood out as landmarks. The jungle appeared a faint line on the horizon but otherwise we were entirely surrounded by water. We were a little over half-way across when suddenly a wind came from nowhere tossing and rolling our boat on steep waves. Dark clouds gathered and we chugged on with all possible speed towards the sunset, a golden glow broken by streaks of indigo. It was a race to get to safety before the full force of the storm broke.

An awed silence fell as we drew nearer Carvoeiro. Four towering palms and a wooden church spire, dark against the evening sky, marked the village set in a primitive landscape of an extensive archipelago of small islands.

As our crew moored the boat, curious villagers came out to gaze at us and the boat. I rapidly pulled a blouse and slacks over my swimsuit and went out into the darkened village to meet an old man, introduced to us as the mayor. We sat and talked with him at a table on the mud-rutted street in the shadow of the church. The only gleam of light came through the open door from oil lamps within.

Not realising how impressed Otis and I were by the wild beauty of the surroundings of the little settlement and its exquisite setting in this unspoiled corner of the earth, the mayor spoke proudly. He told us of the fertility of the soil and how, by clearing the trees, wheat could be cultivated there on a big scale. Much was an old man's fantasizing as he explained how he had even experimented with wheat in an old tin, which, he said despondently, would have germinated had not someone forgotten to water it. Then after more talking, we thought perhaps he could sell us some eggs, but he shook his head, he had none as the hens did not lay for lack of *milho* (corn). In my mind I contrasted him with old Antonio Carvalho on the Gurupi who had developed everything he needed on his little farm by observing and respecting nature, and without destroying the wonderful forest.

Not far west of Carvoeiro a small hut had been constructed on the banks of the Negro by an American church mission, which also served as the headquarters of the *Alpha Helix,* the large boat of an American-backed scientific expedition. The following day I went with Otis to visit the scientists and found that the *Alpha Helix* was away on the river and that the base had been left in the care of a Brazilian, Diego, and an Australian who was in charge of the collected animals. He had a tame young *anta,* two kitten *maracajas,* very ill-treated, a coati so sick he could scarcely stand in his filthy cage, and a lovely *barriguda* (woolly monkey) suffering from worms, who hung on to the flowers of *Galeandra devoniana,* an orchid I had collected, gazing at us appealingly with his dark eyes. Suddenly, inwardly, I was terribly angry and upset when I noticed skins of *jaguatiricas, maracajas,* monkeys, sloths, *onças,* wild pigs and many other forest animals. And this was supposed to be a scientific expedition!

The 'keeper', probably to make his own guilt seem less, told us how the Manaus owner of the boat, finding himself with a surplus of sloths for a film, had them thrown to *onças* to tear to pieces as a spectacle. Later, in front of us, and presumably to show his prowess, the Australian dragged some of the *maracajas* into the river. They emerged terrified, looking like drowned rats, and from that moment I hated the man with intensity.

To my relief Santino recommended we should move on as we had more than a week to go before reaching our base. The journey continued smoothly, past deeply inundated isles until we left the open river and headed through a natural canal *(parana)* between thick forests near the mouth of the River Jarati. When night obscured the landscape I sat on deck watching a great waning moon, red near the horizon, sending a path of light in our wake. I remained there till it was late, enjoying the cool air after the heat of the day before reluctantly going to the cabin to hang my hammock. Five hammocks were crowded into the tiny space, the heaviest occupant above mine and, fearing the ropes might slacken, I slept fitfully. Then soon after midnight, just as I was dozing comfortably, we arrived at Barcelos, a larger village and the mid point along the Negro. I tried desperately to tidy myself and was not a little embarrassed when the village came out to watch my efforts.

Barcelos in the past was an *aldeia* of the Paumari Indians, and is now dominated by the Salesian Mission. The inhabitants are very mixed: Indians (the original inhabitants), *caboclos* and a few people of European descent. I did not find the town very exciting, but it did provide us with a few 'fresh' supplies of eggs and bread. Otherwise I was glad to leave.

As we got further upstream the rivers became more and more fascinating. *Jará* palms grew in humid places along the banks, sometimes almost covered by the high water, their fibrous stems making wonderful homes for dozens of epiphytes. Groups of perfumed orchids, including *Galeandra devoniana,* bloomed profusely. Cerise flowers of another superb orchid, *Cattleya violacea,* were so brilliant they gleamed in the trees beside the delicate white blooms of *Brassavola martiana.* Trees of *Gustavia augusta,* with large pink and white flowers, were frequent and I felt I should have stopped, collected and sketched. But that had to wait, the Neblina was still a long way away.

The day passed pleasantly, and as the sun touched the forest its last rays caught the red and blue plumes of *araras* crossing the river in pairs or occasional threes, while oddly beaked toucans, herons, noisy kingfishers and flights of parrots all on their homeward way kept my attention fixed. This far away from the main Amazon, the forest was a treasure house. Dangling from the highest trees were colonies of *japim* nests, their owners protesting loudly at our intrusion on their territory. Fresh water dolphins played near the boat rippling the still water.

That night I slept peacefully on deck until suddenly awakened by a storm wind. Within minutes a tempest was raging. With a struggle I escaped from the deck and, the wind tearing at my clothes, scrambled into the stuffy cabin where all windows had been closed.

Santino managed to moor in a small bay which we had the luck to be near when the storm reached its height, though even there we were tossed and churned about. These violent storms on the Negro do not usually last for long; this one was true to form and soon abated leaving a rolling swell as it swept on.

The pattern of the days and nights was much the same during the rest of the journey. The motor gave endless trouble and only Otis could manage it and keep it running. Stormy weather alternated with tranquil days and nights. Incidents were

Flooded forest, igapó, *beside the river.*

The fascinating mountains at the head of the River Negro.

The orchid Catasetum discolor.

few, although on one occasion we ran into a sandbank and, when free, the boat spun around in the current hitting the branches of a large tree and breaking the mast and hurricane lamp. I was on the cabin roof at the time and the tree just missed my head, leaving me amidst the wreckage with leaves, twigs and insects in my hair.

In every way the journey up the Negro was undemanding and peaceful. I had long quiet days to watch the wilderness slip by and concluded thankfully that, in the forests, the animals pursued their lives as their predecessors had done before man made his appearance on our planet — or on the Amazon. It was glorious; time simply did not exist. Our first real break came eight days upriver from Manaus at Tapurucuará (now Santa Isabel do Rio Negro), where Father Joao Badelotti from the mission came down to the shore to welcome us. He was a tall, strongly built man, with a thick greying beard. And, as we discovered, he was respected along the river as kindly and tolerant. On one occasion I confessed to him that I was not religious and belonged to no denomination or sect. 'You are religious,' he replied, 'for you love and respect nature.' We were introduced to the Mother Superior who was very friendly when she learned that I had visited the Salesian Mission in Uaupés in 1964/5. At the Tapurucuará Mission I met Carlos, a pilot working for the priests, who was pleasant and recommended as reliable.

Carlos knew the rivers which came down from the Pico da Neblina and the unmapped forest we had to enter. Two rivers needed careful navigation, the Cauaburi, beset with rapids and the route to the mountain, and the canal, or river, Maturacá which skirted the base and led towards the Orinoco river. The canals of this area had long fascinated me, for they are natural waterways connecting rivers flowing in different directions. Which way would the water run in the canal, I wondered? All this was barely known country, home only to a few Indians and the missions. We still had several days to go up the Negro before we reached incoming rivers from

104

Galeandra devoniana *(Orchidaceae)*.

Margaret Mee
June, 1984

Galeandra devoniana Schomb:
Lago Sapucá, Oriximiná,
Pará

mountains in the north. But, as Carlos explained, there was no other large village on the way.

Tapurucuará looked the spot for a base, and I was thankful when the Mother Superior allowed me to leave my plants in the coconut palms which grew in a sheltered part of the mission garden. This arrangement also freed my plant baskets for the collection which I hoped to make on Neblina. Sorting out and restocking with food took two relaxing days. Supplies were purchased in the village, where about half of our needs were met, so we had to trust that we would get fruit and fish on the journey. At ten on the morning of 29th July we left Tapurucuará on our way to the Pico de Neblina.

Shortly after leaving the village, Carlos caught sight of a large bunch of *assaí* palm fruit and climbed the slender trunk of the palm Indian fashion, his feet in a belt of *tucum;* thus we had a store of *assaí* fruit as well as *cucura* — a delicious black fruit resembling grapes from a small tree with a much divided leaf like cecropia. It soon became one of my favourite foods.

Three days upstream from Tapurucuará we left the Negro, still almost a mile wide, and entered the River Cauaburi between thickly forested banks. The mouth of this river was several hundred yards across and we had to keep to the fast channel to avoid awkward shallows. Then we met the first rapids of the River Cauaburi; they were both difficult and dangerous, for the channel narrowed considerably and the force of the water rushing through was tremendous. Our malevolent engine stopped running in the midst of a great eddy, but Otis somehow got it moving, saving us from disaster.

It was on the Cauaburi that we met an Indian paddling his dugout canoe, and we invited him to join us for coffee. As he was about to leave the canoe for the boat, he looked up at me and said: 'I remember — you were in Curicuriari.' It took a moment or two to place him, but as we chatted he laughed about my adventures. 'The Tucános still talk of the day when you faced that *garimpeiro* from Manaus with your revolver — he was our enemy, too, you know. Most people in the village wish you had shot him. No one there would have worried.' So I sent greetings by him to my Tucáno friends, particularly Amelia and Joao Firma, my next-door neighbours there.

The journey was getting harder, and for hour after hour we edged up the sinuous river through the many rapids until late afternoon when we reached Destacamento, the most formidable of all. A river wide barrier of rocks and foaming water, it was a foretaste of the mountainous Amazon. Without the help of the Archimedes outboard motor we could never have overcome those raging torrents, in spite of all the efforts of Carlos, who shone as a pilot.

Just above the rapid we moored for the night beside a small shelter which, to our surprise, was already crowded. We met another boatload of passengers from upriver and the 'comandante' sold us three litres of oil which we needed desperately as our motor was losing oil rapidly. He was a nice, quiet fellow, but other members of the crew were flinging bilge water at random, and their loud radio and graveyard coughs so disturbed us that we decided to move up the river to a quieter spot, which was sheltered by overhanging forest trees.

The beautiful falls of Jacamin were next and passed easily, though the falls of Manajos-açu (*açu* meaning big) which followed presented a real test of navigating skill. Once more, Carlos managed to get us through. The raging waters tried to hold us captive and Carlos ordered us to stamp and rock the boat to free her whilst he ran the motor at full throttle, and in the end we slipped by. Then another swirling eddy held us, and I watched a little tree on the bank as a marker to see if we were making headway against the current. This time the motor, working its hardest, could not move the boat through the overwhelming force of the falls. Carlos peered at the water and,

'I remember,' he said.

*Margaret collected and
sketched in the dark forest.*

instinctively found a channel, shooting through exultantly to calmer waters. After that test we came to the Manajos-mirim (*mirim* meaning small) and other lesser falls which proved no obstacle to our voyage up a glorious river.

In the tense moments of the struggle to pass the rapids I glanced up to see a noisy flight of brilliant green parrots followed by dozens of delicate scissor-tailed nightjars, their long slender tails rippling as they crossed the river. I had hardly looked down when there was a sudden stir and Santino shouted in great excitement that he could see a *sucuriju* on the bank. The enormous creature, which must have been fifteen feet long, lay stretched along a fallen tree, a large bulge in her sleek body, for she was digesting a recent meal. Carlos told me that in the Maturacá canal he had seen one of these snakes almost twice as long.

Otis was very eager to photograph the reptile, so the crew prepared a lasso on a long pole, hoping to trap her in the noose. We had hardly started to move towards her when, like a streak of lightning, despite her big belly, the snake disappeared into the river without leaving a ripple. Disappointed by this lost opportunity, Otis determined to get a record of the next animal that might appear, and very soon Joao shouted that there was a sloth in a tree. With a cord hanging around his neck, and intent on a capture, Joao climbed the tall smooth trunk, but not without risk, for the branches overhung the river. The sleepy sloth refused to move, and continued sleeping, rolled tightly into a ball. Rather cruelly, Joao severed the branch with his bush knife, and the sloth, still clinging to the branch, fell with a mass of foliage on my basket of plants. Unhurt, the poor dazed creature sprawled helplessly on the deck. His long, coarse fur was grey-brown, but between his shoulder blades an orange patch marked him as a male. Santino held him gently by the paws, careful to avoid his long, sharp claws, whilst Otis filmed. Once released, the animal struggled to the mast, before slowly and deliberately climbing the mast itself on which he settled comfortably and promptly fell asleep — or was he feigning sleep? For soon, he came and made towards the river. We moved towards the shore and an overhanging branch which the curious animal clutched eagerly, a strange half-smile on his face. Then from the branch it scaled the

The blue orchid, Acacallis cyanea.

tree to continue an interrupted siesta. While everyone including Carlos was occupied with the painfully slow antics of the sloth, I collected an *Acacallis cyanea,* the unusual and rare blue orchid in full, exquisite flower.

Maturacá

On 2nd September we reached the mouth of the Maturacá canal at the base of the mountain. The way divides nearby, with the Cauaburi and our route coming in from the right, the Maturacá canal leading to the left. According to Carlos, this could be followed via another canal to the maze of rivers on the Venezuelan side of the border. The entire area was a veritable warren of waterways and forest. We headed first into the Maturacá towards the mission of Father José Schneider where we could find Indian help and establish a base.

The black water of the canal must be one of the most beautiful waterways in

A village near the mouth of the Cauaburi.

108

In the forest at the foot of the mountains.

Beside the River Cauaburi.

Amazonia. Its banks harbour a wealth of plants, among them the epiphyte *Aechmea chantinii* with vivid red bracts and silver ringed leaves, and scarlet pitcairnia (both bromeliads) massed on banks crammed with forest plants. Every curve in the river, and they were legion, gave a spectacular view of the forested slopes of the Serra Imeri, the range extending to the Neblina. As we rounded one bend a canoe paddled by two young 'Waika' (now more usually known as Yanomamo) Indians glided swiftly towards us. They were handsome young men wearing the traditional ornaments of their tribe, two scarlet *arara* tail feathers bound on the upper arm and bunches of parrot feathers in the lobes of their ears. As they shot past us they smiled in a friendly way. Clearly they had had little contact with the 'civilizados'.

Father Schneider's mission stood high on the river bank, a modest unpretentious building, from which a large cleared area led down many crudely made steps to the 'port'. No sooner had the boat been moored than dozens of naked Indian children of all sizes rushed down to the water's edge and crowded around talking excitedly. Father Schneider, a tall lean man in a grey habit came down the steps to meet us, smiling kindly. Another German priest, Father Francisco, was with him, 'visiting,' he explained. We were made very welcome and invited to supper with the priests in an austere room made more so by its whitewashed walls. Whilst we conversed at table I observed the two men, complete contrasts to one another. Father Schneider ascetic and saintly; Father Francisco a typical well-fed friar who might have come out of a medieval painting.

The mission building proved large and rambling and was about ten minutes distant from the *aldeia* and *maloca* of the Araribo Indians, whose name comes from their use of *arara* feathers. I met one of the wives of the *tushaua* Joachim, a pretty petite woman wearing only bunches of red, yellow and green parrot feathers in the lobes of her ears. The Indian women did not speak Portuguese and only very few of the men commanded more than a word or two.

'Unhappily many of the children look sick and are suffering from sore eyes and bad teeth, whilst the adults seem healthy and have beautiful white teeth. It seems that the older generation, living according to their traditions, have fared much better, though they too have been and are a prey to the white man's diseases of colds, tuberculosis and smallpox.'

From the Cauaburi I had seen the magnificent Serra do Padre, or Piripirá as it is known to the Indians, and it formed a wonderful contour against the evening sky as I walked to the *aldeia*.

A 'Waika'.

110

Margaret quickly made friends with Indian families at the mission.

A loud chanting came from the village. The *feiticeiro* (shaman) was dancing and singing in the heat of the midday sun. Streaming with sweat, which had partially washed away his serpentine body painting, he careered through the *maloca,* obviously fortified with *parika,* a snuff used in religious rites by the 'Waika' Indians. The snuff, made by powdering the bark of the virola tree of the Myristicaceae family, is blown through bamboo tubes into the nostrils. Though consumed with curiosity I kept my head averted, only surreptitiously glancing from time to time, knowing that women, and above all, strange women, were forbidden to witness these rites. Some hours later the *feiticeiro* was still dancing and singing with the same energy and fervour.

In the village I was besieged by children who hung on my hands, hair and shirt sleeves. They were smiling and chatting to me in the only language they knew, of which I could not understand a word. My replies in Portuguese, of which they could not understand a word, did not deter them in any way. They were the most affectionate and natural children one could wish to meet. The women were mostly petite, their bronze-coloured bodies often painted with *urucu* (a scarlet stain), and *genipapo* (a black dye). Their clothing consisted of feather earrings of various colours.

An Indian taking snuff.

Suddenly there was excitement amongst a group of Indians and a little woman ran towards me and threw her arms around my neck, asking if I remembered her. I thought quickly and recalled that I had met her at the Içana Mission. She even knew my name, 'Margalete', though we had met briefly. She was married now to an Indian of the Araribo tribe and lived in the *maloca* they called Irocaí. She explained how she had moved around with the mission boats, the only means of contact along the rivers. While we were talking one of the men took a fancy to my hair, plaiting it and unplaiting it, but I did not like to protest for blonde hair is a novelty. As he plaited so he let flow a running commentary which kept his audience in peals of laughter. Then my straw hat was passed from hand to hand with the Indians trying it on at various angles. When eventually it was returned it was stained red with *urucu* from their foreheads.

Tushaua Joachim arranged for three men to lead us to the Pico da Neblina, for without guides who were familiar with the *trilho* (way through), the ascent would be almost impossible. Three strong young 'Waika' men who knew the *serra* were chosen from the Irocaí *maloca* — Placido, Napoleao and Rafael. Placido and Napoleao were handsome young men of approximately thirty and twenty respectively, maybe younger. They had very fine features and their figures were magnificently shaped with broad shoulders and narrow hips. Napoleao

The Maturacá canal, dominated by 'Padres' Peak, skirts the base of the Neblina massif.

Margaret and Paulo took great care with the plants, well rooted in their temporary home.

had dark green eyes, an uncommon colour among Indians, but I was to hear later that many of the 'Waikas' who lived in the regions between the River Demeni to the east and the Orinoco were comparatively fair, while some even had blue eyes. Rafael had a sombre, unsmiling countenance, and an unfortunate history which caused him to behave rather strangely at times. Once, when he was alone and unarmed on the slopes of Neblina, he had been attacked by an *onça* which he killed with his bare hands after a terrible struggle. Torn, bleeding and suffering from shock the poor Indian had dragged himself three days through the forest to the mission. Father Schneider cured the wounds on his face and chest, but he remained strange, never fully recovering. It took time, but I got used to his moroseness.

Before leaving the *maloca* I gave presents for the tribe to *tushaua* Joachim who distributed them to the circle of Indians whilst we looked on. He was extremely careful to give them all an equal share, but his own present of a large bush knife had been substituted by Carlos, who had deemed it too good, and had brought along instead a very inferior specimen. I saw Joachim's look of disappointment and sent Carlos back immediately to fetch the bush knife which Joachim accepted with great satisfaction.

Again we supped with the priests in the austere dining room, but this time there was another visitor, Benedito a farmer from the River Negro, who appeared bent on introducing cattle to the region of Pico da Neblina. As he would be the first there he could claim plenty of land.

That evening we prepared for our journey to the Pico. The place was in utter confusion, but somehow we managed to pack in spite of the Indians who invaded our room to watch and eagerly examine our belongings. Preparations for the journey were only finished by morning. Then another problem. Ten hunters from the tribe asked to be towed to the mouth of the Tucáno, a tributary of the Cauaburi, our starting point for the mountain, and five days' hard paddling away. We were desperately short of fuel for the return journey as so much had been wasted through the malfunctioning of the motor, but we said we would tow them some of the distance. We set off along the canal back to the Cauaburi, and then apprehensively turned upstream.

112

Aechmea tillandsioides (Bromeliaceae).

Margaret Mee
1976

Aechmea tillandsioides (Mart. ex Schult.)
Amazonas, Rio Negro

At every curve of the river we imagined we were arriving at the mouth of the Tucáno, and when eventually we did reach it we found the narrow channel completely blocked by fallen trees and branches. It would have been hopeless to try to hack our way through the tangle as it seemed that the barrier continued for some distance. So we disembarked at an old camping site of the Boundary Commission where the date of their stay was inscribed on a sturdy old tree.

The way to Neblina

The beauty of the remote forest was awe-inspiring and my excitement overwhelming. To think that at last I was at the base of the mountain about which so little was known, and at which I had gazed longingly — but always from afar. We slung our hammocks between trees, and after a simple supper around our fire we spent a peaceful night. Carlos and Santino were left at the mouth of the river with the boat and asked to move it downstream to navigable waters if the river level began to fall. Otis, Paulo, Joao, our three guides and I moved on as far as we could by canoe and outboard motor.

Early next morning we were up and about early and eager to start on the climb. We concealed our canoe and motor in an *igarapé* overhung with thick bushes and set out in drizzling rain. Our Indians led the way. Early on in the journey Napoleao shot a *mutum* (curassow, a relative of pheasants). He explained that as soon as we started to ascend the *serra* there would not be any game, news which I heard with concealed relief. So the Araribos dined on game, and we on our dried packet food.

The ground of the forest was saturated by incessant rain and the water-filled hollows made climbing difficult, but we walked on through lofty forests until early afternoon when we prepared to camp again for the night. Then a problem arose: we were short of one hammock, for Rafael had left his behind, feeling that it was too dirty to bring with him on the journey. He shamefully confessed the fact, but Otis drew a nylon hammock from his pack which served adequately, though it was somewhat cold and uncomfortable. As the rain had not eased all day we were soaked to the skin, and to make matters worse it continued with renewed force at night. Snug and dry in my tropical 'tented' hammock, through the dark net windows I could see the rain teeming in the forest. The Indians, accustomed to these downpours and wet nights, had constructed a shelter for their hammocks.

On the following day we stopped beside a small stream where the Indians, who had by now begun to understand the object of my journey, collected orchids and bromeliads for me, even vying with each other as to who could discover the most interesting plants. The rain continued for the greater part of the day, but in spite of it the sultry heat was overwhelming. Rain mixed with sweat ran down my brow, stinging my eyes.

In one place along the way we found strange spirals of black mud on the forest floor. When I stepped on one of them there was a sound like rumbling thunder and I asked Placido what it could be. He informed me that beneath these hummocks lived *minhocas* (type of giant earthworm). Amongst the rotting leaves with which the ground was carpeted I stepped on the still fragrant though faded flowers of *Clusia grandiflora*, the 'queen' of clusias, fallen from the canopy overhead.

Rain, and still more rain, and as the light had faded by four o'clock we camped early, cooked supper and retired for the night. But this time my hammock was not so inviting. It had been hung hurriedly so that water streamed in and I was drenched. Rain dripped in my ears and when I turned over to avoid it, dripped in my face. There was no escape for Paulo either, who shouted above the pelting rain that he, too, was sodden as his plastic cover kept blowing off. When morning came there was no relief, for from wet pyjamas I changed into wet clothes.

'I remained entranced by the beauty.'

'A strange and beautiful tree.'

Our trek continued with the climb becoming steeper. Numerous streams crossed the now almost invisible track and we waded through pools of black mud. In spite of these hardships I remained entranced by the beauty of the surrounding forests, and their timeless aspect dwarfed such trivial things as the pouring rain. Streams which I found difficult to wade, the Indians carried me across, laughing and joking. One particularly steep and slippery ascent proved too much for me and scrambling upwards, exhausted and streaming with sweat, my heavy rucksack seemed to be pulling me backwards. Sick with faint I flopped face down in the mud and signalled to Rafael, who was coming up the slope behind me, to call Otis, Paulo or one of the others, who then came to my assistance, took off my pack and helped me to my feet. At this critical moment a *toçandira* stung me on the wrist and shoulder, an agonising pain!

But then, suddenly, relief. I was cured of all my ills at the top of the slope where the hill opened to a shoulder covered with a glorious array of orchids and bromeliads. Among them was *Aechmea fernandae,* a rarity which I had last seen in the Mato Grosso at Aripuana.

Otis was ahead, though slipping often on the treacherous mud which made the climb more difficult than it should have been, but was certainly not unexpected on a cloud-covered mountain. The rain and fine drizzle blanketed everything and turned the forest into a misty, fantasy land. Suddenly I stood transfixed. At a short distance from the track grew a strange and beautiful tree. Or was it a tree? Or was it a tremendous mass of lianas? The thick rope-like stems writhed and twisted towards the sky where they were lost in the canopy of the forest. There was not a leaf to be seen

Margaret sketches the pitcairnia (opposite) beside a stream at about 1,600 feet up the Cerro da Neblina.

on this curious giant. Not a single epiphyte — absolutely nothing, it was bare. I made some sketches and then took the chance to have a short rest.

As I stood wondering and admiring this magnificent creation, Rafael, who had been some distance behind me passed with a strange lingering gaze and I realised with a start that the rest of the group were out of sight and far ahead. Panic seized me as I realised I was alone on the slopes of Neblina and that soon it would be dark. Following Rafael, who was rushing ahead, I hurried on, pausing only to glance over my shoulder to assure myself that what I had seen was real and not a waking vision.

We came down a sharp slope to the sound of tumbling water. We had reached the mountain course of the Tucáno and it seemed a good spot to camp for the night. This was the place which the Boundary Commission accompanied by Bassett Maguire and a Brazilian botanist, Murça Pires, had reached a few years earlier. The posts were still there, though slightly weathered by the elements. We were almost 3,000 feet above

The pitcairna, a bromeliad.

sea level and surrounded by drenched Amazonian forest. The nearest people were the Indians at the mission a long way below. I took a refreshing bath in the river and decided to retire to my hammock and relax but found it still saturated and my pyjamas wet through. Nothing ever dried in that climate.

With the morning light came bad news. Placido came to tell me that we could not continue on our journey as the incessant rains had washed the trail away. Early that

A galeandra orchid.

morning, the Indians had gone ahead to discover the state of the path and, finding it completely obliterated, felt there was no alternative but to return to the boat. Cutting a totally new trail would take weeks if not months and we were not equipped for that. I was bitterly disappointed and could not restrain my tears, but I fostered the lingering hope that should the weather improve that day we might struggle on.

The kindly Joao seeing my distress and to console me disappeared into the forest and returned with a scarlet flowered pitcairnia for me to paint. In spite of the drizzle I became absorbed in my work until Napoleao ran off with my tube of red paint to which he had taken a fancy. He returned it willingly but only after my protests. We waited in camp for the morning and then the drizzle turned to rain. Then, at last, we decided to abandon the attempt and packed ready for an early start the following day.

Soon after daybreak, I made an unwilling retreat down the slopes of Neblina. As all the camping equipment was so saturated with water, which doubled its weight, we were unable to hurry. We had been on the mountain a week and were anxious about the boat for, despite the rain, August is the time when the river level drops and the sand banks are exposed. The boat could easily be trapped for weeks. We thought it possible that Carlos and Santino might have moved off to navigable water. Perhaps even as far as to Maturacá.

Napoleao and Placido went ahead, carrying our food and most of the camping equipment with them. They raced through the forest as only Indians can. We never caught up with them and that day we suffered the pangs of hunger, only finding a little rice and powder milk in our baggage. However, at an old *maloca* we gathered an unripe *mamao* (papaya) which helped ease our hunger. There I was able to recline in one of the hammocks which had been hanging there maybe for years. Rafael told us that the *maloca* had been abandoned when many of the Indians died of introduced diseases.

As we walked on we reached another of these sad, abandoned *malocas*. We rested there and, without any sign of emotion on his expressionless face, Rafael told us that there most of the tribe had perished of 'catarrh' — influenza, amongst them his father who lies buried beneath one of the huts. I was not sorry to leave this place of tragedy, haunted as it was by sad memories of the dead.

Before nightfall we reached one of our camp sites in the lower level of the Tucáno river. Another day and we would get to the Cauaburi. The men reroofed the shelters which they had built on the outward journey, using the huge rather banana-like leaves of ravenala which grew there in abundance. The fire was lit in the smallest of shelters but only just before the heavens opened, and the torrential rain soon quenched the flames. Joao and Rafael crept into the thick forest, returning with an enormous termite nest, like tough, tinder dry wood, with which they soon rekindled the fire. The nest blazed furiously, giving off heavy, acrid yellow smoke which hung in the trees. Shivering and wet we crowded around the fire in the little shelter waiting for Napoleao who had more baggage and our hammocks. He arrived late having spent a few hours hunting — unsuccessfully.

We left early in the morning, greatly relieved that the heavy rain had turned to drizzle. My plants were becoming an intolerable burden and the ground was tremendously slimy under the rotting leaves; once again I lagged behind my companions. Moreover, I was waylaid by more exciting plants which I had to collect. Once I lost the track by following a dried stream bed which looked for all the world like a path, then I found I was losing grip on the plastic plant bags. I felt the last of my strength slipping away, but as I turned a bend in the path a most welcome sight relieved me — Napoleao standing beneath a great tree. 'I was waiting for you Dona Margalctc', he said with all his charm, and taking my bags he slung them easily over his shoulder.

We walked rapidly until we reached the Cauaburi, though I slipped often in my mud-covered canvas shoes. The launch was still there, but I noticed with a shock that she appeared abandoned, silent, her shutters closed. Moments later I was thankful when the shutters were opened noisily by Carlos and Santino happy to see us again. They complained they had been eaten by *pium,* and had shuttered the cabin to escape the plague of these blood-sucking flies — they were 'red *pium*' they said, much bigger and more venomous than the small black variety.

Santino had prepared a meal of *paca* and rice which we ate hungrily, even before changing our travel-stained clothes, for it was over a week since we had enjoyed a substantial meal. Then we headed back to the mission to land our Indian guides. What a help they had been — I knew that with good weather they would have taken me to the summit.

We started off on our return journey to Tapurucuará after literally extricating ourselves from the 'Waikas' who beseiged us from early morning with outstretched hands: *'Iba! Iba!'* (give! give!), one of the worst gifts of civilisation. We said our 'goodbyes' simply and clambered on the boat. Carlos pushed out into the canal and we turned towards the Cauaburi.

I was sad to leave these beautiful people, dwellers in another world, a world of glorious nature — but for how long?

The return journey was uneventful. Margaret sketched and cared for her plants putting them into baskets for safety. Once back in Tapurucuará, she decided to stay on the Negro and make a journey to the River Marauiá, while Otis returned to Washington. The report of their expedition, with a list of species collected, including one new species (a bromeliad, Neoregelia leviana, *named by Dr. Lyman Smith), was published in a special National Geographic Society Research Report.*

Herons.

Gustavia augusta
Amazonas Nov. 1985

Margaret Mee

JOURNEY FIVE: 1967
To the 'Waika' Indians of the River Marauiá

'Curica'.

The River Marauiá grows from a score of mountain streams nearly one hundred miles from the Pico da Neblina. As a vigorously young river it tumbles through forested canyons before pouring over a succession of rapids into the River Negro. In 1967, the headwaters were unmapped. They were known to only a handful of garimpeiros, Salesian missionaries and local 'Waika' Indians.

The 'Waika' had long held a reputation for being hostile. Their name is often simply translated as 'killers', though in their language its meaning is certainly deeper. These Indians are part of a larger, highly individual group, the Yanomamo, whose territory ranges across the mountainous borders of Venezuela and Brazil. The Indians live near tributaries of the Orinoco and Amazon. One of these is the Marauiá.

Margaret first heard of this intriguing river from Dr. Leopoldo Froes in Belém. He told her of his excitement in 1939, when from the air he sighted large, thatched, ring-shaped Indian shelters. Father Schneider at Maturacá expanded on the story for he knew of the region from another priest, Father Antonio Goes whose tiny mission outpost was far upriver. Armed with an introduction and her ever-present urge to explore, Margaret planned to ascend the Marauiá at least as far as this mission. Her friends at Tapurucuará offered help, but warned that the journey would be arduous. So with a Christmas deadline to meet in London for her Tryon Gallery exhibition and related book launch, Margaret sent a message to Greville saying she would allow herself just two months more.

Indian children at Tapurucuará mission.

16th August, 1967

The Santa Casa — the hospital of the Salesian Mission in Tapurucuará — had not been used since the patients of the last measles epidemic had left. As a room it had little appeal. It was large, rather dark and with sightless windows. I was assigned to these quarters by the Mother Superior, and as I could choose any bed I liked I took one near the door. Outside, a long corridor isolated the hospital room from the main buildings, while at the other end a heavy wrought iron gate led into the open garden with access to the only track in the village. I was warned to make sure the gate was closed as there had been a robbery only the week before.

Indian girls who were pupils at the mission school, carried my rather untidy baggage from the boat, and while they were busy my first thought was to hang the cage of 'Curica', a beautifully coloured, orange-cheeked parrot, on a hook near my

Gustavia augusta.

121

With a tame parrot on the River Negro.

bed. The parrot was a gift from my good friend Sister Elza Ramos and as I could not bear to see the fledgling cooped in that tiny space, I opened the door of the cage.

'Today I worked on the plants collected on the journey to Pico da Neblina. I have planted them temporarily in the leaf sheaths of the palm trees — they make such wonderful natural spots as they gather plenty of moisture. Most of the plants seem to have survived, but a good rain would be a godsend. Paulo helped me and worked well, whilst 'Curica' sat in a little tree, observing and enjoying himself immensely. But after supper, I went to my room and found him hopelessly tied up in the fringe of a towel. I hurried the suffering creature to Paulo, who quickly cut the fringe whilst the parrot screamed loudly. When free, he took water in gasps, then insisted on sleeping under my chin.'

That night we shared an unpleasant experience. In this region of the upper Negro, as well as in Sao Gabriel da Cachóeira, vampire bats seem to be prolific and they are no better now than in the days of Richard Spruce. He mentioned how unwittingly he became a meal for the creatures one night when his mosquito net opened slightly.

I had noticed the night before that there was a bat flying around, but apart from the noise of its wings it did not bother me as my net was secure. But soon after turning down my oil lamp I heard the iron gate rattling loudly, and with the burglary in mind I felt it my duty to investigate. I peered through the high window but saw nothing suspicious. Then, as I returned to my bed, the bat flew close to my face with an almost caressing movement of its wings. I rapidly scrambled back under my net. I shone my torch (which always lies beside me) around the room and, to my horror, the beam shone on the bat hanging under the little parrot's cage. 'Curica', frozen with fear, sat huddled in a corner of the cage. I jumped out of bed and the bat flew off as I seized the cage and thrust it under my net. 'Curica' felt secure and calmed down, but the bat continued to flap around my mosquito net and kept me half awake for the rest of the night. Next morning I searched the room and found the lethargic creature hanging under a bed. I opened the door and windows before prodding the beast into life.

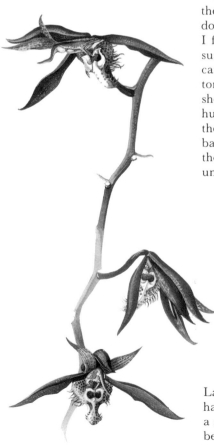

'Dr. Hans Becker, an anthropologist from Hamburg, accompanied by an Indian girl, arrived at the mission today. He has just returned from a journey to the first rapids of the Marauiá with a party of wealthy German birdwatchers and has invited me to their boat to meet them. Frankly most of them do not appeal to me and I am sure the feeling is mutual. My reception there this morning was cold and some of the 'tourists' even appeared hostile. But Dr. Becker was able to tell me about the river which he says is 'black' and relatively free of mosquitoes and *pium*. The group had only reached the first Indian *aldeia*, a village of the Kemeneté, a 'Waika' family, below the rapids. Beyond that point the river becomes progressively more difficult with five bad *cachóeiras*. The Indians have given them delightful names. Bicho-mirim, the small 'bicho', or animal, comes first, then Bicho-açu, or large animal, said to be extremely hard, and followed by at least four more.'

Later that day I was sitting on the hospital terrace. An interesting orchid, a catasetum, had flowered and I had just finished painting it when Adhemar Fontes, the owner of a small boat, came over to talk about sharing the cost of a journey upstream. He had been recommended by the sisters, as at one time he had worked with a Government malaria squad travelling the rivers and spraying *caboclos'* huts with D.D.T. against mosquitoes — hence his nickname 'Dede'. Luckily for me, he had given up that job

Catasetum saccatum.

Below the rapids, the Marauiá is tranquil.

and turned to moving cargo up and down the rivers in his boat, the *Santo Alberto.*

'Dede', with a young Indian boy to help, was taking a sheep and a mule to the mission of Father Goes, so I asked him if there would be room aboard for Paulo and me. We agreed on a fifty-fifty basis and decided to leave early the next day. At the last minute we were delayed when, fortunately for us at least, a mule, true to character, obstinately refused to go. The effort of trying to get the animal aboard took most of the morning and I was relieved when 'Dede' decided to leave without it. We edged out into the Negro and headed upstream. The river was broad and easy flowing between banks lined with unbroken forest. 'Curica' came too, and I arranged his cage in the cool under the roof.

Many of Margaret's pictures were affected by the heat and humidity, like this of the banks of the Marauiá.

Our first stop was not far upriver at Adhemar's house where he wanted to pick up a small canoe. His wife, a pretty Tucáno Indian, greeted us with her two beautiful children beside her. The house was constructed in the Indian style, but had a slightly more elaborate interior. Like the boat, it was spotlessly clean and we were treated to a splendid lunch of manioc and fish while 'Curica' was given *goiabas* (guavas). Adhemar also produced a stronger, more resilient cage built from split cane which he said I could borrow for the parrot. We transferred him to the new quarters, said our 'goodbyes' and went on our way.

The route kept close to the north bank in a *parana* separated from the main river by forest which in high water is half submerged. This *parana* 'de Tapurucuará' led us into the Marauiá where, soon after dusk, we arrived uneventfully at the Indian *maloca* visited by Dr. Becker and his party. Lights shone intermittently among the leaves like enormous fireflies and I could only guess that the Germans had left torches as presents for the Indians. Voices in the local language rang out asking our business and Adhemar, who knew a few words, answered. Some shots came next followed by more shouting which echoed across the dark river. Splashing and shouts came from the bank nearby. The men were hunting *jacaré*. These Amazon crocodilians can grow to over fifteen feet, and we waited quietly to hear if they caught one.

As the noise subsided we noticed the gentle splashing of a canoe paddling. Two of the men had left the hunt and come over to find out what strange animal we had aboard, as they were consumed with curiosity and much amused by the bleating of the sheep on board the *Santo Alberto*, a sound quite new to them.

In the dim light I was able to observe the Indians. They appeared to be around thirty years of age, both had well-shaped, muscular, bronzed bodies, and the only concession in dress to us 'civilisados' were brief shorts. Blue and white *miçangas* (tiny beads on cords) were worn around the neck and crossed over the chest, and in bands around the top of the arms. In the tradition of the tribe they had their ears pierced, though they were not wearing ear ornaments. As I learned later, the German 'tourists' had swapped the torches and other goods for the ornaments which were pretty bunches of parrot feathers. Now the Indians were busy making new ones to replace them.

The two men invited us to their *maloca,* the name we used commonly at the time for the large, thatched shelters covering the communal houses of these Indians. Adhemar explained that we would visit them after we had eaten our supper. Manioc, some rice and fish was already prepared and we ate hungrily. Adhemar then suggested that I should go with Paulo while he and the boy stayed behind to guard the boat. We took our hammocks and my bag with the sketch book. Felipe, one of the Indians, paddled us in his dugout canoe to the beginning of a forest path leading to their *maloca,* which was called Irapajé. The two Indians then escorted me carefully over rough ground which was absolutely black. Trees and undergrowth hemmed in on every side bringing the gorgeous night sounds ever closer. It was a long walk through the woods and, though difficult, it was an entrancing experience with the soft perfume of night flowers and dampness all round us. Only a pungent waft of wood smoke told me we were getting close. Then, quite suddenly, we were in a clearing with an open, starry sky above. The glow of several fires ahead gave a faint outline to the village.

The *maloca* consisted of eleven or twelve houses built in a circle around a large open area. There was also a sprinkling of huts which were not traditional and were inferior in finish and design. The traditional houses were very elegant, with four tall slender poles at the front holding the palm leaf roof which sloped steeply to a wall of leaves from the *paxiúba,* a palm, where the hammocks were hung. The structure was open at the sides and front. As the distance between the front poles and the back wall was relatively great, I imagine that the roof provided sufficient protection against heavy

rains and storms. We were shown a place to hang our hammocks, and we then joined Felipe and his family.

As the full moon appeared in the unclouded sky, she shone between a magnificent group of palm trees. The village was silent as we sat on low Indian stools and talked in Felipe's house until late, while the rest of the tribe slept in their hammocks above the glowing embers of the individual fires. However, Felipe, his friend Domingo and Araripe, a relative, were not very communicative, partly through difficulty with the language, but also, I sensed, because Paulo was asking too many questions about the village, customs and religion. Felipe's wife, nursing in her arms a baby nearly as big as herself, talked more freely with me, in spite of language difficulties. Weary with the excitement of the day, I slept soundly, but in the small hours of the morning I was awakened by a man's voice singing loudly. The song seemed to be interspersed with weeping, and it wailed on, sometimes sad and complaining, sometimes angry with loud curses, when the word *Jurupari* was distinguishable.

Shortly before dawn a soft woman's voice joined the singing. Then the singers must have fallen asleep, exhausted, for silence once more reigned in the *maloca,* a silence broken only by the graveyard coughs of many of the tribe. Later Felipe told me that the singer was a man whose wife had recently died of measles, and who had been lamenting his loss in this way every night since her death. I knew from the mission there had been an epidemic amongst the 'Waika' tribes in the area, and here I felt the fullness of the Indian's dread of diseases brought into their forest isolation by the 'civilisados'.

Next morning we returned to the boat accompanied by Felipe and Domingo who came to help us cross the *cachóeiras.* Truly we needed their help for the boat had to be lifted over the rocks and dragged through the raging torrent. It took over an hour to pass the first fall with much sweating and straining and, as they had said, Bicho-açu was even more of an ordeal. The only way up was among rocks near the bank, and the two Indians used long poles to lever the hull across the obstruction which took until midday to pass. Finally we were over the rapids and, completely exhausted, settled on a group of big stones beside calmer water. A fire was soon prepared and we cooked rice for our lunch. With time to rest I even took 'Curica' out of his cage, a decision I soon regretted when he fell in the river and had to be rescued by Paulo.

It was a splendid place for plant collecting and there I found *Streptocalyx longifolius* — a bromeliad with tremendously long leaves and *Aechmea mertensii.* This last was a bromeliad I had seen in a variety of habitats but always filled with stinging ants. I carefully cut some good examples and put them in my collecting bag for sketching once we reached a more convenient place.

125

A coati.

Their work done and their hunger satisfied, the Indians left us, having been paid for their valuable help with fishing hooks, nylon line, a small knife each, and plenty of cigarettes, which they do not smoke but take apart to chew the tobacco. They headed back to their *maloca* through the forest and, as Paulo told us, would hunt along the way.

The next rapid, which the Indians assured us would not be difficult to navigate, proved quite impassable. After making many desperate attempts to cross, we unloaded the boat and tried once more, but without any success. There was nothing for it but to get help again from the Indians. So Adhemar, accompanied by the Indian boy, paddled off in our small canoe to get help. They did not return and, as it was growing dark, I began to be afraid that they might have met with disaster in the rapids.

Whilst waiting anxiously for their return I sat in the forest and painted the beautiful blue orchid *Acacallis cyanea*. There I also found a *Heterostemon ellipticus,* so fragile it was already wilting, and a marvellous *Pitcairnia uaupensis* in bud.

Much to my relief the two men returned, but they had been unable to reach the *maloca* in time to return before dusk, for after dark they would have been hopelessly lost. That night we had to sleep in the boat with the rapids roaring beside us. In the morning they set off again, and returned with Felipe, Domingo and another strong Indian lad. It was a tremendously difficult task to cross these rapids, and to make matters worse, as there had been no rain for days, the river level had fallen exposing more rock. However, after a stupendous struggle, the Indians managed to heave the boat through the fearsome torrent. It literally inched forward with their efforts, and at one point Adhemar fell on the slippery rocks and was nearly carried into the falls. Whilst the men sweated and struggled, *mutucas* (horseflies) took advantage of our situation to attack us with their sharp, painful stings.

'We did not stop today until nearly dusk, when we sighted a hut which appeared to be abandoned. It belonged to Feliciano, a *seringueiro,* and was perched high on the river bank bounded on one side by an *igarapé*. A long roughly-hewn ramp, weak and precarious, led to the entrance. The cabin itself was clean and pleasant, so Paulo and I hung our hammocks there, whilst the men lit a fire in the primitive fireplace to cook supper.

In the garden, which was being invaded by forest trees and plants, I found a bush of *cubiu* in fruit. This plant is related to the potato and tomato and has tomato-like fruits. They are pulpy and edible so I gathered a few. There was also a well-laden lemon tree (lemons were introduced to Brazil by priests in the early days of Portuguese colonisation). 'Curica' and I ate the *cubiu* ravenously, for there has been a real lack of fruit in our diet. Collecting here is good. Where the

Streptocalyx longifolius (Bromeliaceae).

Margaret Mee

Streptocalyx longifolia
Amazonas, Rio Negro
May, 1982

The black-headed cacique.

trees have been felled by Feliciano they have brought down orchids which are now growing within my reach. I have collected a small catasetum and many other plants. '

We left the hut early next day. The river was falling fast and Adhemar was concerned that on our return journey we could get stuck above the falls. We continued all day, with the river narrowing between rocky banks and made even more perilous by shallows. By dusk we were not far from the mission of Father Goes, our destination, and Adhemar decided to keep going slowly. Experienced pilot though he was, he strained tensely at the wheel, whilst the Indian boy shone a beam from the powerful torch to light the banks. It picked out a scene of curious trees, dark water and rocks. After almost two hours of difficult navigation, Adhemar announced that we must be reaching our destination, as he could hear the voices of Indians. What relief! And indeed, within a few minutes we moored against a steep bank from which hurricane lamps were shone down on us.

We were welcomed by Father Antonio Goes, a tall, heavily-built man with a dark beard beginning to grey a little. His name was legendary all over the Negro as he had experienced many adventures. Once he was lost for three days when his canoe was dashed against rocks in a *cachóeira*; on another occasion he had made the first contact with an Indian tribe. He had settled his mission at this spot six years earlier and now spoke the local language fluently. He soon made us feel at home and invited us to hang our hammocks under the roof of a large covered area supported by posts. These also supported the priest's living quarters on the floor above which were reached by a flight of open wooden steps.

The mission was in the Serra do Chamatá, a range of low foothills to the higher *serras* of Tapirapeco and Curipira. Narrow 'divides' linked the headwaters with the Cauaburi where I had been only a month earlier. As we talked for an hour or two over a simple meal, the priest told me that, as far as he knew, the region was botanically unexplored. The flora, he felt sure, was very rich but to go further upstream or into the mountains would take more time than I had. Furthermore, I would need a canoe with an outboard motor — which he had, and could lend me, except that he was short of fuel. In the same breath he asked if Adhemar could give him a tow when he returned to Tapurucuará.

The night was incredibly peaceful and, though disappointed that I could not get beyond the mission, I slept soundly until dawn. After a simple breakfast of rice and fruit, Father Antonio, knowing I would appreciate a little privacy, showed me to a small palm-leaf hut which had the unique luxury of a lock and key and where all my possessions could be guarded. But the Indians were too quick, and before the rucksacks were stowed, they invaded the hut. Their curiosity was insatiable and each Indian examined everything I had with concentrated interest. Paulo came to my rescue and succeeded in tactfully leading them away. Once they were out of the room I quickly locked the door and began to change my travel-stained clothes for clean ones. It was a marvellous relief to tear off my sweaty shirt and muddy slacks. Totally nude I was fishing about in my rucksack for clean clothes when I thought I heard a whispering and tittering. The thin palm-leaf wall was a-twinkle with pairs of Indian eyes! Discovered, the Indians dashed off, laughing as they went.

After changing and tidying my sketch books I joined Paulo on a walk around the mission and nearby forest. Two Indians who understood a few words of Portuguese

'At the maloca *we were led from family to family.'*

led us to the *maloca* which lay at a little distance from my hut through trees brimming with life. Although people were never far away, the sound of insects, the flash of brilliant butterflies and the bird calls were undisturbed. The Indians and the forest lived simply together. At the *maloca* we were led from family to family, some of whom were reclining in hammocks, many with sick children who were just recovering from measles. The epidemic that had taken its toll in the *maloca* in Irapajé, had swept through this *maloca* too.

We exchanged the things the Indians asked for, such as mirrors, scissors and beads, for feather ornaments, baskets and arrows. The Indian workmanship was beautiful, and I really felt the exchange was very one sided and that we got far more than we deserved for our objects. The two *tushauas* were delightful men, especially the one calling himself Pedro. Like other Indians I had met they did not divulge their Indian language names — even to Father Antonio who had been with them for six years. The reason here, as in other parts of the Amazon region, concerned the Indian belief that a name was a soul which could be lost if it was given to us 'civilisados'. When I was presented to *tushaua* Pedro, who spoke a little Portuguese, he held my hand long and lovingly and stroked my hair then took hold of the tresses, saying 'Margalete, I want to cut your hair'. Suddenly, I felt alarmed. If he did want my hair how could I refuse? I was their guest and he meant no harm. But I imagined appearing at my exhibition in London with short hair cut in the traditional tonsure and stained red with *urucu*. The thought appalled me, especially as The Tryon Gallery was fashionable and there was to be a special reception to celebrate the exhibition and launching of my book.

In the forest beside the river.

129

'My days with the ''Waika'' were always happy.'

Sketch of an oncidium orchid.

How was I to dissuade the chief from cutting my hair? He had already sent a boy to fetch the scale of a *pirarucu,* one of the largest of all Amazon fish whose hard, bony scales can be sharpened and used like a knife. Now he was grasping my hair firmly and clearly had no intention of letting go despite my pleading. The long hair fascinated him; obviously it was the first time he had seen anything like it. In desperation I turned to him saying that when I returned to my home far away if my hair had been cut I should not be allowed to enter the house. At this simple logic, the kind hearted *tushaua* looked grave and said in that case he would not cut it. He must have seen my relief when, with obvious disappointment, he relaxed his hold.

The *maloca* was constructed on similar plan to that of the village of Irapajé, and the buildings were of the traditional kind though loftier. Inside the shelters, I noticed with regret the instrusion of utensils and some hammocks from the sophisticated world. They looked so incongruous amongst the superior hand-made articles of the tribe.

We left the *maloca* to return to the mission, but before we were in sight of the mission huts, we heard a loud weeping and wailing floating up towards us from the river. A heavy grey drizzle had set in and we hurried to find shelter. Father Antonio appeared from his house and signalled, indicating that I should remain silent. He then drew me behind the palings forming the limit of his ground.

At the river bank below, Indians were leaving their canoes and forming a procession which was winding slowly up the path towards the *maloca.* Through the gaps in the fence I watched, fascinated and apprehensive. Father Antonio whispered that I must not be seen, or it could be dangerous. This was a funeral procession mourning the death from measles of a *tushaua's* wife. The small son of the *tushaua* led the way. He was followed by his father whose ceremonial paint had been largely washed away by his flowing tears. The other men of the tribe followed in full tribal paint and adornments, the most highly ornamented being the *feiticeiro,* who danced beside the leading men. His limbs were painted with serpentine designs, two of which ran from

Rudolfiella aurantiaca (Orchidaceae).

Margaret Mee

Rudolfiella aurantiaca (Lindl.) Hoehne
Rio Negro, Amazonas.
November 1971

The Indians followed the feiticeiro.

his shoulder over his chest and down the complete length of his body. He wore bunches of parrot feathers in his ears, and at the top of his arms were fixed bracelets, probably made of monkey skin. Two scarlet *arara* tail feathers gleamed on another mourner. His limbs and torso were painted in the near black colour of *genipapo*, and much of the remainder of his body and face were covered with *urucu*. The women, who did not form part of the funeral procession, carried *xotos* (baskets supported on the shoulders by a palm fibre band resting around the forehead). These closely-woven baskets were so full of plantain that the women were bent over horizontally by the weight. Some of them also carried small children. The *xotos* were stained a red earth colour with *urucu* and painted with snake-like designs in *genipapo*. The Indians wound their way to the *maloca* to continue their lamenting with others of the tribe.

The funeral procession passed and Father Antonio, who was a mine of information, said that the main Indian feast — the Feast of Spring — and the funeral rites would be celebrated the following week. Then the ashes of the *tushaua's* wife would be ground to a powder, mixed with plantain and made into a soup which would be eaten by the relatives. Such was the strength of feeling that the departed spirit of the dead wife should not return that the Indians would dispose of every piece of her and her personal belongings.

I returned to my hut and was soon joined by two Indian women. One, who carried a baby, was wearing a ragged cotton dress, a cast-off from civilisation, while the other, Maria, who was minute, was completely naked. She was not even wearing a *tanga* (simple pubic covering worn by some Indians). Maria and her friend wanted to exchange gifts. I had brought mirrors, a pair of scissors, some *miçanga* and had other simple things in my bag. While we were talking the lady with the baby slipped her dress off one shoulder and began to feed the infant. Maria, who saw this pointed excitedly and tried to make her cover herself. As Maria was totally uncovered, except for her *genipapo* body painting, I was surprised, but learnt some time later that Father Antonio would not allow the Indians to go unclothed in the mission grounds. Maria had been afraid that I would scold her friend.

'Tomorrow we are leaving for Tapurucuará in the company of Father Antonio. I shall be sad to leave the Indians for some have become good friends. They have

'Waikas' and their xotos *(baskets).*

132

'*I was joined by two Indian women.*'

had a bad toll from the diseases of us 'civilisados' and the measles epidemic was serious. Twelve of the Indians and some children, who have legs like matchsticks and can hardly walk, recovered through the careful treatment of Father Antonio.

This morning, after asking the permission of the Indians, I took photos of them receiving their 'ration' of tobacco, which they chew. They keep it behind the lower lip when it is not in use, which gives them a slightly distorted appearance around the lower jaw. When the scanty wrapping paper ran out, they fetched the large leaves of the *embaubá* (cecropia tree) as a substitute. Happily, outside the mission the majority of these Indians have not taken to the habit of wearing the discarded clothes of 'civilisados' which destroy their dignity and grace, and many still used beautiful feather ornaments to decorate their coppery bodies. Unfortunately the *feiticeiro* refused to be photographed and became very angry when first Paulo and then the Father asked if he would allow this. I wondered what the objection could be, and the Father said that the tribe held the belief that their souls could be imprisoned by the portrait. '

In the afternoon I went collecting in the nearby forests, two very handsome Indians, wearing red and white feather armlets, leading the way. They were most helpful, too, and we returned from an *igarapé* heavily laden with plants. We had some exciting bromeliads and orchids with — surprise! — only one scorpion among them. But the trip left me soaked with perspiration which activated all my insect bites, so I went for a dip in the river. Refreshing though it was it did not rid me of the thousands of *mucuim* bites which had accumulated since I left Tapurucuará.

'The *mucuim* drive me frantic with their irritation. The last three nights there have been fierce storms, reaching a climax last night. Another seems to be approaching now, judging by the thunder and flashes of lightning streaking through the heavy clouds. Hopefully it is also raining on the *serra* and this will help fill the river for our return journey. Adhemar tells me that the water level has been rising rapidly, which will help us over the *cachóeiras,* and the absence of a bleating sheep, which has been delivered to its destination, will at least give us some peace.

We left the mission at eight in the morning. Father Antonio is journeying with us for one day and we shall camp together for the first night of the voyage. Three Indians, Felipe, Domingo and Bauari are with the Father to help. His aluminium canoe with a fifteen hp outboard motor and his large wooden canoe are being towed to save petrol.

We have just passed two magnificent *cachóeiras* — the last one so difficult to navigate that it took two hours and caused damage to the hull. We have stopped

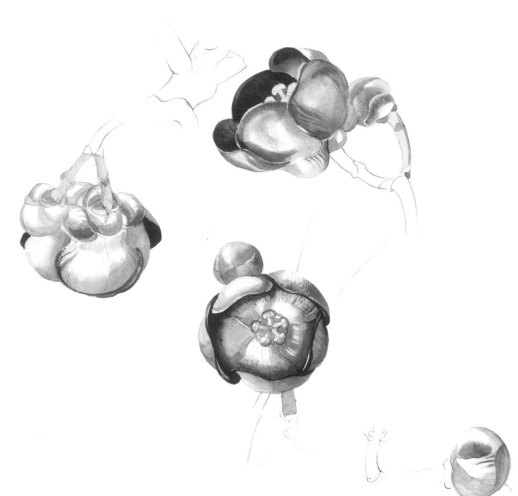

Sketches of Clusia grandifolia *(Guttiferae).*

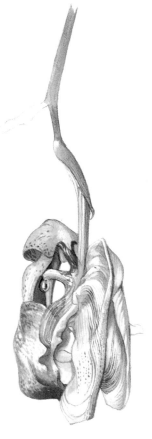

A coryanthes orchid.

for repairs and the night and Father Antonio says he will go ahead in the canoe with the three Indians.

It is the last day on our way to Tapurucuará and we are apprehensively anticipating the passage over the Bicho-açu. This is the last bad rapid and the fatigue from working in the rough water has put Paulo in such a temper. I hope the boat goes through without damage. '

We reached the *cachóeira* and Adhemar chose to keep near to the bank where we could grasp branches and keep the boat from rushing forward. We were hanging on desperately, and the river was sweeping by threatening to take us over the falls, when I caught sight of a long, pendant inflorescence of a somewhat faded coryanthes orchid. It was a dramatic moment to try and halt the boat but the flower was within arm's reach of Adhemar. I begged him to get it for me as it was a great rarity. He tugged at the beautiful plant, then gave a cry as fire ants, which usually live with this plant, swarmed up his arms, stinging ferociously. In one move he flung plant and ants' nest into the river, and plunged his arms in the water. Fearful that the strong currents would carry away my prize, I seized it still full of ants and, in spite of their stings, quickly put it into a plastic bag from which the ants could not escape. This coryanthes was such a prize and for me, at least, it was worth the suffering.

Then the struggle to pass the rapids started. Adhemar who was standing on slippery rocks in the midst of whirling currents, suddenly slipped and fell, just escaping being carried away by the seething cataract. All hands shot out together to help but the damage was done, and without Adhemar's leverage the boat swung sideways, jolting sharply against a rock. The freshly repaired part of the hull was broken again and once more we had to stop for repairs. It was late evening before we left the Marauiá. I was sad to be leaving such an untouched and exciting river, but then it was a marvellous feeling to be back on the River Negro, with a fine collection of plants waving in the breeze!

134

Clusia grandifolia.

Margaret Mee 1982

Clusia grandifolia Endl.
Rio Negro, Amazonas

The return to Manaus, down the River Negro

We left Tapurucuará soon after midday and almost immediately encountered a storm. We were five aboard, Adhemar, the crew of two — Tonika an Indian and a *caboclo* — Paulo and myself. The wind blew up suddenly, as it does in a matter of seconds on the Negro — on other rivers it never seems to break so quickly. White capped waves were soon knocking against our little boat, so Adhemar decided to put into a 'port' serving a small group of huts. We waited for almost an hour, and though the thunder and brilliant lightning passed, the waters remained turbulent. Adhemar chose to be cautious and we passed the night in that sheltered spot.

It was a fortunate decision, for next morning I saw some orchids in the branches above the water. Tonika and the *caboclo* were quickly into the trees collecting and I decided to try the forest. 'Curica' was out of his cage, as I felt he needed native friends, but, for the second time, he fell awkwardly from the boat into the shallow water and almost drowned. He emerged drenched and terrified and I did not have the heart to leave him alone. Instead I put off my collecting until late in the afternoon when we stopped at a sandy strip with the river on one side and on the other a dark *igapó*. Here the strange shapes of dry, dead trees intermixed with the living formed a fantastic world shimmering in the tropical heat. On the trees I found two cacti, one a rhipsalis rather like a collection of boot laces, and the other a broader leaved phyllocactus. I looked in vain for a third species, the rare night-flowering strophocactus which botanists say is special to these places.

The downriver journey was hardly quicker than upstream as the current was insignificant. Already the Negro was over four miles wide here, with *igapó* which, in high water months, would be flooded as much as fifteen or twenty miles beyond the banks.

'We spent last night on a wonderfully peaceful beach, the margin of a long, sandy island between two wide reaches of the river. In the swampy stretches low bushes grow, mostly mimosa and, in the deeper swamp, small palms. I have found the petals of qualea, a glorious gentian blue, but cannot locate the tree from which they have fallen. The forest canopy and lianas form a luxuriant mass of vegetation, with every tree and creeper struggling to reach the sun.

Tonight we stopped at about eight. It is pitch dark with the stars and moon hidden behind clouds. As there are no beaches, we have moored in a small *igarapé* in an area of *várzea* (seasonally flooded land which dries at low water). The large, waxing moon rose over this peaceful haven, silent but for the frogs' chorus and the sad cries of owls and other night birds. For the first time I have heard the remarkable cry of an aquatic night bird, the *saracura* (rail).'

'A cloudy day dawned but it revealed a splendid place for collecting from the small palms, on which there was a profusion of cattleyas and catasetums, some of the latter in bud, promising male and female flowers.

I spotted a very impressive iguana, pale greyish-blue and larger than a full grown *teju-açu,* which measures over six feet when adult. He was basking in the sun on a mass of foliage in the *igapó,* but fell with a tremendous splash into the dark waters when he saw us in the canoe. The name for him in the region is *cameleao.*

Today I made colour sketches of a beautiful clusia which I could just reach on the bank; it was no easy matter, seated in the boat which was rolling in the swell of the river. This is the first time I have seen a perfect specimen of this species, *Clusia grandiflora,* which is a coral colour inside and white outside, looking like a precious piece of porcelain.

I started the day with a fine collection of plants and seeds of the *Bombax*

An igapó *of the River Negro.*

A gustavia (Lecythidaceae).

137

munguba, which has large scarlet pods full of kapok in which nestle seeds very much sought after by parrots. Later Paulo collected a large bromeliad which was so full of ants we had to put it in the canoe we are towing.

We reached the research ship the *Alpha Helix* moored beside the hut which is used as a base, but I have just missed Richard Evans Schultes, the ethnobotanist studying medicinal plants. He is as elusive as the British botanist Ghillean Prance from the New York Botanical Garden. I seem to be following in their footsteps. '

After five days of non-stop travel we were well down the Negro and the river was growing all the time. It was also becoming more dangerous and the storms had a violent effect on the water. One night the storm came earlier. The sky had become inky black from mid-afternoon and then quite suddenly a line of storm clouds came rushing towards us. 'Dede' went full steam ahead, searching frantically for shelter. But the wind and rain caught us. Paulo and I fought the gale and tried to hang a canvas over the side entrance where the rain swept in. However, we were fortunate, for just as a blinding white curtain of rain — the terrifying *chuva branca* — came rushing up the river, completely obscuring the land, we reached a narrow *igarapé*. It was well protected by the high forest on either bank and we moored there until the fury of the tempest passed on.

Eventually we got under way again and passed our last night before Manaus beside a white sandy beach of a steep promontory. Stunted trees grew straight from the sand which was warm, wonderfully clean and was washed time and time again by pure fresh water. Unfortunately it was a case of 'Where every prospect pleases and only man is vile', for there lived nearby a horribly inquisitive *caboclo* who insisted on conversing with us. But when he rambled on with meaningless talk, Adhemar choked him off and he left us to a peaceful night. As the moon rose it illuminated the strange landscape. The stillness was broken only by the sharp cries of night birds and the sound in the river of fish jumping as they were chased by larger fish. River dolphins played and sighed, easing out of the water within a few yards of the boat and it was late before I fell asleep, swinging gently in my hammock.

It was an enchanted spot, but Adhemar insisted we left before dawn so we would reach Manaus early in the morning. After six hours on a choppy river like an inland sea we arrived in the filthy, unsavoury port and picked our way over black sludge, refuse and decaying offal. This was my first contact for over three months with one of the worst aspects of the outside world.

I had to wait for a flight to Sao Paulo and this gave me the chance to see the way Manaus was growing. The city was spreading into the forest. The glorious Ponta Negra was being cleared and a road north was planned. Suddenly, this great Amazon forest which had captivated so many naturalists, one of the loveliest and most valuable gardens of nature, was being reduced to ashes by a gang of know-nothings. I was appalled.

Margaret returned to Sao Paulo with only days to spare before she was due to fly to London. She had felt unwell for part of her return down the River Negro and assumed she was weary from the long journey. But in London, where she was staying at the home of George and Joy Rainbird, Margaret realised she had contracted infectious hepatitis. 'I woke one morning, looked in the mirror, and found to my horror I was the colour of the gold brocade bedcovers.' The infection was serious and she was admitted to hospital where doctors warned she had to rest to avoid complications. This, of course, was anathema to Margaret but she obeyed. Too much was at stake. George Rainbird had designed her book Flowers of the Brazilian Forests, *a folio edition of thirty-one paintings, The Tryon Gallery were the publishers, and H.R.H. The Duke of Edinburgh the patron.*

On 3rd January, 1968, the day before the reception to launch the book and exhibition, Margaret's specialist agreed to let her attend and she was given strict instructions not to tax her strength. It was a grand occasion, with the art critics praising the paintings and the press unanimous in wonder at her adventures. She remained in Britain until she was fit to return quietly to Brazil.

Margaret arrived home with a fresh ambition. By the end of the 1960s some people in Brazil were already aware that the Amazon forest was threatened, but open criticism of Government policies was not easy as the press was controlled. Margaret and Roberto Burle Marx were among the few who spoke out. They faced almost daily announcements of massive road schemes to open up the interior, and watched helplessly while trees were cleared. As her strength returned Margaret knew she must devote the rest of her life to the Amazon. The skills mastered in her earlier political life could be redirected, and she would paint a lasting record of the forest

Another oncidium orchid sketched by Margaret.

Margaret Mee
1977

Catasetum saccatum Lindl.

Amazonas

JOURNEY SIX: 1970

To the 'Upper Amazons' and the Twin Rivers of Sorrow

Almost two and a half years passed before Margaret could return to the Amazon. In 1968, when Sao Paulo was growing visibly, Margaret and Greville decided to move to Rio. There they found a quiet house above the city in the old, wooded district of Santa Teresa. The forest reached from the hills to their garden, delighting them as birds, small monkeys and other animals passed through the ever-open windows. A new studio was added overlooking the trees, and Margaret enjoyed the time she took to recover fully from hepatitis.

She continued to paint, using as models living plants she had sent to Roberto Burle Marx and referring to sketches made on her journeys. At this time, too, she began working with her old friend Guido Pabst who was preparing two massive volumes describing Brazilian orchids.

For her next journey Margaret had already decided to return to the River Negro to follow the course of the Demini, a large tributary coming from the north of Amazonia. The Demini rises in forested serras marking the eastern limit of 'Waika' territory. According to the botanist/philanthropist B.A. Krukoff, the flora of this region was extremely varied. Furthermore, Margaret was looking for a chance to visit for the first time the main course of the Amazon. She had flown across it many times on the way to Manaus and had seen the sharply defined junction of the 'black' River Negro and the muddy Solimoes, or 'River of Poisons', the early Portuguese name for the Amazon above the mouth of the Negro.

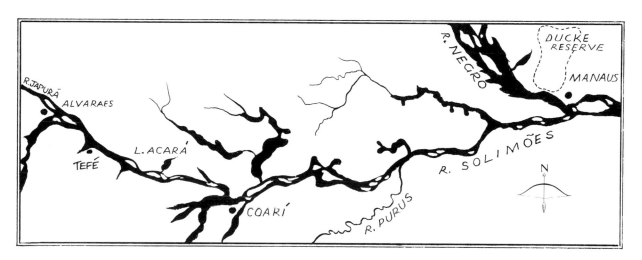

30th June, 1970

The military plane bound for Manaus was more luxurious than the others I had flown in, with individual upholstered seats instead of the wooden benches to which I was accustomed. The flight left in good weather and took us via Cuiabá in Mato Grosso, then north to Porto Velho on the Madeira river. When the pilot turned low over the water, I saw great tree trunks rolling along with the brown current, washed down from far inland. Beautiful forests of palms and hardwood trees grew right up to the Porto Velho runway where we ran to a stop in light rain.

I had been given permission to have a room at the National Institute of Amazon Research (now I.N.P.A.) in Manaus. On one side it overlooked the port, where boats were always bustling along the Negro, hooting above the constant sound of motors. Soon after my arrival an opportunity to visit the 'Upper Amazons' of Henry Bates was presented by a friend, Dr. Heitor Dourado, who was going by boat to Coarí, a small riverside town, about three full days away upriver. (Bates who spent eleven years on the Amazon from 1848 to 1859, wrote the classic *The Naturalist on the River Amazons*.)

Catasetum saccatum (Orchidaceae).

'The strange moonlit landscape slipping by.'

Dr. Dourado had organised a small medical expedition up the Solimoes to carry out research on malaria. I was introduced to the members of the team: Dr. Prata, of Salvador (Bahia) on the Brazilian coast, Dr. Phillip Marsden, of the Hospital of Tropical Diseases, London, and three Brazilian medical students. Dr. Dourado collected me and my baggage and drove me down to the team's beautiful boat. It was the best I had ever seen on the river, being scrupulously clean with bunk cabins, bathrooms, hospital and a dentist's room!

We left the mouth of the Negro and turned upstream into the turbid, pale brown waters of the Solimoes. Floating vegetation and grass patches streamed by, so without a further glance I could see it was a different river. After a hearty meal in the cabin, beside the powerful motor where no one could speak for noise, we sat on deck, watching the strange moonlit landscape slipping by. A labyrinth of small islands and trees, of which only the canopies remained above water, lay along the river, for the water is high during June and July. Our searchlight scanned ahead picking out huts (which were completely submerged in spite of being built on stilts) and searching for a way between floating isles of grass and logs. Some trees were in flower and I could see through the dark the big white blossoms of *Bombax munguba,* which was also in fruit with scarlet seed pods. On many stretches of the river ghostly *embaúbas* lined the water's edge, hopeful pioneer trees to protect the forest.

We sat talking far into the night, but next morning I was the first to rise, curious to see the passing landscape. Many of the cattle from the narrower strips of pasture flanking the river were on *marombas* (rafts), built to save them from the swollen river. A few were grazing on swampy grasslands between lakes and forest. Chickens, from a hut still above the water, were living in a canoe. The river was alive with dolphins, and enormous gourds of calabash trees dangled over the water.

Soon after passing the town of Manacapuru on the right bank, our pilot made an unfortunate short cut. The river had so many inviting channels, and he chose one where the boat became entangled with a large island of floating grass which took an hour to clear. But it was hard to blame him, for the Solimoes and flooded forest becomes over thirty miles wide at this part of its course.

Cochleanthes amazonica.

Margaret Mee
September 1948

Cochleanthes amazonica
(Rchb. f. & Warsc.)

At the mouth of the River Purus, a tributary coming in from the area of Acre in the west, the tremendously wide Solimoes and the vegetation flanking it became more varied and spectacular. The golden panicles of cassia, a type of leguminous vine, covered the trees like massive cloaks, hung between with the delicate white flowers of lecythids. Richly green aroids and bromeliads were grouped on the lofty limbs of *sumaúmas* (silk-cotton trees) emergent from the forest canopy. Everything seemed larger than on the Negro, and the scale was hard to imagine as this rich, humid forest stretched for a thousand miles or more in every direction. We kept mostly near the banks which had been cleared of original forest many years ago, a fact which became more obvious as we travelled past margins cultivated and planted with mangoes, cacau and citrus fruit trees.

A *festa* (holiday) was in full swing when we reached Coarí and the people were strolling around the nearly finished church of Santa Ana. They appeared to be predominantly Indian; some could have been pure Mundukuru (an Indian tribe from south of the Amazon). The main street of packed earth was lined with modest wooden and wattle huts through the open doors of which I caught glimpses of hammocks, in many cases the only furniture. Near the river banks the huts were half under water.

'We have been moored in Coarí for two nights and a day, on top of a rubbish dump crawling with cockroaches. The stink is just horrible. To make matters worse our pilot left the boat and went off to make merry. We have run out of oil and diesel and in order to get more supplies the pilot should have obtained a permit from the mayor's office; this he has failed to do, presumably because he is too drunk. Following a conference between the mayor, his secretary and Dr. Prata, our pilot was finally dragged out of a bar, red in the face and scarcely able to stand. The mayor, a most courteous man, decided to travel upriver with us to the next port, Tefé, to ensure that law and order were observed. The captain is still red in the face, but is somewhat calmed down by the threat of dismissal.'

At Coarí an old *fazendeiro* (rancher) embarked. He had been travelling up and down the Solimoes for many years and knew every tree on the river banks. He lamented to me the fact that recently all the mahogany trees, which once were plentiful in the forests of the Solimoes, have been cut down. All the hardwood trees were disappearing, he said, to be sawn into planks. As a cattle farmer he was most preoccupied about the flooding of the river, which had been much higher than normal, leaving the cattle almost without pasture. He had a keen appreciation of nature, and was genuinely upset by the destruction of the forests, which, he assured me, was becoming worse daily.

Further upstream we passed through a swampy area where a small boat was moored, from which emerged three men, obviously hunters, for one was armed with an old *springada* (shot-gun). Near to their boat a beautiful pair of *jabirú* (storks) waded, gracefully picking their way through shallow water. As the armed hunter made to cock his gun the *fazendeiro* shouted angrily that no good could come of shooting *jabirú* and I joined in the protest. The birds, alarmed by the noise, slowly spread their wings and flapped away, whilst the furious hunter struggled with a half-cocked gun.

The scene hardly changed from an endless forest and ocean of fresh water. Most of the flooded forest was now on our right but there was no sign of high ground anywhere.

We reached Tefé another day and night later and, before disembarking with the mayor, the *fazendeiro* gave me a Tukuna Indian necklace, telling me that if ever I passed his way, he would take me to see an Indian funeral urn which he had found in the river bed about two hours' journey from Tefé.

In the flood season, many riverside houses stand in deep water; the people leave and their chickens take to the roof.

River boats at Coarí.

Tefé is built beside a large lake joined to the Solimões by a broad natural canal. Originally called Ega and described by Henry Bates as being a semi-Indian village surrounded by 'perpetual verdure', Tefé was still small. Perhaps two or three thousand people instead of the 350 in Bates' time. The little town was without shade, as the mayor, who did not like the great trees which shaded the village square, had them cut down to the roots, an action which had met with no opposition in spite of the antiquity of the trees and the shelter which they gave to what was now neo-desert. And the surviving trees had had their canopies shorn to look like *piaçaba* (palm fibre) brooms. I left Tefé without regrets and, shortly after, we moored outside the sleepy, peaceful village of Alvaraes on the Solimões opposite one of the mouths of the Japurá river.

Stories about the Japurá have fascinated me, as tributaries in its upper reaches have connections with my favourite river, the Negro. In Alvaraes I met an old Dutch priest, Father Antonio, of the Order of Espirito Santo, who had long experience of Indian ways and a good collection of artefacts. He said he would be able to help me if I wanted to explore the Japurá, and one afternoon he introduced me to some Baptist missionaries from Britain. We had tea together and they told me about the connection in high water season between the Japurá and Negro by way of the Rivers Uneiuxi or Urubaxi which empty near Tapurucuará, the connecting region being known as 'Primavera'. The route has been known for a long time and the journey from Alvaraes is about three hundred miles. According to the missionaries, few people ever went to 'Primavera' and it seemed to be an area which was completely untouched and uninhabited except by Indians. Locally they were called Piranhas who, according to the Maku tribe, live in the trees. I had heard this story before but never had a chance to follow it up. One day I would get there. A spectacular tree grows in the region, its pale violet flowers attached directly to the tree-trunk. Could this be a heterostemon which flowers in October and November?

The Baptists had a boat, a creaking vessel belching diesel smoke. At their suggestion they took me a little way out of Alvaraes to meet a *tushaua*, the last of his tribe. We drew alongside his hut and the missionaries departed, leaving me with the waiting Indian. By each hand he held one of his finely built sons and he greeted me with pride and dignity: 'Welcome to our territory.' Later he told me that he had been moved by farmers from his land, which was forested and fertile, to this miserable *capoeira* (wasteland), where he had built a hut in the Indian style of bamboo and palm leaves. It was cool and clean inside, though harbouring a tragedy. In a hammock lay his little granddaughter, only seven years old, dying as the result of measles. She had a black patch on her forehead and her eyes were dull and so lifeless that they left her tiny face without animation. She could eat nothing, her mother explained, sadly saying she had not been able to move from her hammock since May (it was now July). The *tushaua's* small family was the only remnant of his once large and independent tribe.

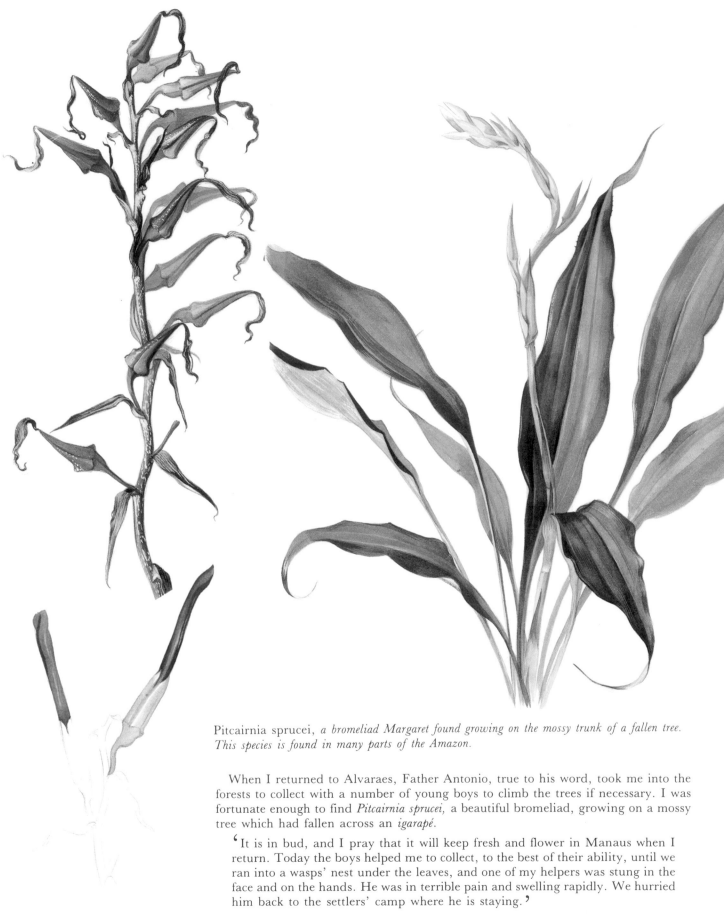

Pitcairnia sprucei, *a bromeliad Margaret found growing on the mossy trunk of a fallen tree. This species is found in many parts of the Amazon.*

When I returned to Alvaraes, Father Antonio, true to his word, took me into the forests to collect with a number of young boys to climb the trees if necessary. I was fortunate enough to find *Pitcairnia sprucei,* a beautiful bromeliad, growing on a mossy tree which had fallen across an *igarapé.*

'It is in bud, and I pray that it will keep fresh and flower in Manaus when I return. Today the boys helped me to collect, to the best of their ability, until we ran into a wasps' nest under the leaves, and one of my helpers was stung in the face and on the hands. He was in terrible pain and swelling rapidly. We hurried him back to the settlers' camp where he is staying.'

Encyclia randii.

Margaret Mee
1983

Encyclia randii (Barb. Rodr.)
B. Porto & Brade
Amazonas

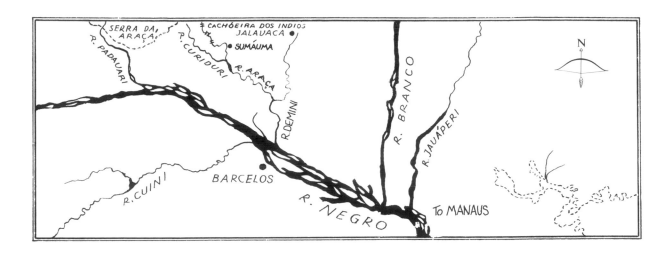

Manaus

So far it had been an interesting but sad journey, for the Solimoes was like an old highway which had been spoiled over a long period of time. I was more anxious now than ever to get to the Demini and the quiet upper reaches of the Negro.

My first thought was to get a boat from Manaus to Barcelos. Then I heard from the Salesian Fathers that the Mayor of Barcelos would be returning there in a couple of days and that he had agreed to take me. After some difficulty I found the boat in the 'port' and a little official, whom I gathered must be the mayor, indicated that I should walk the plank to the boat if I wanted to speak with him. Having got my feet soaked in filthy water I explained that the Fathers had recommended me, and that he had agreed with them that he could take me. But here he blankly said that he knew nothing about the arrangement and that his boat was loaded to capacity already. He could take no one. He was quite rude, did not shake hands, and would not even suggest an alternative boat. I was almost in tears as this chance of getting to Barcelos suddenly faded. Then, with great good fortune, I was able to book on a commercial flight to Barcelos. In fact I was told by the airline that the flight leaving later in the week would be the last to use that route!

When I returned to the Institute to pack for the journey I had a day to spare, so that afternoon I took the local bus to Ponta Negra and the *igarapé* Leao where I hoped to find flowers to paint. But there was little in bloom, for the river had so flooded the forests for miles around that many plants were under water (the seasonal rise in this part is over twenty-eight feet). A local man, who had been settled there for many years, led me to an area of *caatinga,* on leached, sandy soil, where two tribes of Indians, now extinct, once dwelt. I picked up fragments of their pottery beautifully engraved with key patterns, along with coloured Dutch beads, reminders of the seventeenth century Dutch settlers. In this cemetery I could feel the spirits of the Indians watching me as I walked sadly across their now desolate territory.

Wherever I went I saw great changes. Ponta Negra was to be turned into a resort and the river was polluted, for an oil refinery had been built on the banks. But I found the Lake of Januaria still alive with spectacular birds and aquatic plants flourished. The *igapós* were overhung with *aninga (Montrichardia arborescens)*, an aroid whose latex is so poisonous it blinds. If a jaguar is being hunted and escapes into a mass of aninga the hunters never follow. I always pray that the jaguar will find a safe place!

The high waters had washed the giant *Victoria regia* lilies away from the main lake, but on a macrolobium tree, a relative of the acacia with fine foliage, I found a beautiful orchid to paint, *Oncidium cebolleta*, with its gorgeous spray of large yellow flowers. A sloth hung like a large brown leaf on a dead *embaúba* tree; on another was a colony of *japu* (oropendola), the black and yellow birds calling noisily.

I had returned to the Institute and was lying in my hammock when I felt it begin to swing violently; doors banged, windows rattled. I got out hurriedly and nearly lost my balance on the rocking floor. The movement was soon over. At the time there were serious earthquakes in Peru, which presumably were reflected as far away as Manaus. [The date and time in Margaret's diary match the major earthquake — 6 on the Richter scale — which was recorded in many parts of South America, but her experience of the event is remarkable as earthquakes or tremors are rarely felt in the Amazon.]

The plane for Barcelos left early next day and I was elated to be flying over the jungles and maze of waters of the Negro. When we landed on the airfield my old friend Sister Elza, who had come down from Uaupés, greeted me warmly. The Mayor of Barcelos was also there, and I coldly looked the other way until Sister Elza formerly introduced me. He appeared to have lost some of his bumptious arrogance, I observed.

Arriving at the Salesian Mission, my first care was for my plants, and the birds. The local *caboclos* frequently brought birds from the forests in tiny cages as presents for the sisters. So, I started a tour of inspection, and found a fledgling olive oropendola, in a sorry state, and a small blue bird which was new to me with a broken wing. These I fed with *mamao* (papaya), dozens of grasshoppers and caterpillars, collected by a group of small boys, only too eager to help this way.

‘ But there is a little aquatic bird, a *jacana,* who will eat nothing that I can find, and I despair of saving her. She runs frantically round the garden, searching for her proper food. As a result of my complaints the *curicas* are all moved into much larger cages, but the *jacana* is still hungry. ’

My first venture to collect plants was to the Parana do Piloto, a forested branch of the Negro. A Malaria Service boat took me up the river where, after passing a few huts, we entered a narrow *parana* bordered with *jará* palms, small trees which, during high waters, are half or even completely submerged. On their fibrous stems clung *Galeandra devoniana,* an orchid with bell-shaped blooms of purple, brown and creamy white. Their perfume filled the air. We paddled in the small and very unstable canoe over the dark water between the half submerged trees. The silence was eerie. Frequently the trees were so close together that we could not use the paddle at all, but pushed and pulled ourselves through between the yielding trunks.

Further afield we encountered an *igapó* of a very different character; gaunt, dried out trees, some of considerable height, reared amongst a tangle of vegetation. They were laden with epiphytes, but some of the trees were so rotten that it was impossible to climb them. In spite of this I brought out a fine collection of plants, including catasetums, brassavolas and a marvellous cattleya orchid — *Cattleya violacea,* with fine blooms.

On the return we made a stop at an old *fazenda*, with a house in bad need of repair, owned by a Portuguese of about eighty called Albino. He sent his son, Atenau, to talk with me, a middle-aged man with dim eyes, who might have been handsome before heavy drinking had coarsened his skin and features. He wrote poetry, he said and, by his eagerness to converse, rarely had visitors except those from the locality. I felt sorry for this lonely, hopeless man, but when I told him I intended to travel up the River Demini his attitude changed. He told me in a dictatorial manner that this was forbidden. 'Impossible!' He was almost threatening. Surprised at his reaction I questioned why, and after a long pause, whilst he obviously searched for an excuse, he replied that there were dangerous Indians in the upper river. I laughed incredulously, telling him that I did not believe him, and that I had met newly contacted tribes and never had any problems.

I left with some misgivings about this middle-aged *fazendeiro,* which were confirmed on the homeward journey when the boatmen told me that the father, Albino, had a

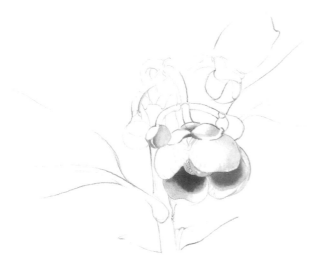

Sketches for Clusia nemorosa *from the Araçá river.*

reputation for being a slave-driver and maltreating his workers. They said that the Demini and Araçá rivers were 'owned' by Albino, who took, among other things, *piaçaba* from the forests. It was clear that, in the tradition of one of the legendary 'river kings', Albino had the monopoly of the boats trading along those rivers. He also controlled the sale of any produce, for which he charged excessive prices.

As we talked, the crew of the Malaria Service boat spoke freely about the 'ownership' of the Demini and its sister river, the Araçá, which enters the Demini from the west. The Indians up these rivers were working for Albino, who supplied them with necessities at a cost far above normal. As debt-slaves to him for life, they worked for a mere pittance. It was an example of the cruel debt cycle which fuelled the nineteenth century rubber boom and destroyed so many lives. For these reasons, Albino was very loath to allow any strangers behind the scenes and had already turned away many would-be visitors. The tales of injustice and excitement begged me to go and look.

But first we had to get back to the Barcelos mission where a boat bound for the Demini was expected any time. A black sky threatened a storm and we had covered no distance before the tempest was raging around us. In a few minutes the smooth surface of the river was transformed and black waves, topped with glistening white crests, were lashing our boat. The wind swept across the river, driving heavy rain before it, and we frantically closed all the screens as the boat lurched violently, almost overturning as waves hit her alongside. But our pilot struggled with the steering and headed into the waves.

At this critical moment the towing ropes of our canoe snapped and, as it was cast adrift, the Indian boy on the poop was blown into the river. Swimming for the canoe

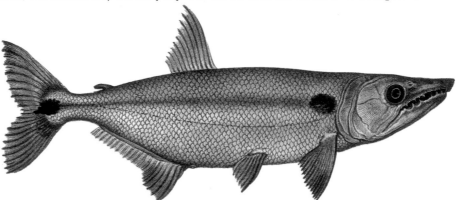

The peixe-cachorro 'dogfish' of the Amazon.

150

Clusia nemorosa *(Guttiferae)*.

Margaret Mee
1973

Clusia nemorosa G.F.W.Meyer
Amazonas, Rio Aracá

with all his force, he struggled in and then paddled after us, catching up just as we crashed into the submerged trees of an *igapó* where we waited for the storm to pass. The wind eased and then torrential rain lulled the angry waters into a heavy swell. It had been the worst storm I had experienced.

Sister Elza had arranged for me to travel up the Demini with a Joao Soares who lived on the Demini almost two days' journey from Barcelos. However, without the permission of F.U.N.A.I. — the Government controlled Indian Agency, I would not be allowed to go as far as I had planned, nor to go to the Indian Reserve at the headwaters of the Demini. Luckily for me, the F.U.N.A.I. inspector, Gilberto Pinto, was due to go to the *Posto Indigena* (agency camp) of Ajuricaba, which was more than half way to the Indian Reserve. I could wait for Gilberto in Joao's house, and then proceed to the *Posto Indigena* on his boat. Sister Elza kindly offered to care for my plants, which were already filling several baskets, while I was away.

The arrangements were better than I had dared to expect. Joao's boat was a small, very primitive palm-thatched craft with a closed wooden cabin and an inboard motor which made explosive noises and gave trouble even before we reached the Demini. The motor stopped frequently and then refused to start until it had been almost completely dismantled. It had obviously been badly neglected and the fumes were suffocating.

From Barcelos we headed upstream to the Negro, crossing the river through islands and *igapós* towards the mouth of the Demini on the opposite bank. There were four aboard beside me. The owner, Joao, and three lads who appeared to do little but steer the boat. One of them came aboard completely tipsy, bringing with him a sick kitten, which once must have been white. Later, it threw fits, poor thing, and insisted on coming to me. Sorry for the creature, I was at the same time worried to death that it had rabies. Up the river there would be no possibility of getting serum should it be infected, so I wore my long collecting gloves and tucked my slacks into my socks, but the kitten, sick with foam, climbed all over me and my luggage. The owner of the pitiable animal said that he was taking it as a present to his wife who had just given birth. As he was too drunk to be open to reason, I did not discuss the matter with him.

We only stopped that night when we came across a motorboat in midstream. Smoke poured from its exhaust pipe and the fumes stifled me in my hammock. The boatmen asked for a tow and Joao obliged. He seemed to know them as they were 'Waika' Indians from the headwaters of the Demini. It was early morning when we moored briefly on the north bank of the Negro to leave one of the passengers from the boat we were towing. We moved on slowly with frequent motor delays, reaching the south of the Demini by mid-morning. Undamaged forest and *igapós* lined the banks and I saw to my surprise that the water was black. This was a relief, for it meant insect pests would be fewer.

We passed the inviting mouth of the River Araçá on the left and continued up the Demini, reaching the clearing of Jalauaca and Joao's house about five hours later.

'Dona Claudinha, the mother of the family, works harder than anyone. She is a very kindly woman, rather heavy, with Indian features. She has three sons, two of whom are absent at the moment, though their families are here in Jalauaca. Two of the small boys are very sick with measles, their stomachs distended and their skin yellow; one of them screams in delirium at night. All the family, except the old people, have graveyard coughs.'

During my stay, two of the boys of the family paddled me into the superb *igapó* beside the house in their dugout canoe. It was full of *jauarí* palms, on whose robust trunks

were circles of long black thorns, quite a menace to the plant collector. Macrolobiums laden with orchids hung elegantly over the black water. From a branch I collected a *Catasetum saccatum* in bud, and nearby I found a charming little red and white clusia. I was busy painting the catasetum when I heard a motor coming up the river. It was the launch of the *Posto Indigena* and I listened to it with some relief, for though my stay in Jalauaca had been quite productive, I was eager to go further afield. Besides, food was becoming scarce and I did not like depriving the family of the meagre amount of fish and *farinha* that it was able to produce. Everyone was most hospitable, but it was clear to me that food was not plentiful.

A man from F.U.N.A.I. handed me a letter from Sister Elza explaining that Gilberto Pinto had been detained on business in Manaus, but that I was authorised to proceed to the *Posto Indigena* . I bid farewell to the kindly Soares family, thanking them for their hospitality, and gave them as much of my meagre supplies as I could afford to help them.

The F.U.N.A.I. boat was spacious and spotlessly clean, with the added luxury of a lavatory and room for my three baskets of plants to be stored safely. Besides the pilot there was a crew of four men, two of them Xiriana Indians, another group of the 'Waika' I believe.

On the first morning of my voyage I nearly met with a watery end in the dark waters. My hammock had been hung to the fore of the portside, and, to keep me sheltered from the cold night wind, the heavy canvas awning along the side of the boat had been unfurled. We moved on non-stop and I was frozen. The night air is always cool and I wrapped myself in everything available in a vain effort to keep out the humid cold. I dozed uneasily until just before dawn, and then, half asleep, tumbled out of my hammock to wash and clean my teeth before the crew was astir. I bent down over the dark water to fill my tin mug, holding a roof post as there was no side rail. But the post was greasy. I lost my grip and overbalanced, falling between the canvas awning and the hull, into the deep black water.

With despair I noticed the boat moving away at a good speed as I came up in a cloud of tea-coloured bubbles, gasping and dragged down by all my drenched clothes. I attempted to swim, but failed, as I was completely exhausted and full of water. So I trod water, screaming my loudest for help. The inboard motor was very noisy, I thought, and I was afraid that no one would hear my cries. I pictured myself struggling in a riverside *igapó*, hanging on to branches for a week without seeing a single living sole. With intense relief I saw that one of the Indians had heard my cries and was running to turn the boat.

I was nearing my last gasp when I saw the boat coming towards me and one of the men holding out a long pole for me to grasp. I heard a shout from the boat saying there was a canoe to my right, and turning I saw an Indian boy paddling frantically to the rescue. My strength had just gone when he caught me by the arm and dragged me half into the canoe. Like a sodden log I fell into the bilge, noting the smell of rotten fish, but completely beyond caring for such trifles.

When the men hauled me into the boat they were amazed to see that I was still grasping my toothbrush and tin mug. The only things I had lost were my toothpaste,

'I found an orchid, new to me, which I think is batemannia.'

soap and slippers. My mirror remained in my pocket and, with a shock, I saw my ghostly face with water oozing out of my nose, ears and mouth. I felt terribly sick. It must have been after an hour when I suddenly felt my blood rushing through my body. My colour returned and I started to laugh, more with relief than amusement. The boatmen came running to my side to see if I had been mentally affected by the accident then, finding me back to normal, they joined in my laughter. I achieved some fame for this escape, and for not having been eaten by *piranhas* (the voracious Amazon fish), with which, the crew assured me, the river was infested.

'I am sitting in my hut at the *Posto Indigena* of Ajuricaba in a raging storm, having arrived here early in the morning. Last night in the small hours we

A 'black' pirana, one of many similar species, of which four are dangerous.

A clusia species.

Margaret Mee
November 1987

Clusia sp.
Alto Rio Negro, Am.

moored outside a hut where the men lingered for a long time; just as well, for a terrible storm broke a little later, and now the rain is pouring through the straw roof, though I will not grumble as it is good for my plants. When we arrived we were met by all the Indians here who gathered to see us land. At first I thought they were waving to greet us, but discovered very soon that they were brandishing cloths to keep the *pium* at bay. Before I realised what was happening I was well and truly bitten by this pestiferous insect, and at the moment look like a bad case of measles, except for face and hands which have miraculously escaped.'

I was introduced to the chief of the family of Xiriana Indians drawn to the *Posto Indigena* by F.U.N.A.I.: *Tushaua* Mattos, a tall dignified man of about forty, and his pretty little wife who was a 'Waika'. They had a son, Diego, of about ten who, with his young friend Bernadino, paddled me for half a day up the *igarapé* Carnao to a beautiful *igapó* to collect. After pushing our way through the trees I found an orchid, new to me, which I think is batemannia.

Sketching in my hut was difficult. It was impossible to keep the Indians away. They fingered everything and were constantly asking for tobacco, clothes, mirrors... I had presents but, at the request of the Government appointed 'head' of the *Posto Indigena,* Sr. Paulo, I handed him everything. He promised to distribute them later, but the procedure surprised me, for previously I had always given my presents to the *tushaua* who knew the needs of his people and was scrupulously fair in sharing them equally. I decided to ask *tushaua* Mattos about the presents. He was obviously offended at being subordinate to Sr. Paulo on what was his land and told me that he had been forbidden to accept or distribute presents.

'The baskets for my plants arrived today. The Indians have made them excellently. They are openwork and well ventilated, to let in rain and dew. I sat with my *cabocla* neighbour Zeta, who is a devout Crente. Her husband is even more ardent about his little religious sect. They live in one of the tree huts which were abandoned by some American missionaries. I have one of them now — just habitable, and with the luxury of a screen over the window, so I am free of *pium* inside the house. Of course the dust of years lies on everything, but it is fairly wholesome dirt. The river nearby is spanned by a little bridge from which I bathe, though this is only possible at night, for during the day there are hordes of *pium*. My staple diet is *farinha, pirarucu* and bananas, and there is a lemon tree outside my door, so I have at least one lemon a day (I have no sugar) which is keeping me fit, though very thin. My companions are a pair of *graúnas* (chopi blackbirds), beautiful birds who watch me curiously and chatter to one another, eyeing me every morning through the little window. They seem to live in a tree which looks like a *goiabeira* (guava), although it is not in fruit at this time of year.

The *igapó,* in whose black waters grow hardwood trees and a sprinkling of palms, is very silent. Small bats, no larger than hawk moths, flit around when disturbed by the lapping water. The birds are shy, hiding in the dark foliage or darting swiftly to cover. There is no sound but the faint splash of our paddles to disturb the tranquillity of this shadowy forest...'

Yon, another Indian boy, Bernadino and I paddled in his father's canoe along a narrow *igarapé*. It was partly open to the sky and was marvellously free of *pium* and other insect pests — apart from ants in every plant and tree. We arrived at a dark *igapó* where the trees stood in deep water with no current and which was silent apart from the splashing of our paddles. We collected some beautiful plants — an *Epidendrum*

Catasetum species (Orchidaceae).

Catasetum sp.
Natural hybrid ?
Amazonas, RioNegro — 1972 ?

Margaret Mee

nocturnum with large white labellum, a deep red clusia and a batemannia bearing both flowers and seed pods. We spent the whole morning in an *igapó* where the boys told me in broken Portuguese of the time when their families were lost there for three days with nothing to eat, sleeping in the trees at night. 'The young survive without food, but the old ones die,' Yon observed. We paddled into tangles of trees and bushes and I feared that we had lost our way, but after struggling through the vegetation, ducking under low branches which barred our way, we saw the daylight over the *igarapé*.

I was fascinated by the problems facing these Indians on the edge of civilisation. One of two Paqueda Indians, who had been brought by F.U.N.A.I. to the Xiriana land in Ajuricaba, became very ill one night. The Indians said he had been poisoned as he had been making advances to the wife of one of the Xirianas; this was bad enough in itself, but being of another tribe made matters even worse. I was told that the jealous Xiriana mixed a deadly herbal poison with earth, wrapped the mixture in leaves and left it on a path. When the Paqueda trod on the poison it would penetrate his skin. The story seemed hard to believe, but I had heard a similar account when I was on the Içana. That night, as the Paqueda was dying, Mattos called together his tribe of Xiriana to discover the culprit and to find out what antidote to use against the toxic herb. So the life of the Paqueda was saved, but he had to leave the village.

Almost immediately I had another experience of the Indian knowledge of forest drugs. Zeta had gone to a neighbouring clearing and left me to look after her house. She had left me some *bejú* which I was eating when a group of hungry Indians wandered in. I shared the *bejú* with them and, as they left, a lone Indian appeared. He wandered around the house trying to get in. He was behaving very strangely and aggressively and was muttering all the time. I suspected he was under the influence of some drug. His eyes looked through me into the distance. Very tactfully, I persuaded him to leave and I was thankful when Zeta returned with three Indian women and several small children.

The women squatted on the earthern floor of the hut playing with the children and feeding them in turn. One of the girls was nursing at the same time both the minute infant of her sister, who had recently died, as well as her own child. I enquired how her sister had died, and from the symptoms described realised that it must have been tuberculosis. The girl, who could not have been more than fifteen, complained that she did not have enough milk to feed two children and asked Zeta's daughter to feed her sister's coughing, wizened infant. Zeta immediately refused, obviously aware of this dreaded disease of the 'civilizados' which has decimated so many Indian tribes. It was a sad life at the *Posto Indigena* and many of the Indians were in bad shape through malnutrition.

'My store of food is at an end and there is nothing to eat here except *bejú*, a few bananas and lemons, so I am quite desperate to return to Barcelos, but I learned that there is yet another delay as Sr. Paulo has to make his accounts balance, reporting back to his superiors in Brasilia. Many of the sacks of rice, corn, sugar, and so on, which he was bringing to Ajuricaba, disappeared *en route,* and he is juggling with the figures, as he refuses to try and trace the missing food. The Indians will suffer as they are completely dependent on the supplies.'

To my distress I almost left in bad odour with two of the tribe. The couple came and sat on the boat whilst I was waiting endlessly for Sr. Paulo to embark — he was still muddling through his accounts. The Indians looked at me aggressively repeating '*Shamin!*' (bad). I soon discovered their grievance. They thought I had given no presents to the tribe and, as their knowledge of Portuguese was practically non-existent, I could not make them understand that I had left gifts for Sr. Paulo to distribute. Luckily, just as they became quite threatening, *tushaua* Mattos appeared and I asked him to explain the situation. Very kindly he led them away and bid me a safe journey. The Indians who gathered around the boat also waved farewell in a friendly manner. Sr. Paulo had not distributed any of my gifts.

The gloomy mood into which this threw me soon passed as I enjoyed the glories of the river banks, for all the flowers seemed to have opened: I saw *Gustavia augusta* with white blossoms; a pink-flowered bignone trailed over bushes into the water, losing its little trumpets in the stream; the yellow panicles of *Oncidium ceboletta* hung below a bromeliad with scarlet bracts, a symphony of colour and form. When we reached the mouth of the Araçá on the right bank, I decided to visit it one day, but first I had to return to Barcelos to find a boat going that way. We stopped briefly by the Araçá where the boatmen picked up two *tracajas*. The poor creatures were left lying at my feet, bound and suffering — St. Francis of Assisi is not respected here.

To the River Araçá

I arrived in Barcelos to be greeted with news I half expected. An old friend from Rio, Mary Auni, had arrived from Manaus on the *Acuario,* a river boat. Mary had had plenty of experience with boats but had never been to the Amazon before. It was marvellous to see her again, and to have her sharing my room at the mission. Sister Elza took an instant liking to her and soon was arranging a trip for us up the Araçá. She told us that Father Schneider and the anthropologist Dr. Hans Becker had been to the headquarters of the Araçá and were due to return to Barcelos soon. They had been looking at the situation facing the few remaining Indians in the area, as F.U.N.A.I. was planning to put a *Posto Indigena* well upriver, at Cachóeira dos Indios, although there was much local opposition. Apparently there were few Indians there, all the others having disappeared into the forests. Dr. Becker and Father Schneider would be able to advise us about our trip.

When they arrived they recommended we should take an acolyte, Paisano, who had been with them on their journey and who knew the language, people and region well. Sister Elza found us a boat belonging to a Sr. Alberto, who had a hut near the Cachóeira dos Indios, which would be leaving Barcelos shortly, together with other boats and *piaçaba* collectors, so we had time to spare before we left; time to prepare my plants, and collect more. We purchased stores and presents for the Indians, all approved by Paisano.

I was eager to send the plants I had already collected to Rio before embarking on an expedition to 'Cachóeira', and I hoped that Dr. Becker, who was going to Manaus, would take them that far. He was to leave on the *Acuario* but, to my dismay, when I was ready with my boxes of plants, I heard that everyone had already embarked and that the boat was imminently about to leave. As I ran from the mission I was confronted by an inky sky and white-topped breakers on the river. The wind heralded a storm, but I hoped that I had time to beat it and reach the boat before it broke. It was not to be. The wind reached gale force, a ribbon of lightning struck the ground in front of me, and the tempest raged with such fury that I feared I should be blown into the river. The rain swept over in gusty, white clouds. I ran frantically for the nearest shelter, a little hut on stilts, where I remained until the storm had abated. Then I hurried down to the *Acuario* which had been waiting for the storm to subside. The plank had already been pulled away, but a small boy took my boxes aboard.

At the mission, turmoil and confusion reigned. During the storm a girl had been struck by lightning and had lost her speech and ability to walk, one of the patients in the Santa Casa had died, and the buildings were flooded. It was the season of storms, but nevertheless Sister Elza wished us godspeed and a safe journey.

We left Barcelos in the afternoon. Scarcely had night fallen, when we were

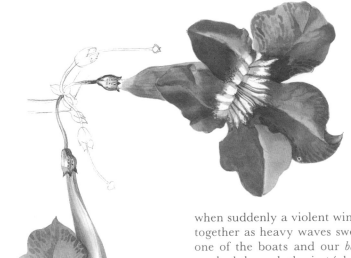

A bignonia from the River Negro.

overtaken by another terrible tempest. We were five boats and two *batelaoes* (cargo boats). All the boats were lashed together and, with canoes in tow, it made a most unwieldy raft — but a customary way to travel on the Amazon and its tributaries. Mary and I were in one of the *batelaoes*, swinging in our hammocks, when suddenly a violent wind drove the rain through the openings. The boats ground together as heavy waves swept us deep into an *igapó*. A giant tree collapsed between one of the boats and our *batelao*, its trunk disappearing in the raging river. As we crashed through the *igapó*, branches came hurtling through the side openings, and the crew, frantically working in the dim half-light, for all our lamps had been smashed, seemed like ghosts in the forests. Then some of the boatmen came dashing into our *batelao*, scrambling to rescue baskets of *farinha*, worth a month's wages to them, and the sole payment for their work collecting *piaçaba*. Meanwhile, Mary and I stayed firmly in our soaking hammocks, the rain lashing us and soaking everything. Each storm seemed to be worse than the one before and Alberto said we were fortunate to have been in the shelter of a *paraná*. Had we been on the open river we would have sunk.

By dawn the boats were cleared of debris and we were on our way to the Demini. The day was clear without a sign of rain as we headed upstream and turned into the Araçá. The river was broad, sometimes well over a hundred yards, with many *igapós*. We glided by the Curiduri, a large tributary, and before reaching Sumaúma, our destination that night, we passed through low *caatinga*. The 'port' of the settlement consisted of one hut and no *sumaúmas*, which had been cut down many years ago. There most of the noisy *piaçaba* collectors left us with their boats and we were free to wend our peaceful way up the Araçá in Alberto's boat, which we christened the 'Ramshackle', a perfect description of the skeleton left by the storm.

At the mouth of the next river, the Matari, we picked up the wife of one of the crew.

'The boats were lashed together.'

160

Sarcoglottes, one of seventeen orchid species found in Central and South America.

She was a very primitive woman and brought aboard a huge tin basin which leaked. It was full of sour *anta* flesh, the smell of which was so repellent that I had it moved from the prow to the poop. Yet she was a good-hearted person and later gathered a bouquet of flowers from the forest for me.

'One of the *piaçaba* collectors has influenza, and during the night lay groaning and spitting near the head of my hammock. I had to move around to get my head as far away as possible and my rucksack was a sight to behold in the morning — having been in the direct line of fire! The kindly Alberto moved it into his boat after cleaning it. Today is glorious, and here the glassy river is fringed with graceful palms, dark *buriti* and *jará*, on the white sandbanks and beaches exposed by the rapidly falling river. Mary and I took our baths in the canoe, pouring buckets of water over each other.

Today we are on our way to Benedito, 'centre' of the *piaçaba* workers, after passing through one of the most beautiful parts of the river. From the mouth of the Javari there is a magnificent view of the Serra da Araçá and the distant Pico Rondon. Bacuri trees, covered with pink blossoms, line the river banks. This tree bears a small fruit, not unlike the Chinese lychee in flavour.'

By midday we were in Monteiro, a 'village' with one hut, where we bathed in the black water, taking care not to tread on sting rays which lie in the muddy beds of streams, or even in the sand. Alberto and Paisano occupied themselves by renewing the *toldo* and walls of the 'Ramshackle' with fresh, green palm leaves. Making a *toldo* is becoming a lost art, for unhappily plastic and canvas now replace the picturesque *sapé toldos*. The men worked well and rapidly, and transformed the boat which had been reduced to a mere skeleton by the storm.

The Araçá has more *terra firma* than the Demini which is all *igapó*. Sandbanks and forest extended to a tremendous width. One *piaçaba* collector, Aristides, was persuaded to act as guide when I wanted to explore the forest. He insisted on taking his rusty old *springada* with him, but as it was loaded and he handled it so carelessly, I suggested that he should lead the way. He became very excited on seeing a great *jibóia* curled asleep around a *jará* palm. His predatory instincts were foiled, happily for the snake,

A clusia and a weathered trunk.

Vriesia heliconioides *(Bromeliaceae)*.

Margaret Mee

Vriesia heliconioides (H.B.K.) Hook. ex Walp.
Amazonas, Rio Deméni
January, 1975

Catasetum appendiculatum
Rio Negro, Amazonas

Margaret Mee
May, 1955

as a steep bank and deep water lay between them. I stopped by a humming-bird's exquisite nest of moss and roots, with two minute white eggs inside, whilst a *japuzinho* (small oropendola) screamed a warning nearby. Aristides was no *mateiro*, for on the return trek he completely lost his way. True, the sun was overhead and it was midday, but he led us round in circles, so that I noticed we were passing the same plants and trees again and again. Eventually Mary and I decided to lead the way, and made straight for the lightest area of the forest where, as expected, we found the river.

Back in Monteiro, Mary and I were offered the hut where we passed a peaceful night whilst the *piaçaba* collectors and crew slept under a large shelter of *sapé*. At dawn we parted company with the remaining *piaçaba* collectors and crew, although one, Joao, remained, for Alberto realised that he and Paisano would not be able to handle the boat unaided in the rapids.

The 'Ramshackle' looked very smart in her new attire, but just as we were leaving port her rudder fell off! Will she be able to pass the rapids? That evening Paisano became eloquent and kept us entertained with his inexhaustible fund of stories. He recounted how he had met Indian tribes for the first time in this region in 1937. There were large tribes in those days, and they lived well from their plantations. He had observed their customs and witnessed, and even joined in, their celebrations and feasts, and he described their tribal dress and ornaments. These stories ran through my mind as I lay in my hammock that night. The Indian tribes of which Paisano had told us no longer existed — they had gone with epidemics, by being used by the *piaçaba* collectors, or simply by losing the will to continue. They were memories of the past. The utter cruelty of the situation struck me with force.

The night was cold and a brilliant half-moon shone into the river. *Guaribas* roared from the forest; *cutias* (agoutis) cried, alarmed by an ocelot or other cat. Night birds called plaintively just as they had for centuries. These sounds had been part of the lives of those Indians, and now they were no more. Perhaps their spirits linger still in the shadows of the forests, waiting to return.

Many of the inviting *igarapés* we passed rise in the Serra de Imajaí, and on the curves in the river I caught a glimpse of these magnificent mountains. They are not tremendously high, but between their forested slopes shone enormous faces of wet rock, silver in the rays of the sun. Alberto said it would take two days by canoe up the Igarapé de Imajaíto to reach the *serra*, and one day of strenuous climbing to reach the summit — a wonderful, mouthwatering possibility for another journey.

The river narrowed considerably and we found the way blocked by a wall of rock. Huge stones confronted us over which the river cascaded in a raging torrent. We had reached Cachóeira dos Indios, or Sao Francisco de Assis, as it is sometimes called after the patron saint of the nearby village. It is a small settlement of huts built by *caboclos* leading a typically rough life. Soon after our arrival I was watching a charming pair of sandpipers running beside the river, busily picking up food. One of the miserable settlers picked up a stone, threw it and killed one of the birds, bursting into unholy laughter as he saw the little bird's body fall limp and lifeless. He was preparing to kill the bird's mate when I called on Paisano to stop him. Paisano reprimanded the man furiously before all the settlers' families, who by this time were crowding out of their huts to see what the commotion was about.

Paisano told me that there had once been an Indian *aldeia* here, but that all that remained was one small *maloca,* and even that was being abandoned. Only very few of the tribe, 'Waikas', remained, including *tushaua* Araken and his wife Joanna. They were to leave 'Cachóeira', the ancient home of their ancestors, to join their tribe in the middle of the forests, far from the 'civilizados'. No one knew definitely why these Indians were leaving, though some of the settlers assumed it was because they wished

The River Araçá from Margaret's notebook.

Catasetum appendiculatum *(Orchidaceae).*

Araken and Joanna leave Cachóeira dos Indios.

Jauarí *palms.*

to be independent of F.U.N.A.I. and the proposed *Posto Indigena.*

I asked *tushaua* Araken if he would take me into the forest before leaving, and he agreed willingly. We set off in his dugout canoe to thick forest lying behind a wall of rocks, over which roared the cascading falls. Araken manoeuvred the canoe skilfully into calm waters, and we landed on a rocky shore where we found ourselves in the lovliest glade, green with ferns and mosses, sparkling with little streams trickling through crevices. Here I made a wonderful find: a small green-flowered orchid, *Clowesia warczewitzii,* was growing on a moss-covered branch. The species had not been seen by botanists for eighty years.

Next morning whilst mist still veiled the river, Araken and Joanna and their family were loading their canoe in preparation to leave Cachóeira dos Indios. Two boys were to accompany them on their journey which would take ten days of constant paddling eastwards up the Deminizinho river. Much had been prepared the previous night, and as we watched silently they bid us farewell, insisting that we must return one day and stay with the tribe — and if we brought presents, canvas shoes would be very welcome. Little did they realise the problems to be faced, and the great distances to be covered if we were to reach them in their forest fastness.

Joanna looked very regal holding a branch crowned with scarlet *arara* plumes. She and Araken treated the parting with impassive solemnity. How many generations of their tribe had looked upon Cachóeira dos Indios as their territory and permanent abode? What did the future hold in store for them? Such thoughts probably accounted for the sad eyes of these homeless Indians.

Clowesia warczewitzii (Orchidaceae).

Clowesia warczewitzii LDL.
Rio Aracá, Rio Negro, Am.
April. 1971

Margaret Mee

Downstream

There was nothing further to stay for in 'Cachóeira'. The handful of local *caboclos* were not very likeable. But for some reason the crew wanted to stay, and incessant rain provided them with a good excuse for not leaving. But at last a fine day came and I insisted on departing by midday. We made a rapid journey to Rialú, a one-hut village, where we passed the night. On the way, I was fortunate to find the beautiful blue orchid *Acacallis cyanea* in flower. And that night in the nearby forest *guaribas* roared in chorus, the most haunting and unforgettable sound of the jungle.

We reached the River Jaua which flows through an *igapó* as far as the eye can see — the preponderance of black-spined *jauarí* palms probably gave it its name. The river rises in the distant *serra* known as Tula-Tula, and soon after passing the mountains we nearly met with disaster. The skies darkened early and storm clouds filled the sky as we rushed for the shelter of an *igapó*. Torrential rain delayed us and when finally the sun came and a rainbow dipped down into the river it was late afternoon. We continued downstream towards Sumaúma as darkness obscured the land. It was a harrowing journey as the night was starless, and the river black, shallow and treacherous, and in certain areas sandbanks rose above the river surface. And, indeed, we did run straight into one, from which we managed to extricate the boat only with much difficulty. Straining our eyes to penetrate the blackness, we eventually sighted a glimmer of white coast where we landed with great relief. It seemed to be part of a small *campina*, so we lit a fire and supped there. Mary and I decided that it would also be an excellent spot to pass the night but the crew was loath to stay and, in spite of the obvious risks, wished to continue on their way. But we prevailed, insisting on remaining until daylight.

Sumaúma came into view at midday but we did not stop there, preferring to make up for the time lost the day before. But at the mouth of the Curiduri river, Paisano became quite excited, knowing that we were near the site of an old Indian cemetery. It was also the site of an ancient Xiriana *malcoca* where Paisano found two black ceramic jars in the cemetery; how I wished I knew something of archaeology and the history and origin of those earthenware pots. The region must have been the territory of many Indian tribes not so long ago.

The distant Serra do Demini came into view in the east soon after passing the mouth of the Curiduri, where on the journey upstream we had left our convoy of boats. During the two weeks we had been travelling, spring had arrived here, with trees in flower, pink and white gustavia, pale purple *pau roxo* (a legume), and countless rose-to-white clusias, the stranglers.

Later on in the day we arrived at a very small settlement, Nova Esperança, where Paisano, who seemed to have friends in all the huts on the river, arranged shelter for us in a large open barn belonging to Dona Bonifacia and Sr. Maricio. In this outhouse I watched the women preparing *farinha*. To extract the poisonous juice from manioc, the grated roots were squeezed in a *tipiti*. Then the pulp was roasted over a stone oven in a huge copper pan, being stirred and turned constantly. It provided their staple diet and was frequently accompanied by fish or fish soup.

In Lebom, the next stop, a deserted, decaying hut served as our living quarters. The ground was full of ant holes, so we hung everything, including hammocks, on the rough hewn wood of the walls. The night proved hot and peaceful but at dawn a storm wind brought heavy rain, which poured through the dilapidated *sapé* roof.

We spent our last night at Carapanatuba, 'place of many mosquitoes' — which lived up to its name, and where I spent an hour exploring the nearby *igapó*. It was densely wooded with enormous trees and *jauarí* palms. Epiphytes in abundance clung to all the branches. To get through this *igapó,* Mary and I had to use our hands more than the paddle, pushing aside branches which trapped the canoe, forcing us at times to find another channel. Whilst we were struggling in the darkness of this swamped forest, the boat of Atenau, son of Albino, passed by, the first craft we had seen on the river since Cachóeira dos Indios. But it was not the last, and another boat coasted in and moored beside us. Gone was peace and seclusion, for passengers and crew talked long and loudly, and when dawn came they were still talking. There was no alternative. Mary and I had to have a rapid and indifferent river wash in full view of a throng of curious *caboclos.*

The mission at Barcelos gave us the chance for a welcome clean up and a brief rest. Then on to Manaus. By bad luck we chose the first boat to leave which was a regular passenger 'liner'. It was crowded and my precious plants were crushed and smothered with gasoline — even soup! Our sleeping conditions were appalling: hammocks in tiers above beds on deck, dozens of children and non-existent hygiene. The journey was supposed to be non-stop to Manaus in twenty-four hours, but we had motor problems and were delayed for a long time. Then came the inevitable storm which was a moment I had been dreading. We suffered when all the shutters had to be closed and we stifled amongst a sea of bodies. Luckily I managed to push my foot against a shutter and open it slightly just to get some fresh air.

Soon after we had passed the River Branco we stopped near the mouth of the River Camanaú where I talked with an old *caboclo* — a *sertanista* (backwoodsman). He had worked with Colonel Rondon, a Brazilian, and the first supporter of the Indians. The *caboclo* had been with Rondon from the age of twelve and had learnt Indian attitudes the hard way, on foot for months in the forest and away from home. We talked about a disaster, some eighteen months ago, when some 'civilizados' arrived on Indian land. The Camanaú was the traditional fishing territory of the Atroari-Waimiri tribe which had killed this group of ten 'civilizados' led by an Italian priest, Father Calleri. A F.U.N.A.I. *Posto Indigena* was near the fishing land and most of its functionaries had left in fright as about three hundred Indians were expected in the area at any moment for it was the turtle egg season. The old man was not surprised by the story, as the 'civilizados' had intruded where they were not wanted. He said he was going to stay at the *Posto Indigena* and meet the Indians in the way he had been trained by Rondon. I often wondered if he had managed to make friends with any of them.

Once in Manaus, Mary left ahead of Margaret who continued collecting in the nearby forest and the Ducke Reserve. Her journeys had been very productive. One of the batemania from the Demini was probably a new species, the pitcairnia from the Solimoes was rare, and the Catasetum saccatum *she painted in both the male and female form. These discoveries and her determination to continue her work in the Amazon, led Margaret to create a collection of her work and another book.*

For the future she envisaged she would need financial support and Dr. William Rodrigues, a botanist with the National Institute of Amazon Research, suggested she should apply for a Guggenheim Fellowship. He backed her application enthusiastically, adding that her work was of the utmost scientific importance.

Margaret Mee
August. 1981

Catasetum galeritum
Rchb. f. amazonas

To the River Maués
and the Land of Guaraná

Margaret received a Guggenheim Fellowship in 1970 and used the funds for two journeys. The first, in late 1971, became a reconnaissance of the Amazon below Manaus and subsequently led to her return to public affairs.

People have been settled for many years in small clearings along the Amazon, but in many of these places the natural aspect of the forest has disappeared. At the time of Margaret's visit large areas were still undisturbed though massive plans were well ahead to open up the region south of the river. Among many developments affecting the forest was a new road being carved from the coast over a thousand miles away. Settlements, agricultural centres and Government offices were to be set at regular intervals along this Trans-Amazonic Highway. Brazilian botanists were justifiably concerned. As the Amazon's forests have many faces, certain plants are restricted to small areas and are doomed to extinction when the land is cleared.

The area Margaret chose to visit was approximately 150 miles south-east of Manaus and the centre of two long-established industries. One was the 'farming' of a liana, guaraná, *the seeds of which are used to make a beverage like tea. The other involved crushing every scrap of a tree, a relative of the sweet bay, to make an oil base for perfume.*

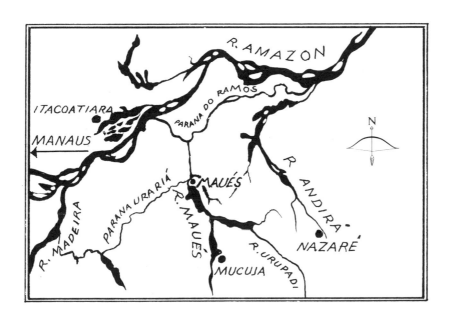

A sketch for Aechmea meeana, *a species discovered by Margaret and which has not been found again.*

September, 1971

I arrived in Manaus at the end of September to begin a journey to the lower Amazon. Originally I had planned to travel further afield but I was warned of a strain of malaria, resistant to the normal treatment, which plagued certain areas. Boatmen avoided these places or charged very high prices, so I settled for the River Maués which I could reach on a fairly regular river boat service.

After so much trouble with motors on previous journeys I felt I should have my own motor which would be well maintained. Accordingly I bought a small outboard which could be fitted to any hired local canoe. The extra baggage meant I also needed a helper, and Waldemar, a boy of about nineteen, was recommended to me. Together

Catasetum galeritum (Orchidaceae).

we boarded a crowded *gaiola* (regular passenger boat — literally a 'birdcage') bound for the tiny port of Maués about two days' non-stop travel from Manaus. The boat had two cabins, one for the 'comandante', and the other available for a passenger, which I was fortunate to get. It was ideal stowage for my motor as the rest of the boat was filled with people, hammocks and luggage.

We chugged down the Negro into the Amazon, past the port of Itacoatiara on the left and across the river, at that point about three miles wide, to a region of canals, small islands and *igarapés* through which only a good pilot could find the way. At night in shallow places the *gaiola's* light picked out the phosphorescence of fish darting in and leaping from the water. Well before dawn I awoke to find we were sailing up the Paraná do Ramos, famed since the days of Richard Spruce for its clouds of mosquitoes. This channel, up to six hundred yards wide, winds through land and flooded forest on the southern side of the Amazon and bypasses a great bend of the river of more than a hundred miles.

Daylight revealed a landscape typical of this part of the river. *Sumaúmas* towered above groups of large-leafed *embaúbas*; the feathery foliage of macrolobiums trailed low over the margins of the river. Where people had settled, the exotics they had introduced, such as lemons and avocados, stood dead and withered, for the annual flooding had been exceptionally extensive and the water level was still high for September. A few poorly *seringas* (rubber trees), *Hevea brasiliensis,* lined the mud-washed banks and a handful of bony cattle grazed on the small patches of grass beside huts. Others stood lean and drooping on rafts. Many huts seemed to have been abandoned and the forests were faint in the distance.

Before noon we left the Paraná do Ramos and turned south into another channel, the Urariá, which links the River Maués with the Madeira. Here the whole region was studded with canals and lakes joining the *paranás* to the main rivers. It was then only a few hours to the town of Maués, my first stop, where my arrival was ill-timed. The small town was as overcrowded as the *gaiola,* and a room in a hotel was out of the question, the only one in the town, the Vitoria Regia, being packed with ministerial personages following in the wake of a new regional governor. Loudspeakers were pouring out his speech at top volume to a background of religious music.

The Covent of the Sacred Heart had a school attached where, as the pupils were on holiday, I was kindly given hospitality in a classroom. Here I was able to hang my hammock and enjoy a few peaceful nights before the journey up the Maués.

In former times, according to Richard Spruce, who visited Maués in 1850, the town was Luzêa or Aldeia dos Mauhes (village of the Mauhes Indians), founded by the Portuguese in 1800 with a population of 243 families. Three years later the settlement had 1,627 souls, of whom 118 were whites. Spruce said: 'The progress of Luzêa has been entirely due to its being the great centre of the cultivation of *guaraná.'*

When cultivated, this stout twining plant is kept more in the form of a low bush. The black seeds are pounded and roasted before being made into hard, chocolate-coloured sticks. The *guaraná* beverage I was well accustomed to drinking is made by powdering the stick and mixing it with water. Without adding sugar the flavour is mildly astringent, not unpleasant, and always refreshing. The outstanding Brazilian botanist, Adolpho Ducke, was supposed to spend his days of research in the Amazon forests sustained for hours solely on grated *guaraná.*

Before long I met a scoundrel — I'll call him Jeronimo — who had been proposed as a guide by friends of the local lady judge, and was described to me as being indispensable on such a journey, as he knew everyone up the rivers and tributaries. Perhaps I should have been more cautious, particularly when the wise old priest at the mission where I was given hospitality looked askance when he learned that this man

Neoregelia eleutheropetala *(Bromeliaceae).*

Neoregelia eleutheropetala (Ule)
L.B.Smith
Amazonas, Rio Urupadi
Nov. 1971

Margaret Mee

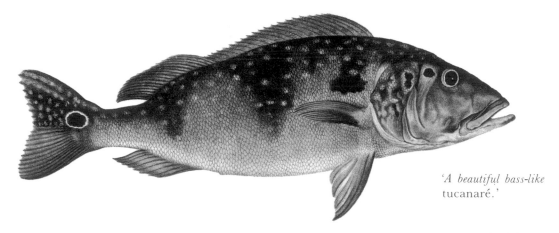

'A beautiful bass-like tucanaré.'

was to accompany me on the journey. He warned me that Jeronimo had been forbidden to enter Indian territory due to some scandal involving an Indian. Unfortunately, Jeronimo already considered himself engaged for the journey, so I decided to speak with him frankly to discover if there was a problem which could prejudice my work — in which case I would not allow him to travel with me. When I questioned him he protested innocence and persuaded me to accompany him to speak with the judge and hear her opinion. For some reason he took me to the judge's landlord instead, an important functionary in Maués who spoke of Jeronimo in glowing terms.

However, I was still hesitant about him, and a little later my doubts were confirmed by an official of F.U.N.A.I. My permit to enter Indian territory presented no problem, he told me, for it had been signed by a general, but when Jeronimo appeared the officer recognised him immediately and in no uncertain terms refused him a permit while Jeronimo listened with a face of thunder. At this point I should have been firmer, but that is easier said than done in an Amazon town. Jeronimo had powerful friends who could have upset my plans and even delayed my departure. I had already hired a small boat, and each day's delay would cost me more, so reluctantly I chose to take Jeronimo as arranged. So it was that, with a paid crew, a small canoe in tow and my precious new motor, I set out into the River Maués, for the first time in charge of my own expedition. I headed upstream, or directly south, into a river which was more like a lake and over two miles wide, with the intention of following the course of the River Urupadi, a tributary of the Maués. We continued between forests which gradually became more distant as the river widened. In this expanse of water, hundreds of *biguás* (cormorants) were diving for fish. As the boat approached they immersed themselves either completely or with their heads just showing above the water watching our

Logging the pau rosa *tree, when every scrap is used to extract an oil base for perfume.*

Bento (standing) with bromeliads he had collected from the forest.

course. The leafless trees which stood deep in the river were alive with these fascinating creatures.

'My doubts about Waldemar's character have been growing for some time, as he and Jeronimo seem to be ganging up. Today, while I was occupied, he took the canoe and outboard motor and sped around in circles, wasting precious fuel. I shouted in vain, for my voice was drowned by the noise of the motor. At last my frantic signals caught his eye and he returned, but not before I had seen him chase and run down a cormorant with the canoe. My anger blazed as I saw the poor creature hanging limp and dying in his grasp, and as he stepped into the boat I seized the bird whose sharp beak tore my finger and made the blood flow. Realising that I could do nothing to save it, I carefully rested it on a tree stump in the water, just above the surface, so that at least it could finish its life among natural surroundings. Waldemar has just shamelessly confessed that he killed the bird for 'sport'!'

It was afternoon when we reached the quiet *igarapé* where Jeronimo's brother, who was about forty, had built a hut and lived with his fifteen-year-old wife. The men fished and caught a beautiful bass-like *tucunaré;* it is a lovely fish with spots of gold and dusky stripes across its dark body and far too beautiful to eat. I found a striking bromeliad with a long inflorescence of six radiating spikes, already dry with fruit forming. It was so unusual that I felt it would be worth returning in six months when the flowers would be in bloom.

Our visit was brief as it was already growing dark and we still had to find a place to moor for the night. Furthermore, the men were desperately keen to find some *farinha,* which they had forgotten to bring from Maués, so we searched for a hut where this staple food could be brought. Eventually Jeronimo led us to a small *caboclo* settlement at the mouth of the Urupadi. Amongst the group at the settlement was a very unpleasant man who lost no time in asking me for sugar and petrol. I gave him a tin of sugar but refused petrol, as I had a minimum supply for the journey. He became quite aggressive and, rather than staying there, I decided we should move on to the mouth of a small river nearby, the Cuiuni. The night was wonderfully cool and we supped on a little beach by the light of the full moon.

In the morning I took my dip from the beach and had hardly got into the water when

Ionopsis utricularioides (Sw.)Lindl.
Rio Gurina-Mirim, Pará

Margaret Mee
August, 1984

I realised I was being watched from the bushes. The unpleasant man from the settlement had followed us and was now peering at me. Quickly I returned to the boat and gave orders to head immediately into the Urupadi.

The days passed and I lost count of them, which is not unusual in the wilds where the only timekeepers are light and darkness. But as the days passed my troubles grew. I was losing time for work and, among many other delays, nearly a day was lost in giving a tow to a family of *caboclos* — it became a lift rather than a tow, for everyone came aboard, bar the man, and sat on deck hungrily eating the only food I had to offer them, dry biscuits and *farinha*. The whole family looked sick, and the children, though pretty, were very yellow. At the end of the 'tow', after accepting a few tins of conserve and worm cures, they wearily went their way up a dark forbidding *igarapé*.

For some reason my boatmen decided they wanted to pass the night on a beach of the *igarapé*, but I did not like the cramped and sombre place, and we retraced our way back. This proved fortunate, for day had scarcely dawned when, as I lay in my hammock, I heard the most glorious melody, the song of the *uirupuru* (musician wren), *Cyphorhinus modulator*. This is a small bird of sombre colouring but with the most beautiful voice of any Amazon bird. Unfortunately the belief that the possession of a dead body of the bird brings luck to the owner results in many of them being killed and sold in the open market of Belém and other towns in Amazonia. The melody continued for sometime, always varied and incredibly beautiful. It is said that creatures of the forests, on hearing this song, listen in rapt silence, then follow the bird far into the jungle.

It was about this time that one of my crew, Bento, an Indian who had been living in Maués for many years, warned me that Waldemar and Jeronimo 'were up to no good.' Bento had been the most helpful of the crew with my collecting and respected the fact that I was a woman travelling alone, always offering to stay with me when Waldemar and Jeronimo were around. This comforted me considerably, for I had evidence that my fears about these two were not imaginary. On returning from collecting by canoe with Bento I noticed, as I boarded the boat, a cartridge from my revolver rolling on the deck. Immediately I examined my unlocked suitcase where I found all in confusion — bullets mixed up with clothes, a shirtsleeve shut in my paintbox. Obviously the two fellows had been looking for my revolver, which fortunately I had left rolled up in my blanket inside a canvas bag; they had not managed to get that far before our return.

That night, as I lay sleepless in my hammock, I heard faint movements behind me and flashed the powerful beam of my torch in that direction, after which dead silence followed for some moments; then someone crept silently away.

Bento did not escape the aggression of the two conspirators, and constant quarrels ensued. The climax came one lunchtime when Waldemar complained that Bento refused to eat the food he had prepared. I found the Indian in a rage, '*Eu sou Indio! Eu sou Indio!*' (I am Indian), he repeated, obviously challenging their malicious goadings. I managed to calm him and asked what the trouble was, but he gave no reply, and I then realised Bento suspected the other two had tampered with his food. The number of poisonous plants in the Amazon are legion and many of the inhabitants are familiar with them and their effects. Indeed cases of death through the administration of these toxic plants are legion. After this confrontation the enmity between Bento and Jeronimo intensified.

These dissensions played havoc with my collecting and painting and I decided that if I were to get any benefit from the journey I would have to ignore them. Fortunately there was a profusion of interesting plants. On the banks of the Urupadi I found some lovely orchids. One, *Ionopsis utricularioides,* was a mauvish pink and had a cluster of

Ionopsis utricularioides *(Orchidaceae).*

flowers. Another, *Mormodes amazonicum,* was larger and yellow. Inspired by these finds I decided to investigate a smaller river, the Amoena, a tributary of the Maués, which Jeronimo said had a waterfall at its source. We pressed on with such speed for the Amoena that I wondered if Jeronimo had any other motive than the approaching dusk for such haste. It was not long before I heard from Bento that Jeronimo imagined he would find diamonds and gold at the *cachóeira*! He was intent on making money at any cost, as I saw when we moored at a lonely beach where some accultured Indians had settled. Jeronimo went ashore to talk and returned with a roll of skins under his arm. Knowing that they were the skins of forest animals, I refused to have them on the boat, insisting angrily that he leave them in the forest. He was livid with rage. Then, whilst this incident was still rankling, we moored at a devasted, god-forsaken beach, where the men, having no respect for forest animals, made one concerted rush to find turtles and their eggs. It is no wonder that the unfortunate river turtles are nearing extinction, for afterwards, at every little beach where we moored, this senseless scramble was repeated.

We chugged on for some distance looking for the mouth of the Amoena, and with the approach of night I asked Jeronimo to draw into the bank and moor. But he refused, saying that we were less than half an hour's distance from the river. So on we glided, twisting and turning through *igapós* clogged with trees and up *igarapés,* until the tunnel of forest through which we were passing became denser and darker making it impossible to see without the aid of a torch, for which I had no spare batteries, Waldemar having forgotten them in Maués. I had been sensing for some time that Jeronimo was lost. He never admitted it and just kept going until it was too dark to

A mormodes orchid from beside the River Urupadi.

A tayra, one of the forest's most agile carnivores.

Mormodes amazonicum (Orchidaceae).

Margaret Mee
September, 1975

Mormodes amazonicum LDL.
Urucará, Amazonas

proceed. Now we were really lost, and had to pass the night in this isolated, unknown spot. In the morning I had to make the decision, after much disagreement from the men, to abandon reaching the *cachóeira* and to return to Maués owing to the shortage of fuel.

'There is a most beautiful *igapó* at the mouth of the River Acoará which I saw today by the light of the setting sun. Through the years, the waters and winds have shaped the trees with such fantasy that each individual was an exquisite piece of sculpture, and as the wash of the boat reached them it lapped softly around and through them, for many were hollowed out like shells.'

The following night we moored beside a low *caatinga* within sight of a distant hut and Jeronimo promptly demanded to use the canoe and motor so he could go and get cigarettes from the occupants. In view of our shortage of fuel I refused, pointing out that we needed every drop for the return journey. The night was very black, but Waldemar and Jeronimo left the boat and made their way on foot through the forest, returning in the small hours of the morning with much noisy shouting. Primed with *cachaça,* they did not hesitate to wake me up to tell the story of how a sick girl, a relative of the owner of the hut, who lived in a small settlement, Mucaja, needed a lift to Maués. From all accounts she suffered from epilepsy and when in a fit, they recounted, four strong men could not hold her down. The two men insisted that I should fetch the girl from Mucaja and take her to Maués. They became insolent and aggressive when I declined, asking them who was to man the boat while they held the girl to stop her throwing herself into the river.

Once they saw my reluctance harden they changed their story. They said I must give her antibiotics which would cure everything. After this ridiculous remark, I said I would seek medical help in Maués for the girl and that was my last word. They then became so abusively unpleasant that, tired of being harangued and tense with the problems of the journey, I shed a few tears — hopefully hidden behind my dark glasses. Indeed, I longed for the end of the expedition but, as I had not collected my usual quota of plants, decided to devote the last few days strictly to collecting.

This time my attempts were thwarted by bad weather. Once I paddled the canoe with Jeronimo and Bento through waves which broke over the prow and made landing impossible. The next day was not much better and, with the sky thundery and overcast, I made another attempt to cross the turbulent river for I was quite desperate to find more material before leaving what was clearly a good collecting area. Then, at last, on the day before returning to Maués, I made a successful trip, for I found and Bento collected a magnificent bromeliad, *Neoregelia eleutheropetala,* its rosette a brilliant scarlet merging to olive green, with florets ranging from violet to white.

We reached Maués safely though I was exhausted by all the frustrations. For some unknown reason, as a parting gesture I invited the crew to a farewell dinner at the Maloca Restaurant, though only Bento and Waldemar accepted and the meal was a complete disaster. Waldemar got drunk on beer and kept demanding more throughout the meal. When it was over, Bento quietly went his way, while Waldemar accompanied me back to the convent for he was lodging with the priests. We had been walking for just a few minutes when he began shouting that he 'refused to sleep at the mission.' His language became abusive when I tried to quieten him — all this in the main street of the town. I was so overcome with shame at being seen in his company I told him angrily he could sleep on a bench by the road for all I cared, and that first thing in the morning I would buy him a ticket to Manaus, as I wished to be rid of him. I did not remind him that he and Jeronimo between them had relieved me of fifty litres of petrol and much of my equipment, but instead walked briskly away and

left him bellowing. In the future, I decided, I would pick my own crew and not be influenced by recommendations from other people.

My journey would have finished there except for an offer by one of the priests, Father Izeu, who suggested I should join him on a visit to Nazaré, at the head of the River Marau. It would only mean another two weeks' travel and the Marau was one of the tributaries of the Urupadi I most wanted to visit.

Villagers gather to be treated by the visiting doctor.

It was a dark morning when we set out in the mission boat with Father Izeu at the helm. The route retraced my earlier journey up the Maués towards the Urupadi, turned into it and continued for another day until we reached a *Posto Indigena* of F.U.N.A.I. and some huts of Maués Indians.

Here we met a Dr. Carlos Otto who was working with the F.U.N.A.I. Malaria Service and would accompany us upriver. After resting for one night we changed boats to the smaller *Dona Rosa* which could navigate the narrow Marau. This boat was a real chugger, the motor spluttered horribly at times, and the rudder failed on various occasions, landing us deep in an *igapó* and crashing us against trees in the forest.

As we journeyed on the river grew more and more beautiful, and many times as we swung around narrow curves in the river we brushed against the foliage of the forest trees. Then the way led through an *igapó* of twisted, dry trees, many of them only hollow shells. Once we emerged to find a marvellous forest fringed with *jará* palms (*Leopoldinia pulchra*) and small blue palms covering the water just as ferns cover the ground of a *caatinga*. It was one of the most extraordinary places I had seen.

We reached Nazaré late one afternoon. Steep banks of white sand led up to the group of huts around the modest church of bamboo and palm leaves. Two *tushauas*, Paulo and Emilio, were standing on the shore, ready to welcome us. Paulo, a man of about forty, strong and well built, Emilio some years his senior, an ageing man, tall and thin with one eye completely white. I wondered if this was the result of river blindness, an insect-transmitted disease common among the Indians, and which I had seen before.

I hung my hammock in the priest's house, which was clean and spacious and impregnated with the pleasant scent of dry palm leaves, and swam in the black water of the river, rather fearful of the strong currents.

Whilst Dr. Otto and his assistants from the Malaria Service attended to the villagers, I went collecting in a canoe with two young Indian boys, Gilberto and Francisco. With amazing agility Gilberto climbed high into a tree and, from a rotting branch which I feared would fall with him, threw down a strange bromeliad. It was shaped like a Greek amphora, and from their red bases the leaves turned back sharply, sword-shaped and deeply serrated with black thorns. The plant was not in flower, but I had no doubt that it was a new species. I was elated — the find made up for all the nightmares of the earlier journey.

Dr. Otto's medical examination was attended by *caboclos* who arrived from near and far. Amongst the Indians there had been little illness, but the *caboclos* who had settled in the region were suffering from numerous diseases — the doctor calculated that as many as seventy-five per cent were quite sick. After a day's hard work the doctor surprised me — for relaxation he suggested a trip in the canoe to collect plants! A *caboclo* paddled us into a fascinating *igapó* where we landed and waded through the swampy ground before returning to deeper waters where the dipping of the paddle

'Philodendrons filled the trees along the river.'

181

A red-headed woodpecker.

seemed not to disturb the birds. The forest was alive with highly coloured jacamars, woodcreepers and a woodpecker with black and white plumage and a large red crest, who, unafraid of the intrusion, continued tapping a rotten tree.

To my horror, Dr. Otto suddenly picked up a gun and cocked it despite my protests and entreaties, taking careful aim at the beautiful bird. In utter desperation I rocked the canoe and twice he fired and missed his mark. The woodpecker was scared and, sensing danger, flew off while the doctor was angrily silent for a long time.

Unfortunately it turned out that the 'kindly' doctor was, in fact, a confirmed predator who, aided and abetted by the ignorant *caboclo,* decided to go on a killing spree. His gun was raised at anything which moved. The *caboclo* waved an arm, pointed at an animal climbing through the trees and became animated, shouting *'macaco'* (monkey). It was not, however, a monkey, but an *irara* (tayra, a large otter-like animal with long silky-black fur and tail). Unobserved in the excitement, I rocked the canoe again, and the shots all went astray. The men were so agitated that they had not seen the *irara's* mate approaching through the trees. When she saw what was happening she made a detour, carefully concealing herself in the foliage, and it was with great relief that I saw the pair meet well out of range and disappear into the forest together.

The display of senseless bravado had surprised and sickened me, so I enquired of the doctor why he was so intent on killing the *irara.* All he could say was that he wanted the skin to keep, and was silent when I pointed out that the animal itself had greater need of it. As I was discovering, the once lovely Amazon was already tainted by intrusion.

We returned to Maués and before leaving for Manaus I took advantage of an offer to spend a day in the forest with an old ex-hunter, Raimundo. At the beginning of our excursion we were caught in a heavy rainstorm from which we sought protection, only to find that the only shelter was already occupied by a snake in a large hole. So I ate my *merenda* of soaking bread and banana, feeling icy cold, and suggested returning. But we persevered, though it was one of the most disappointing journeys I had made. The forest was destroyed for miles around. Burned giant trees, stripped of vegetation and epiphytes, stood gaunt and white-scarred-black on arid soil. The only area of green and living forest was being hacked down to make way for a rice plantation. A little further afield stretched a miserable *capoeira,* once a plantation of *pau rosa* — by law since 1937 for every *pau rosa* tree cut down another had to be planted. But in this spot the law meant nothing. The trees had gone long ago and only maimed stumps remained. As I looked on this desert I tried to block from my mind a vision of the Amazon of the future.

Margaret had not only discovered a new species — the bromeliad which Gilberto collected for her was later named Aechmea polyantha, *and it has never been found since. She also realised she had discovered a rich, new collecting ground, one which sadly was being damaged, so she planned to return as soon as possible. Her plants, carefully packed in Manaus, were flown to Rio where some went to the Botanic Garden and others to Roberto Burle Marx's sitio.*

Aechmea polyantha *(Bromeliaceae).*

Aechmea polyantha Pereira & Reitz
Rio Manac, Maies, Amazonas

Margaret Mee
January, 1975

JOURNEY EIGHT: 1972
Through the Cradle of the Red Desert

Less than four months after completing her reconnaissance of the Maués, Margaret Mee was ready to return to the Amazon. But first she took up the suggestion of Dr. Richard Evans Schultes to attend an 'Orchid Congress' in Medellin, a city in the forested Andes mountains of Colombia. After a very successful Congress, Margaret travelled from Colombia to Manaus where she spent some days arranging her next journey. Using her Guggenheim Fellowship funds she bought a small boat to use with the motor she had kept from her earlier visit to Maués. She had made friends with the local representative of the Brazilian Forestry Development Institute, Vivaldo Campbell de Araújo, who felt Margaret was someone he could rely on to report objectively about the current problems of intrusion into virgin areas. A local view was badly needed as the emotive issues of Amazon devastation and the threat to the Indians were beginning to reach the international press, whose reports upset Brazilian political circles.

In some places of Amazonia when the trees were felled the red, tropical earth was exposed to rain and sun and the possibility that the entire forest might disappear and leave a 'red desert' had been mooted. According to some authorities it was just a matter of time before the land would harden and then, devoid of vegetation, become a dust bowl. To find more plants before they were lost and to see the threatening changes, Margaret planned three journeys to places both old and new to her. The first was to Autazes; the second back to the Marau, and the third to rivers of the Upper Negro.

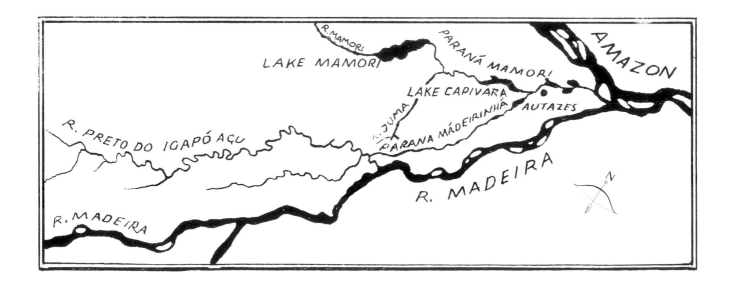

14th March, 1972

I was now the owner of a little boat almost thirty feet long and four feet wide, in excellent condition, only lacking a *toldo*. Manaus harbour regulations did not permit the use of palm or grass thatched shelters as they frequently caught fire in the port, but I decided I could get a shelter made somewhere along the river. Most importantly, this time I chose my guide, boatman and pilot, Severino, who was getting on in years, but still capable of manning my little boat single handed. He was a kindly, trustworthy man, small but tough, with many years of experience of Amazon rivers.

My friends at the Forestry Development Institute suggested I should go to the River Preto-do-Igapó Açu (black river of the large *igapó*). The name was enough to whet my appetite for interesting plants, but the officials wanted to hear about any infringements of the hunting and forestry laws. The request was important as the institute's office in Manaus was preparing a report for the Government's Planning Ministry.

The morning had been frustrating as my boat was moored far from the port and transport was a problem, but this was forgotten as soon as we began loading. The boat was beautiful, spacious and ran at a good speed with my 6hp outboard motor. In fact, the only problem was the lack of a *toldo,* and when it rained heavily, just as we were heading out into the River Negro, we stopped at a *flutuante* (floating petrol store), and sheltered for an hour before setting off again. I was full of *joie de vivre* — my own boat and a competent boatman. At last!

We had left the Negro and been travelling down the Amazon for about five hours when black clouds piled up, threatening a storm. Severino decided to take shelter as soon as possible. This was not easy as the banks had been denuded of trees, but fortunately we were not far from a couple of huts on stilts. The *banzeiro* (storm) blew up in minutes and a raging wind was tearing at all our possessions in the boat. There was not even time to moor, but we dragged it up on to land with the help of the family from one of the huts. Numerous children ran to and fro rescuing our belongings, and we had just climbed up the steps of the hut when the fury of the tempest increased and it seemed that everything would be swept into the river.

When the storm had passed we continued our journey until, in the waning light, we decided that, as the night promised to be dark, we would search for a house in which to shelter. As we motored on we spoke with two fishermen, eating their evening meal from an iron pot, who advised us to make for the 'Zinc House', a landmark with a shining galvanised iron roof. According to them, the house was about an hour distant but it turned out to be more. Some three hours later we saw the roof gleaming from afar. The house was large and impressive for this region, but almost impossible to approach, for it stood on stilts on land which was mostly under water. We had to paddle the boat through grass and then carry the baggage along a slippery path of slime-covered giant tree trunks which must have been felled many years ago. In the large, depressing house lived a widow, Dona Mariá, with a hacking cough and two sons. She kindly invited us into the bleak interior which was even drearier than the exterior. It was completely devoid of sanitary arrangements and as a lavatory I was offered the cracks between the palm wood kitchen floor where fish was being prepared.

Dona Mariá was a hospitable woman and served us a fish supper at a long table in company with her two sons. After partaking of fish soup and fish we were offered *macaxeira* (a drink). As this is made by chewing manioc in order to mix it with saliva, and the liquid then allowed to ferment, I politely declined! That night I slept on the terrace in my hammock where the air was fresh and cool, having decided that Dona Mariá's cough could be infectious and, in any case, disturbing. Outside the only sound came from hordes of mosquitoes buzzing with hopeless longing around my mosquito net.

With gratitude for the hospitality, I left this sad, isolated family whilst there was a break in the rain-filled sky, but soon had to seek shelter again in another *flutuante.* This time we seemed to be stuck forever with shower after shower blowing towards us. Eventually these turned to a continuous, fine drizzle and we decided to press on downstream. We made our way through the grey weather, expecting to reach the Parana Mamori, and a small settlement, Autazes, that afternoon. This hope was dispelled when three *caboclos* sitting on the bank told us, between gulps of *macaxeira,* that Autazes was at least three hours away. After we had been travelling for an hour, we drew into the bank where, at a riverside hut, Severino asked how far it was to

Two lecythids from the Mamori river.

Autazes. The owner suggested considerately that, in view of the bad weather and distance, we should pass the night in this hut or that of his neighbour. As I had noticed numerous children looking from the neighbour's window I judged that we should be crowded there and that this man's house would prove more tranquil. I was to regret this choice, for during the night and until dawn a wretched cat hunted the swarms of *pererecas* in which the place abounded. The animal, sensing my hostility, clawed at my

The highwater season in the forests near the mouth of the Madeira river.

hammock whilst the cries of the poor tortured frogs drove me frantic. I smacked at the beast with my shoe, but in the complete darkness could not rescue the suffering victims, and only in the morning was I able to drag them away and fling them far towards the river.

The lack of *toldo,* the struggle, often in the burning sun, to extricate the boat from islands of grass which clogged the mouth of every river and *igarapé,* in addition to a strong wind which lifted my enormous straw hat's brim, combined to give me burns on my hands and the lower half of my face. Early in the afternoon we turned from the main Amazon into the Paraná Mamori and by dusk were moored at Autazes. Although small, with just a few huts in a clearing on the left bank, Severino knew the mayor who offered us generous hospitality of the kind only found in the backlands. We had coffee, supper and I was offered a little shelter. I was desperately eager to get a *toldo* made, for protection against sun and rain, and was greatly relieved when I found a man who could make one. In fact he made two, a large fixed one and a smaller extension. Townspeople had not learned the art of making these screens from palm leaves and not many men in the country still knew the craft.

The mayor's brother, who knew the region thoroughly, advised me to travel up the River Mamori rather than the Preto-do-Igapó-Açu, as the former was much nearer — only half a day's voyage compared with twenty hours to the mouth of the Preto. He described Mamori as being rich in epiphytic plants which, as I had already lost much time due to the weather, decided me to change my plan.

Autazes had a poor vegetation, many areas having been stripped and burned so that few birds were to be seen. Cattle and a sawmill seemed to be the town's most treasured possessions, and horrible groaning sounds came from the trees in the sawmill as they were reduced to planks and sawdust. There was a prefabricated hospital imported from England being assembled under the watchful eye of an expert, but the medical equipment was to be carefully guarded until such time that the village could afford a doctor. Autazes was on the verge of becoming a commercial centre.

Margaret's boat on the River Mamori.

This part of the Amazon is a maze of lakes, *paranás* and small rivers. The whole region is crossed by waterways and *igapós* linking the Amazon and Madeira. I had been away from Manaus for six days and was still travelling towards the River Mamori by a round about way. First up a dull river with little of interest, the Autas-açu, or Parana Madeirinha, then into the Juma which flows into a large lake where I longed to collect from the banks. But the wind was too strong and drove us into an *igapó*. Indeed, just after the *toldo* had been made up we were crossing this turbulent lake and I had to hold on to it since it was flapping violently and I feared it would be blown into the river. Severino was too nervous to stop as he was unsure of the direction of the river and there was not a soul of whom we might enquire. At last we found the way and headed downstream into another large lake, Lago Capivara, with many outlets, our channel confused by islands of floating grass. But eventually we reached the mouth of the Mamori.

The night I passed in the tiny god-forsaken settlement of Itaúba on the River Mamori was disturbed. My hammock was hanging in the very primitive open hut of a young cowherd who was trying to breed cattle. The smell of cow dung in the shelter and all around was overwhelming, and when it came to starting before dawn I was obliged to pick my way carefully over the ground. A cool drizzle began early in the morning and I wrapped myself in a Colombian *ruana* (type of poncho) in an effort to get warm. However, with the sun came warmth and once more I longed for the welcome shade of the forests.

On one of the enormous trees on the other side of the river, about two hundred yards away, a mass of dark leaves hung in a heavy wreath around the trunk. Severino turned the boat in its direction, and on reaching the bank I could see the pendant white flowers of a beautiful white orchid which I had not seen before (*Stanhopea grandiflora*). It appeared to be too high to collect, until I noticed a natural ladder formed by the roots of an *apuí*, a strangler, leading up to the cluster of plants. Severino muttered that he was too old and stiff to climb to that height, besides there was a danger of snakes,

so I suggested he should cut a crook from the nearby wood, but he took so long in selecting and cutting one that I had nearly reached the plant when he returned. Seeing me with my head in the leaves he became alarmed in case I should fall and break a limb and begged me to come down. Using the crook he detached a plant with flowers and, seeing how beautiful they were, then wanted to pull down the whole cluster, but I restrained him and instead he got me two plants with blooms.

Night comes suddenly in the tropics, and because the rain continued I decided to look for shelter for the night. At a neat looking hut a pleasant woman came to the door and welcomed the two of us. She led me to the room where she said Severino and I could hang our hammocks. It was large and dark. All the windows were covered and it was some time before my eyes became accustomed to the gloom and I could distinguish a hammock already in the room and a figure reclining there. With a shock I saw a man with a gaunt, cadaverous face, his eyes sunk in huge dark sockets, and around him on the floor and beneath this hammock an indescribable confusion. I looked away quickly from the sordid scene lest my horrified expression should upset the man. Then I heard the woman's distant voice calling to suggest 'that of course the visitors would not mind sharing this room with the invalid.' I was horrified and my mind cast over all the usual illnesses — tuberculosis, leprosy, countless fevers and parasite problems. When I regained my speech I explained politely that I was accustomed to sleep in the open and would appreciate being allowed to hang my hammock on the balcony — which thankfully I had noticed on entering. Severino, who had followed me into the invalid's room, looked embarrassed as he told our hostess that he could not stand the cold, and might he hang his hammock by the open oven in the kitchen?

We left before dawn. As the sun rose I moored my boat to a white limbed bignonia, *pau-d'arco* (bow wood tree), Tabebuia species, which was covered with purple, bell-shaped flowers, but quite unconscious that I had tied the rope to a branch within a yard or so of a snake, who lay half hidden in the shadows. Completely motionless, I suddenly saw her watching me with her yellow-green eyes. By the design on her body and large head I recognised her as a *surucucu,* one of the most feared and aggressive serpents in Amazonia, with a deadly venom. Severino, who had seen her as he peered into the shade, was in a panic to leave and was roaring the motor. I begged him to run the motor as silently as possible as I released our rope, knowing that vibration would upset the snake. Very gingerly I released the cord, all the time gazing fascinated at her eyes with their slit pupils. The beautiful creature did not stir, fearless in the knowledge of her power. As we reached midstream a lifeless *surucucu* floated by, a great gash, possibly from a propeller, showing on her body on which feasted the most magnificent butterflies.

The sketches of the stanhopea on the Mamori: 'new roots white; bracts pale beige — speckled; new leaves light and y. green.'

'I had seen many vines of the same family — Bignoniaceae.'

Fearing further encounters with 'cobras' — the general name for snakes, of which he had a horror, Severino had to be persuaded to cross the river to the opposite bank where I had noticed a group of brilliant yellow flowers. I had seen many vines of the same family — Bignoniaceae, for during June many species come into flower. I retrieved trails of the trumpet-shaped blooms of this plant being borne downstream by the current, and as I unravelled the tendrils of the vine, impressive blooms fell in a golden shower. I painted the plant seated in my boat.

Heading back toward Autazes, we were crossing the broad, grey expanse of Lake Mamori when a storm threatened and, as the light was already failing, we looked for a hut in which to pass the night. But that night all the *caboclos* were celebrating the Feast of Judas and so had no time or room for us. One woman was even hostile in her refusal. We turned around and headed back to the open river. It had been difficult enough to moor in the little harbour used by this small group of hut dwellers as waves were beating us into the shore, and the wind had kept us imprisoned amongst a maze of tree roots, but it was even more of a problem to get clear again into the turbulent, open river. At last Severino succeeded.

We motored in heavy wind through blackness until a distant light gleamed faintly ahead. Hopeful, yet fearful of another refusal, we made our way in its direction. To my great relief, when I knocked on the rough door it was opened by a pleasant young man who bade us enter and led us to a large airy room where we were able to hang our hammocks and to retire, exhausted. There was no furniture in the room, and

The boat was loaded with plants, all packed in moist palm fibre in baskets.

A sketch of Catasetum gnomus *(Orchidaceae) from the River Mamori.*

through the open window I could see the dark shape of my moored boat. I slept fitfully listening to the wind and rain, anxious about its safety. *Mucuim* bites were torturing me. Suddenly I woke with a violent storm wind blowing in my face. When I looked out of the window to check my boat, to my horror I realised it was no longer there. I fell out of my hammock and rushed down to the windswept bank. No, the boat was not there and must have drifted away in the gale! I hurried back to the hut and with much effort awakened Severino, who, more asleep than awake kept on repeating *'Ja guardei!'* (I've looked after it). Eventually I prevailed on him to go down to the river with me where he explained that whilst I was in a deep sleep he had become fidgety about the safety of the boat and had moved her to a more sheltered mooring. Poor man! It was with apologies to Severino and tremendous relief that I saw it in the protected spot, well out of danger.

We left at daybreak in the wake of a larger wooden boat manned by a *caboclo* whose family peered curiously at us. A handsome cockerel strutted on the roof and a parrot screamed from a window. As our boat came alongside, Severino and the *caboclo* chatted together and Severino discovered that the man had seen the hostile refusal for shelter we met during the Feast of Judas. Interspersed with laughter he told the story of why

191

the woman was so aggressive towards us. Apparently she had heard over her transistor radio that two thieves were fleeing from Manaus to the interior of Amazonia, and she was convinced that Severino and I fitted the descriptions perfectly!

After sailing through the Paraná Mamori we headed for the small river, the Castanha-mirim, a region of strong contrasts. Here I saw spectacular birds in old forest, followed by a ghastly area of hideous devastation. The forest had been cleared to make way for a confusion of huts, tanks and barrels, all of which I guessed was in preparation for oil drilling. Fate was unkind enough to force me back to that scar in the forest, to stay the night in a house nearby, not with the smell of petrol in the air, but of manure of pigs, hens and cattle. We left early next morning to paddle through a beautiful *igapó* on the way to another lake. There spreading trees with adventitious roots some sixteen feet above the water formed arches and twisting ladders. Clovis, the son of a *caboclo* there, and I paddled away in his leaking canoe to collect, leaving old Severino to snooze in the boat. I returned with a worthwhile collection of brassias and catasetums and Severino and I left the lake and entered the fast flowing 'Furo', Castanha-mirim, eventually reaching the well-established Casa Fonseca, the grandest house in the area.

'I am to spend the night in a spacious room with the luxuries of a chair and two long mirrors. This is not very consoling as I am able to see my *mucuim* bites to advantage, which gives me quite a shock. I should be used to them now as I seem to get them on most journeys in the forest.'

After a few more days collecting and painting, we left the *paranás* and lakes, entering the Amazon along another *paraná*, and returned to Manaus by way of a most depressing water slum.

Return to Maués

A return to the River Maués had been a dream after I had found so many wonderful plants there. Among the many I hoped to find in flower was the bromeliad which I had collected in Nazaré and which was later confirmed as a new species (*Aechmea polyantha*). I delayed my departure for a day or two when I heard that Guido Pabst was due to arrive in Manaus on a visit in his capacity as a Director of Varig, the Brazilian airline company which was building the hotel and holiday centre at Ponta Negra, just outside Manaus.

In the richly forested hotel grounds, Guido Pabst was kneeling beside a pile of recently collected plants, busy pressing them. He was so intent on this work that I stood watching him for some time before he was aware of my presence. Then we sat together chatting over our drinks, and Guido told me many disturbing things that were happening to our fauna and flora without any preventive measures being taken by the authorities. I was in despair for our glorious Amazon forests, for I had already seen much of the destruction. This conversation convinced me more than ever to keep my collection of paintings of Amazon plants intact as a record for the future, and I resolved I would do all I could for the conservation of the Amazon forests.

After my experiences on the slow journey to the Mamori, I decided to travel to Maués by passenger boat with my small boat in tow. So Severino and I went down to the port to book two passages on a Linha Maués boat. Unfortunately a storm was blowing up, lifting the *toldo* of my boat, whilst craft nearby were batting against its sides making me feel quite uneasy. It looked so frail amongst the tough, rough hulks around. Severino stowed the baggage then, looking at his watch, told me he had some urgent business to attend to and disembarked hurriedly. The Linha Maués boat was due to leave Manaus at midday, yet ten minutes before the hour there was still no sign of Severino. I enquired anxiously whether the boat would leave on time and was assured it would. It did, and still there was not a sign of Severino. I felt sick with worry about my boat in tow and our plans for Maués. Perhaps Bento would be there to help? How could I disembark alone in Maués? Dozens of questions arose in my mind.

We had been sailing a good half hour when I sensed that something was happening. All the passengers were gazing intently at a rapidly approaching speedboat. It came alongside with a flourish and to my amazement Severino came aboard, bowing and smiling like a super star! With great relief I heard his story. His appointment over, he had hurried to the port just in time to see the Linha Maués sailing away. By a stroke of luck he met a friend with a speedboat who offered to follow and catch up with me.

'This passenger boat is grossly overloaded and the lower deck a nightmare. People in hammocks hang cheek by jowl over pools of dirty water, and the stench is unbearable. Severino has had a chain attached to our boat in addition to the rope. The tow is now secure and I feel more tranquil. Even the *toldo* is not lifting.'

Even so it was with relief that I disembarked in Maués. In the town I searched for and found Bento who had proved so loyal and helpful on my previous visit. Severino, who seemed to be ageing rapidly, needed assistance. With my crew and provisions ready I set out once again for the River Marau.

After two days travelling steadily up the Maués it was dark when we reached Piranga, a small settlement rather spread along the bank. We had been advised by friends of Bento to pass the night at the house of Monteiro da Sousa, but in the darkness it was impossible to find. Tired of searching, we moored at the bottom of dozens of rough wooden steps where Severino and I hung our hammocks whilst Bento slept in the boat.

Leaving early, we ran into a confusing maze of *igapó* where I saw many bromeliads, but dared not stop to collect as we were desperately seeking an outlet into the Marau. This tremendously extensive *igapó* stretched fully across the mouth of the river, and had we not met an Indian lad in a dugout canoe we should never have found our way out. He was the son of the *tushaua* Emilio, a former chief of the Maués tribe, whom I had met in 1971 in Nazaré. The lad led us through a forest of small trees, *molongó* (oleander relatives), to his father's *laranjal* (orange orchard) and dwelling at the mouth of the river.

In pleasant shade the *tushaua's* wife was peeling *mandioca*, preparatory to grating it to make *farinha*. Across the river a burned-out area and remnants of a construction camp marred the scene. It appeared that the gang who bore responsibility for the ugliness was still in the area, for there were reports of some two hundred men followed by a number of women, a crowd that Father Izeu in Maués warned me of: 'Keep well in front of them, or far behind them, for they are rough types without respect for man or nature.' It did not surprise me when later I heard that three deaths had resulted from their brawls, and that the local people demanded their expulsion. At the time of my visit no one knew of the whereabouts of the gang, but I was apprehensive when I learned that two rivers not far distant were swarming with *garimpeiros*, reminding me of my most unpleasant encounter with gold washers in Curicuriari.

The three deaths happened near the F.U.N.A.I. *Posto Indigena* on the Maués, but strangely the official there seemed unaware of the incident. Or so the *tushaua* explained as he directed my boat through a spectacular *igapó*. He was setting us on the way to Nazaré and, like all the *tushauas* I had met, he was dignified and courteous. As he paddled we heard he had quite a history.

As a young man the *tushaua* was living with his tribe, his grandfather being the chief

A Mauhés (Máuha) Indian.

of the Maué Indians. The *feiticeiro* in the village, apparently a scheming man, eventually persuaded and convinced the young *tushaua* that his grandfather was the source, or 'mother' in the terms of Indian belief, of the much-feared illness influenza. At the time many of the tribe were dying, and the spirits had to be called to stop the disease before the tribe died out completely. The *tushaua* told us how he had most unwillingly yielded to the evil *feiticeiro's* persuasion and killed his grandfather, the old *tushaua,* to eliminate the source of the illness. He was arrested and tried by a local court in the municipality and acquitted, but not before the entire tribe had been completely disturbed.

The *tushaua* left us close to the mouth of the Marau where we spent a peaceful night. Soon after dawn the next day I went collecting in the wonderful *igapó* and filled my boat with bromeliads including species mostly unknown to me. One was a magnificent aechmea in flower. Bento swam to the tree where a huge group of these plants grew in a forked branch just over the water. He put my bushknife between his teeth, climbed nimbly into the tree, tipped out spiders and scorpions with the point of the knife and hacked at the hard woody roots. At the first slash he was black with ants which swarmed over him and I called to him to stop, knowing how painful the stings are. But he only smiled stoically and continued hacking. When he could bear the stings no longer he jumped into the river, washing off scores of the troublesome creatures. Smiling with relief and success, Bento swam across to me with two plants, one in full flower. Realising that it could be a new species, I knew I should require another specimen for the Botanic Garden, but my search was in vain, for I could neither find the species again nor the host tree.

At no great distance away, in a lighter area of the *igapó,* stood a tall, slender *pau-d'arco*, the canopy a mass of purple-violet flowers. Just below on the white trunk clung two massive bromeliads with coral inflorescences. To climb up the smooth trunk was impossible, for there was not a single branch below the canopy, and no liana nearby from which Bento could swing to the tree. I was sure the bromeliad was *Aechmea polyantha* which I had returned to the Marau to find, but it was completely out of reach. We searched back and forth through the *igapó,* keeping to the lighter, less shaded parts until eventually I found three plants of the same species, all without flowers. I collected them carefully so they would have a good start in the Botanic Garden.

This *igapó* was one of the most exuberant and undisturbed that I have seen and explored; *jará* palms spread their fringed leaves between *pau-d'arco* and other hardwood trees. Humming-birds found a paradise there and, though we were always conscious of the myriads of insect pests which enveloped and tormented, their sounds merged to become an incessant murmur of life.

Leaving this fascinating region we had to shelter from a fierce storm, and took refuge in a hut occupied by a man and boy. The small fenced enclosure near the hut was occupied by a pack of dogs snarling, yapping and a picture of misery. All of them were scabby, ribby and half-blind, and their diet was — unspeakable! Fortunately the hut was some way from an open shelter where Severino and I could hang our hammocks while Bento slept in and guarded the boat. It was a glorious moonlit night; owls called from the forest and I could hear the distant replies of their companions.

By contrast, the following night was spent in Maués, in the most insalubrious port,

Aechmea meeana (Bromeliaceae).

Aechmea meeana Pereira
Amazonas, Rio Marau
March 1978

Margaret Mee

where we moored close to the Malaria Service boat. But for all the horrors of stench and noise it was convenient, and next day I embarked on the *Andrea,* a river boat bound for Manaus on which I enjoyed the luxury of a small cabin. Severino put his hammock where he could watch our boat, once more in tow and carrying all my plants.

In spite of my anxiety and constant vigilance for my plants, I saw with horror that the movement of the smaller boat in our wake was throwing them around. Soon they were in a chaotic state, the baskets of specimens toppled in confusion, and I asked to be helped down at the next halt to put them in order. But worse still, as the next disembarking passenger managed to scramble off while the boat was moving, the 'comandante' did not stop. There was no alternative and I tore off my shoes, stepped over pigs, hens and such until, with the help of a tough Indian lad, I reached my boat. Severino kept a firm hand on the towing rope but just how I managed the crossing with the pitching and slippery wood, I cannot imagine. The chaos was worse than I had seen from afar, but the Indian boy helped me adjust the plants, and secure the baskets. That done, my main fear was that petrol might have got into them.

Satisfied that order had been restored I began to climb back, this time from my boat several feet lower than the *Andrea.* We were plunging along now, crossing the Amazon which, from my level, was an ocean of brown water. I could not get a firm foothold on the hull of the *Andrea* and suddenly felt myself falling backwards. Instinctively I flung myself forward against the bulwark which I hit with some force as the boat pitched into me at the same time. I heard a sharp crack and the pain which followed told me I had broken a rib. The pigs snapped at my feet as I clambered over them avoiding their snouts, for they were famished, not having eaten for days. Eventually I sank exhausted on a pile of luggage. At that moment Severino announced that the 'tough' nylon rope securing my boat had broken a strand and was unwinding. He said it would soon snap and all would be lost. The most I could do was to ask him to replace the rope which he eventually did, expertly. After such traumas and frustrations it was a relief when we landed safely in Manaus.

To the River Negro

In Manaus I carefully sorted my plants, putting them into palm fibre baskets where they would stay until I returned from the River Negro. The rib was troublesome so I fixed strong bandages around my chest for a few days and kept my fingers crossed. Then I was ready for the second part of my journey, this time to the Upper Negro tributaries on the left bank which could be reached from my old base at Tapurucuará.

Nazarene, a young inspector in the Malaria Service whom I had met in Maués, had

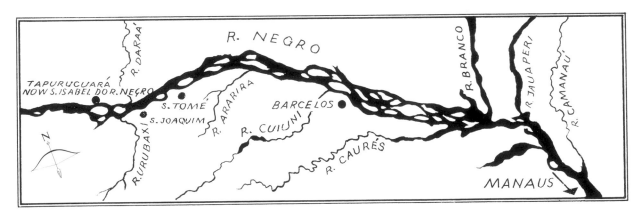

said he would tow me from Manaus to Barcelos and then onwards to Tapurucuará once he had finished his work. We set out in the evening, my boat in tow, and began with a 'tour' of the *igarapés* near the city where Nazarene had to deliver medicines at various houses, for as Manaus grew the only place for many people to live was along the banks of the *igarapés* where they kept boats and animals. The wooden houses on stilts were packed together with slatted walkways between them and the aspect of some of these *igarapés* was horrendous. In the past they must have possessed the charm of some of the streams in the deep interior of Amazonia with the huts surrounded by bananas and tropical vegetation. A few still had the remnants of lush greenery around the sad, decaying dwellings but the charm had vanished. The fires in a slaughterhouse glowed red through the darkness, like a scene from Dante's inferno. Beneath a huge roughly-built shelter of posts supporting a frayed straw roof, dozens of dark bodies were wielding great pestles in steaming cauldrons. Piles of bloody meat stood around, and the stench of blood was nauseating. A real Witches' Sabbath. I was more than thankful to return to the open river where clean, fresh air was blowing.

It was two years since I had travelled the Negro. Then I had moored beneath great trees, had seen enormous *figueiras* (Moraceae), which could have sheltered a village beneath their spreading branches. But in that short span of time, the destruction on the banks of the river had to be seen to be believed; small, miserable huts stood in the midst of large, burned areas, producing nothing or at best a feeble crop of *mandioca*.

Rain was falling heavily when we passed by Paraná Sumaúma, the mouth of the Camanaú River and Ilha do Jacaré (Caiman Island). In fact it had not stopped for two days; everything in my canoe was sodden and I had to bale constantly. But I was not the only sufferer, for passing Ilha do Jacaré, I caught sight of an old friend from Sao Paulo, Adolfo Richter, an orchid collector, sitting in his small canoe in a grey hooded raincoat, smoking a pipe and gazing up into the trees with such concentration that he did not hear my greeting. He was a noted professional collector and good friend of Guido Pabst. I called again but he appeared to be in a dream world, shrouded in the mist hanging over the river.

Westwards, beyond the River Jauaperi, the Negro widens and becomes like an inland sea, reaching its maximum width at the mouth of the great, 'white' river, the Branco, which rises in Serra Parima on the Venezuelan border. I was looking out for the four tall palm trees and church spire marking Carvoeiro. A vast expanse of river lay before us, studded with isles of tangled bushes and contorted trees, the trunks grand, impressive and white with lichens. On the left bank we passed the River Caurés, where many cerise flowers of *Cattleya violacea* gleamed in the dark trees.

I was in a deep sleep when we reached Barcelos long after nightfall. Nazarene brought the boat into the tiny 'port', I secured my craft and walked over to the Salesian Mission where I was greeted by the nuns and invited to stay in a little room with the luxury of a bathroom. Nazarene had warned me that malaria was very prevalent both in Barcelos and Tapurucuará, so I hung my hammock with its built-in mosquito net in my room, resolving to sleep in it rather than the bed so kindly offered. The malaria epidemic was one of the chief subjects of conversation for it was in the minds of everyone at the time. One of the nuns, Sister Anna, told me bitterly of her terrible experiences during the last epidemic, and how with high fever from malaria she had to attend stricken villagers, some at death's door. Many of her patients were working for a 'River King' whose sole ambition was to make money, to which end he used the most brutal methods. Like other 'River Kings' he was said to 'own' several tributaries. His workers were living in unbelievable conditions, housed in a huge barn with an open cesspool in the centre, around which hung the hammocks of the sick and

Raimundo and his helper Deolindo.

Oncidium lanceanum *(Orchidaceae)*.

A dry trunk from the igapó *in the River Cuiuni.*

dying. In that horrible place, with the exception of the father and one small child, a complete family had perished. The man was taken to the Mission Hospital and when the 'River King' spoke with Sister Anna he told her that her patient was only feigning sickness. The sister turned on him furiously, saying 'No, he is not just sick. He is dying!' Next day the man was dead.

All the news seemed bad. I was most distressed to learn that my beautiful bird, 'Japu', an oropendola, had died shortly after I left him on my last visit to Barcelos. Poor creature — although free I suppose he died of starvation, though I briefed two girls to look after him.

Barcelos had been modernised since 1970, and on the road, where asphalt had just been substituted for earth, I met the mayor, who obviously remembered our encounter on his 'official' boat in Manaus. He walked by, turning his back on me, but I responded with a friendly greeting, forcing him to be moderately civil. The changes in the little town were not aesthetic improvements, and the three or four shops were now selling articles which seemed quite incongruous to the region. I searched in vain for canvas shoes, and found only high-heeled slippers. The attempts of some of the villagers to assume a sophisticated air were quite painful to see.

I returned to the boat to find that Nazarene was to be delayed in Barcelos for a few days due to the serious malaria epidemic. But he had met a friend who had a friend, Raimundo, who would take me to the nearby River Cuiuni while we were waiting to move on. The Cuiuni, whose headwaters were to the south near the Japura, was one of the rivers I had long wanted to visit as it had many *igapós* which extended to the mouth and the verges of the Negro.

Raimundo appeared to be a pleasant, steady young man but I was far from impressed by his choice of a helper, Deolindo, a much older man. I informed Raimundo of my doubts, but he said that he had already asked Deolindo to accompany him. Hesitant, and with painful memories of my experiences with Jeronimo, we set out. The river was four or five hours away through a long, forested channel. At the mouth of one *igarapé* I asked to moor awhile. Deolindo became nervous and agitated saying that up the *igarapé* lived a terrible man whom it transpired was the same 'River King' Sister Anna had mentioned. Deolindo assured me that the man was the 'owner' of Cuiuni, and to prove his point recounted how a *caboclo* had been

Billbergia decora *(Bromeliaceae)*.

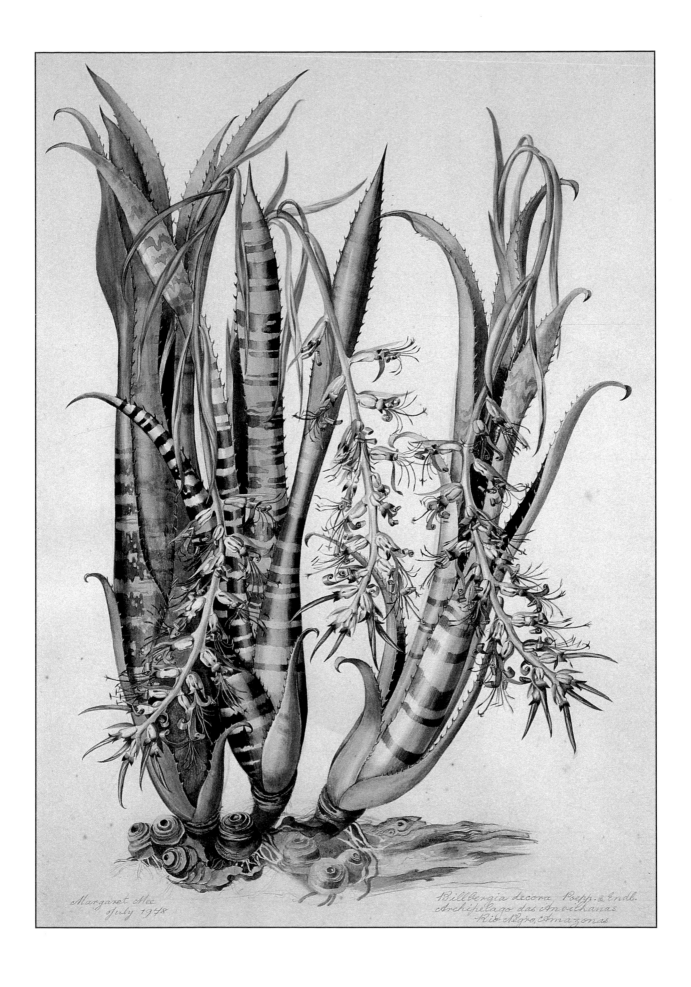

Margaret Mee
July 1948

Billbergia decora Poepp. & Endl.
Archipelago das Anavilhanas
Rio Negro, Amazonas

'A snake skin was draped in trees filled with philodendrons.'
Igapó, *River Cuiuni.*

gathering *castanhas* in the adjacent forest and was later charged with theft and imprisoned at the demand of this 'River King.'

The vegetation was somewhat monotonous, being scrub and low forest, until we reached the mouth of the Cuiuni itself, the Boco do Rio Cuiuni por Cima which was a wonderful region of great trees. There I made the best discoveries of the whole journey and collected a much prized orchid, *Oncidium lanceanum,* and a wonderful bromeliad, *Billbergia decora*, out of which jumped a large frog to be followed by two red scorpions and swarms of ants.

'Deolindo, very stiff in the joints, today climbed with difficulty to get the orchid and bromeliad specimens, though he cannot be more than sixty. People here do not wear well, probably due to poor health and lack of good food. There seem to be remarkably few birds in the *igapó* of this river, and I imagined it had been burned until I realised the extent of the strange vegetation. They say that in 1925 there was tremendous heat and spontaneous combustion which started forest fires. Only the forests bordering the river escaped the conflagration. Presumably man did his utmost to continue the destruction.'

I asked Raimundo to keep the boat moving slowly so I could scan the banks for plants. Suddenly a commotion startled me and I turned to find Deolindo leaning over the side of the boat, his arm outstretched in an attempt to catch a male *guariba*, swimming across the river. The poor creature was completely exhausted and his expression, full of fear and despair, was touching as he looked up at Deolindo. I ordered Raimundo to run the motor, which he had stopped for Deolindo, and to keep moving slowly past the monkey. I was rewarded by seeing the *guariba* clutch limply at a *jará* palm and slowly make his way into the obscurity of the forests.

Curious to know what Deolindo intended to do with a captive *guariba,* I enquired of his intentions, and was horrified when he replied that he would have killed it and sold it for meat in Barcelos. Having heard this, and in view of the fact that we were running out of supplies of macaroni, our staple food, and that there were two hungry men to feed, I decided to return downstream to Barcelos.

Here the malaria epidemic persisted, and when I landed I was told by the sisters that families were arriving hourly from distant rivers by canoe for treatment in the mission. Sister Anna said that there was no hope of the situation improving for the services were inadequate; indeed, malaria was likely to spread. Nazarene agreed. He needed help for such an epidemic in such a large area.

His next stop was to be a Tapurucuará, about 170 miles up the Negro, and on the third day of the journey after leaving Barcelos we had ample evidence of the epidemic, for a family of *caboclos* signalled us to stop, and came aboard our boat, a mother, father and two small boys. The children were puffed and yellow, and I imagined they must have had hepatitis as well as malaria, or some other terrible illness. The parents looked unhealthy and sick too. Nazarene, who was accustomed to such problems, embarked the family immediately. He put the canoe on our boat telling the man that he would take his family to the mission in Tapurucuará.

I retired to my boat which was being towed and from where I was able to watch the wonderful forests. Opposite the magnificent coast near Tapurucuará lay a long island where dark *jauarí* palms flourished among the hardwood trees and giant erismas. The view changed as we neared a settlement; along the banks the big trees had been cut down leaving a gaping confusion, for the smaller trees had collapsed when the giants were torn away. Then we passed two rivers. Entering on the right bank I saw the Daraá which, like many of the rivers I had travelled earlier, rises in the north along the ranges extending to Pico da Neblina. On the other side of the Negro, hidden in

Howler monkey.

the distance, was the Urubaxi, one of the rivers with a connection to the Japura and Solimoes. It was a river I had planned to explore since meeting the Baptist missionaries near Alvaraes two years earlier.

My thoughts were rudely interrupted as we came to a sudden stop, fumes pouring from the motor. Fortunately Nazarene and his helper were good mechanics and managed to get it running again, but not for long, and the second break-down was more serious; repairs could not be done on the river. The only solution was a tow and, using my little boat and outboard, Nazarene brought us safely, but at much reduced speed, to Tapurucuará.

On arrival I found that the mission was full, and an unpleasant sister from the south of Brazil (a *Gaucha*) sent me to hang my hammock in the infirmary which was crammed with sick people. I politely refused. The alternative that she offered was the girls' dormitory and again I refused, saying I would look for lodging elsewhere. On seeing me preparing to leave the Director Sister who remembered me intervened and promised to arrange a room. I was happy to see her again for I had met her in the missions of Taraquá and Içana. She told me that my friends Father Schneider and Father Goes were expected any day.

Whilst wandering round the village, reviving memories of the journey to the River Marauiá, I ran into Adhemar my pilot of those days. He called out to me by name and we chatted about the happenings there since 1967. Sadly his beautiful Tucáno Indian wife had died, but his daughter still lived with him in the little house attached to his grocery store and *'barzinho.'* I would have asked him to pilot me again had Nazarene not already engaged Leonardo, a Tariana Indian and brother of Carlos, the skilled pilot who took me up the Cauaburi to Pico da Neblina.

Acacallis cyanea, *the blue orchid.*

The leaves of the cactus Strophocactus (Selenicereus) wittii *'growing as flat as a scarlet transfer against the trunk.'*

Leonardo was already working on my boat, preparing her for a long voyage and fixing the troublesome *toldo.* I was very impressed by his apparent reliability and independent manner. He was around forty and stockily built, with high pronounced cheek-bones and long, sloping eyes common to many Indians. Above all, he was proud of being an Indian. His wife, who was badly disfigured by burns, kept herself hidden away in their hut on the banks of the Negro. Leonardo would have nothing to do with any organisations such as F.U.N.A.I., and became extremely irate when they were mentioned for he valued his independence.

He chose a Tariana boy, Joao, to help him on the journey, a shy lad who spoke little Portuguese and, unlike Leonardo, did not regard himself an Indian. When I asked him if he was a Tariana he denied it until I expressed disappointment and mentioned some of the best Indian qualities I had met. Then his face brightened and he said, rather proudly 'Perhaps I am an Indian.' I understood his attitude, for the *fazendeiros* and many *caboclos* speak very disparagingly of the indigenous people.

I chose the River Daraá for my first journey. I particularly wanted to find the rare *Strophocactus (Selenicereus) wittii* which I had seen near Tapurucuará in 1967. Then it had been late in the year and it was without flowers or buds. I hoped that at this time of year it would be in flower. We had not gone far into the river when we found a beautiful *igapó* and within moments I saw the cactus. I paddled right up to the tree on which it grew, and by standing in the boat could just reach it. It was growing flat as a scarlet transfer against the trunk, for the roots which grow from the back of the leaf secure it to the bark. The broad leaves were fringed with tiny, sharp spines but there was no sign of fruit or flower and I searched the *igapó* in vain for more of the strange plants. Not far away grew *Acacallis cyanea*, the blue orchid, and a very pale yellow orchid, *Scuticaria steelii.*

Scuticaria steelii *(Orchidaceae).*

Scutacaria steelii Lindl.
Amazonas, Rio Negro
May, 1972

Margaret Mee

A clusia from the River
Urubaxi.

Leonardo and Joao found a deserted hut at the top of a steep bank and that night
I slept in my beautifully prepared canoe, my hammock hung between two posts which
Leonardo had fixed. The night was marvellously peaceful, the only sounds the sighing
and splashing of dolphins.

Morning found us coasting further upriver until we heard the first of the thunderous
falls. Spume was blowing across the river and, as no channel existed, and because with
only a small crew there was no possibility of passing the cataract, the only way to the
higher reaches of the river was to drag our boat around the fall. So we walked through
the forest passing the deserted hut of the 'keeper of the rapids' but, finding little of
interest except a *toçandira* which stung me painfully on the hand, I decided to return
downstream.

So we set out with a fresh wind blowing and the sun hidden by clouds, which was
good for the many plants already filling the prow. And I welcomed the cooler weather,
as it soothed the aching and burning of my swollen hand. On the way we met two
caboclo fishermen from whom I purchased *tucunaré* and *surubim* (large catfish). Leonardo
said the fish would keep as the weather was cool, which was just as well as for the only
food the Urubaxi river had to offer us was a bunch of unripe bananas. I was surprised,
as I had been assured there was *muito fartura* (much produce) there. The fishermen also
had a spare small canoe which I bought at a very reasonable cost as it would be useful
for getting into dense *igapós*. We arranged a rope to tow our new acquisition.

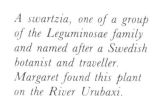

A swartzia, one of a group
of the Leguminosae family
and named after a Swedish
botanist and traveller.
Margaret found this plant
on the River Urubaxi.

To reach the Urubaxi we had to cross the Negro and head to the west, slightly upstream. But as we neared the bank our view was obscured by blinding sheets of rain driven by a raging wind. Leonardo held the boat steady and we reached the mouth of the Urubaxi just as large waves were forming on the river. When Leonardo had put my new canoe in tow, all the plants which I had collected on the journeys were transferred to it from the prow of my boat, thus making room for the petrol tins. Fuel was getting low and I hoped desperately that it would see us through to our return to Tapurucuará. Leonardo was extremely good and took advantage of the strong currents and eddies to eke out our supply, but it was, sadly, insufficient to take us to the mysterious headwaters of the Urubaxi. But the river proved a marvellous one to explore, and I added many interesting plants to my collection. Among them, the orchid *Gongora quinquenervis,* which I found growing on an ants' nest in a dark forest, as well as many bromeliads including aechmeas, billbergias, araeococcus, neoregelias and guzmanias. Then, sheltered by dark-leaved *buriti* palms (Mauritia), in which the river abounded, I found a small tree deep in the water, covered with bunches of cerise-coloured fruit. Between the brilliant pink bracts hung black and green berries. I made a rapid painting of this plant in the boat, then sketched a red clusia flowering nearby.

The glories of this river, however, were overshadowed by the senseless destruction of the *buriti* palms which, as Leonardo said, were originally the most plentiful trees along the banks. Not many were now standing, for the majority lay in the river, their massive trunks just below the water's surface. I was told that *caboclos* from Tapurucuará went up the river for a few days, slept in the leaf-thatched shelters that Leonardo and Joao used, and then collected the natural products including *buriti* fruit, *piaçaba* and *castanha* (the *buriti* fruit being easier to get by cutting down the entire tree). The *coboclos* also took hardwoods and cleared forests by burning. The results were plain to see — patches of wasteland with blackened stumps and felled *buriti* in the river. Some of the local riverside people with whom I spoke were quite cynical about this destruction, and when I pointed out they would end with nothing if they took the fruit of the *buriti* by cutting down the tree, they replied: 'Then we will go to the other rivers where there are plenty of *buriti.*'

The nights on the Urubaxi were peaceful. A sense of security and peace enveloped me when I moored my boat. One night I slept in the boat under a group of dark trees standing deep in the river, rocking gently with the lapping water. The men had found a small shelter out of sight, four posts with a palm leaf roof on the slope of the nearby river bank. Opposite lay a beautiful *igapó.* We were far from any habitation. Next morning the men were about very early, looking a trifle pale and jaded. Enquiring if the shelter had proved adequate and if they had slept well, they replied that they had not slept for a moment, for all night long they were listening to an *onça* roaming in the forest. Laughing, I reproached them for not warning me of the danger, to which they replied in all seriousness that they could not guess whether the animal would decide to choose me or them!

Homeward after four months

Tapurucuará behind us and replenished with a small supply of petrol, Leonardo, Joao and I set out in my small boat for the long journey back to Manaus. Though I was well used to the sudden storms on the Negro, I was always somewhat apprehensive about them. And, sure enough, we had not been travelling long before a terrific wind driving blinding rain before it came sweeping with fury through the forests and across the river. We were in a *paraná* where there was no protection, so Leonardo hastily made for an *igapó*, driving the boat firmly into bushes to secure it. We sat out the tempest clutching the *toldo* and watching the rain lashing the grey trees. The last heavy

On the River Urubaxi; Joao and the boat loaded with plants.

Gustavia pulchra.

shower opened the sky to a glorious sunset such as I have only seen in the Amazon — indigo clouds against a fiery background.

The following day, too, proved tempestuous, but in spite of wind and rain I was able to collect and paint a pure white *Gustavia pulchra*. The large tree, obviously a victim to a recent storm, had fallen into the river and was floating with the flowers on branches above the water. Leonardo navigated the choppy waves and handed me the spectacular flowers, which I painted in the boat, in spite of the harassing wind, before they had time to wilt.

Three stormy days had passed since our departure from Tapurucuará, during which we had continued travelling during the night when the water became considerably calmer. When we reached the mouth of the River Ararirá, about half way to Barcelos, we moored and I examined my plants and thought they looked a trifle sad and unlikely to survive the long journey ahead. Leonardo was exhausted and decided to have a well earned rest. The break gave me a chance to paddle with Joao in the small canoe through an *igapó*. As soon as we had reached the shadow of the trees we heard a tremendous crashing noise, and I imagined that Leonardo was signalling for us to return by banging on the side of the boat. Joao laughed heartily at this idea, saying simply *'guaribas'*. Immediately above our heads the howler monkeys set up a tremendous roar which was quite deafening. They were so near that I could

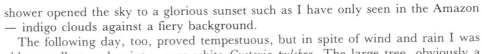

An unidentified species from the River Urubaxi.

Margaret Mee

Ochna
Amazonas, Rio Jurubaxi, June, 1972

The sketches of Scuticaria steelii.

distinguish individual voices, and the leader's husky tones above the rest. Joao looked at me enquiringly to see if I was alarmed, asking whether I wished to return to the boat. Should the *guaribas* object to our presence, he explained, they might pelt us with branches or, worse still, relieve themselves on us. But, they proved friendly and left us in peace. We continued our search and, suspended from twisted branches, I found a lovely bromeliad, a neoregelia, formed like a delicate candelabra in whose little cups blue crystal florets bloomed.

On this long journey our small supply of petrol became a worry, for there was little hope of buying any before Barcelos. But at one small settlement I noticed a river boat unloading cargo and some fuel drums. I asked the people if they would sell some petrol which they agreed to do at double the usual price and I bought two full cans which would be sufficient to get us to Barcelos where the mayor was supposed to have plenty. When we arrived, while Leonardo repaired a part of the motor I went in search of fuel.

I waited hopefully to see the mayor. Forty-five minutes passed whilst I sat on the balcony with his family, who first said that he was sleeping and then said he was eating. I ignored these obvious excuses and swallowed my pride as I was desperate. Without petrol we would have to wait for a boat and a tow. The climax came when the mayor sent word by a servant that he had no petrol to sell. I left angrily with my dislike of this arrogant little man intensified. Fortunately I had made friends earlier with one of the traders who offered, at a reasonable price, enough fuel for our return to Manaus.

We kept going that night, Leonardo navigating through a dense mist, keeping his head above the *toldo* so he could see, and driving the motor with his right foot. He had few landmarks in the river which was ten miles wide and more in some places. Joao scanned the river ahead for obstacles such as sandbanks which glowed white even in the pitch darkness.

Early one morning we approached the maze of islands and *igapós* known as the Arquipelago das Anavilhanas where, by common knowledge, the Negro can be turbulent, although it is worse nearer Manaus. The waves tossed my little boat about like a cork. As time passed the waves became rougher and the sky was grey and overcast. But this did nothing to alleviate my sadness at the thought of leaving the beautiful River Negro, the good companions of my voyage and the glorious forests of the Amazon, though I was rather weary and battered after four months of travelling through the wilds.

By this time my boat resembled a floating forest, for plants were hanging around the 'eaves' in baskets bursting with leaves and flowers. Many buds had opened during the voyage, though the humming-birds, which had come to take nectar from them, were left far behind. Instead, *urubus* (vultures) wheeled overhead and quarrelled over scraps of refuse on the banks. The smell from the slaughterhouse wafted across the water. We were approaching the noise and pollution of Manaus. Small craft dotted the water, cargo ships were in the harbour, a thousand miles from the sea. As we entered the port a speed boat shot by and turned sharply, its wake almost overturning my boat as the owner shouted loudly '*Tem peles da onça*' (Got any jaguar skins to sell?) Leonardo in true Indian style replied angrily in ringing tones '*Vai embora, contrabandista!*' (Push off, you smuggler).

These journeys were some of Margaret's most successful so far. When the plants she returned with were identified, she was credited with the discovery of three new species. Two were named after her — the aechmea she had found on the Marau and which Bento had cut for her in spite of the stinging ants, was named Aechmea meeana, *and an orchid identified by Guido Pabst was named* Sobralia margaretae. *The aechmea she found on the Marau on the* pau d'arco *was, as Margaret had thought, confirmed as an* Aechmea polyantha. *The three species are known only from Margaret's paintings: they have not been recorded since.*

Later Margaret wrote a report for the Forestry Development Institute which was widely quoted in the major newspapers of Rio and Sao Paulo. Her findings brought attention to the devastation which could be seen around Manaus where the trade in skins and forest products was unregulated. Margaret Mee, the papers said, had seen all this during a few months in the Amazon. In fact, she had seen the problem growing for far longer, for her travels already spanned fourteen years.

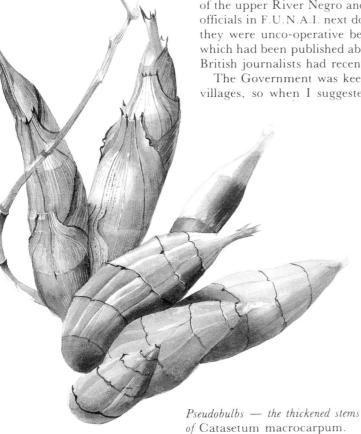

JOURNEYS NINE & TEN:
1974 & 1975

An Interlude with Friends

An orchid, Catasetum macrocarpum, *from the Andirá.*

After completing her work for the Guggenheim Fellowship, Margaret travelled to Britain in 1973 for hip replacement surgery. After the treatment she spent some weeks recuperating at a friend's home in the wooded Gloucestershire countryside before returning to Brazil. Her objective in the Amazon was unchanged and she planned more journeys. The River Negro never lost its appeal, but after the successes with new plants near Maués, Margaret began to consider more areas of the lower Amazon. She arrived in Manaus in July 1974 to find her canoe missing and the motor, which she had lent to a friend, was no longer reliable. Despite these problems she decided to continue.

23rd July, 1974

The diminutive Hotel Paris is tucked away in the older part of Manaus in Avenida Joaquim Nabuco, cheek by jowl with F.U.N.A.I. headquarters. I called at the hotel to have a chat with the owner, Capixaba, an old friend of many years. The Paris was always an 'open door' for me and somewhere cool to rest in the town. Weary, I sat down and was enjoying a *cafezinho* (small bitter coffee) when I saw a British airline bag swing by. Capixaba fetched the hotel register and I realised that the arriving guest was Christopher, a tall, blond and typically English young traveller I had met in far more luxurious surroundings in Gloucestershire.

Although a surprise here, I had half expected to see Christopher somewhere on my journey as we had talked at length about the Amazon. As we sipped coffee he told me he was trying to obtain a permit from F.U.N.A.I. so he could visit the Indian *aldeias* of the upper River Negro and River Uaupés. Christopher was drooping a little as the officials in F.U.N.A.I. next door had refused him entry to the Indian territory. He felt they were unco-operative because of photographs and articles critical of F.U.N.A.I. which had been published abroad. Without accusing anyone directly, the officials said British journalists had recently visited that region.

The Government was keeping tight control over any foreigner's access to Indian villages, so when I suggested to Christopher that he should join me, he accepted

Pseudobulbs — the thickened stems of Catasetum macrocarpum.

Catasetum punctatum *(Orchidaceae).*

Catasetum punctatum Rolfe
Amazonas, Rio Mamori

Margaret Mee
July. 1974

enthusiastically. But I had problems, too. The beautiful little canoe I had bought on the Daraá had either been lost or stolen from the *flutuante* owned by the Amazon Research Institute (I.N.P.A.). Fortunately, the Institute scientists lent me another, though somewhat inferior, canoe. I also needed a boatman and I had arranged interviews with three men. Only one, Carlos Tadeu, seemed suitable and even he did not arrive on time. I had to send a taxi to fetch him!

I was preparing to leave for the River Andirá, a tributary which enters the Paraná do Ramos about fifty miles downstream from the Maués. The first part of the journey, to near the mouth of the Madeira, about a third of the distance, was to be a tow behind a boat owned by an uncle of Carlos. He had a fifty hp engine so we would make good speed.

'Christopher has been busy fixing my *toldo* using palm leaves to disguise midblue plastic. It really looks quite pretty and he is tacking down the sides now. I shall be glad to get to the wilds as there is quite a lot of destruction on this section of the Amazon, though the change is not as great as I imagined... We left at about half past three this afternoon, ran into a *banzeiro* and were drenched, mainly because Carlos and his uncle did not slow down.'

The night was wonderful, with a star-filled sky, glassy water and a waxing moon. We were preparing our meal when, to my dismay, I discovered the·stove I had been lent was worthless, no — worse — a liability, for it caught fire when we lit it and, but for prompt action, the boat might have been on fire too. I decided to buy one in Itacoatiara (a port on the north bank of the Amazon, thirty-five miles from the Madeira), or starve. We slept, I in my small boat and the others in a *flutuante*. Large boats were passing all night long.

At the agreed place we said goodbye to Carlos' uncle and set off alone. Slower, but Carlos was a good boatman. We did not reach the Paraná do Eva, a very narrow channel and highly populated, because the motor gave trouble; it stopped dead thrice but, when the plugs had been changed, ran well.

In Itacoatiara, I searched in vain for a little gas stove and eventually came away with a wretched alcohol burner and two bottles of spirit. The stove cost thirty cruzeiros. Blackmail! I bought it, from a very grasping woman, at a small cottage outside the town.

'We have entered the Paraná do Ramos and will spend the night at a small hut. There are more mosquitoes than I can ever remember. Agonising! As we stopped only at ten everywhere is shuttered and dark. So our three hammocks have had to go up on the new frame in my canoe, which fortunately is standing the test! Unfortunately, the mosquitoes are biting me through the thick cotton hammock and a cat got on the boat and clawed Christopher's net.

We are now heading along the Paraná do Ramos — it is tremendously long. In eight hours we should reach Barreirinha. Magnificent birds are appearing, much to Christopher's delight — *araras*, parrots, *mergulhaoes* (grebes), *garças* (herons), and an aquatic bird which I have seen pictured in Zimmerman's book of birds — there was a large flock of them with young, and they set up a screaming at us as the boat passed by. There are hundreds of dolphins popping up from time to time.'

Barreirinha on the *paraná* is an unexciting, quiet port. There was a small Catholic mission and school beside the river where I asked for shelter for one night. As Carlos decided to stay there, I also asked if they knew a boatman whom they could recommend to take us up the Andirá. The sisters suggested Manoel, a small but sturdy

The bromeliad Neoregelia leviana, *a new species.*

man of Indian descent, and I agreed thoroughly with the choice. So after a peaceful night, supper and breakfast in the Mission we set out again at half past eleven the next morning. The sisters and a crowd of onlookers were there to see us off, but the motor failed before we were even out of the port!

The gasoline was at fault; it must have collected some water in the tank, so we changed it and got along splendidly until we stopped to collect some catasetums in the *várzea.*

The flooded banks of the lower Amazon, near the mouth of the Madeira river.

The next day began with more motor trouble. It refused to start, so Manoel paddled away in the canoe to fetch help and, just as night was falling, returned with a lad from a nearby village, though he had not a clue as to what was wrong with the motor. So Manoel and the lad paddled us through the dark forest to the next village where we moored for the night in a small inlet. In the morning they tried the motor again, but it refused to start. We took a tow with a river boat to Parintins. Not a good start to our journey.

Parintins, with a Malaria Service office, is a small port on the Amazon surrounded by *igapó*, lakes and the Paraná do Ramos. It is the point where river traffic moving upstream on the Amazon can enter the *paraná*. Here a mechanic at the Malaria Service office repaired the motor. After we left we went first through the *paraná*, and then through a narrow channel and *igapó* which formed the mouth of the River Andirá.

I collected in the *igapó*, which had some interesting plants — various orchids, catasetums — and was stung by a wasp but without any reaction. I wondered if I could be immune after my many stings. From the narrow channel the river opened into a broad lake which we crossed quickly as a *banzeiro* threatened, much to Manoel's alarm. The rain and wind caught us and we ran for shelter where we found good collecting. The *igapós* there were just magic, with the water so still that I could not distinguish the image from reality. To my joy I found *Catasetum macrocarpum*, the male and female forms. All around the forest seemed so rich that I resolved to return some time.

The Andirá continued more as a lake than a river and gradually turned to the southeast. Small inlets and *igapó* broke the line of forest for almost a hundred miles. We passed deserted houses, and some nights we even stopped beside them. Then, as the river narrowed, we reached the settlement of Ponta Alegre and the F.U.N.A.I. *Posto Indigena*. Above this point was the territory of the Maués and Satere Indians. We spent a night at the *Posto*, after handing over cameras, revolver, etc., for the regulations had to be observed at the insistence of Daniello, the youth in charge. He was an Amazonense, local to the region, and appeared to have better relations with the tribe than other officials I had met. I had a somewhat heated argument with him about relinquishing my camera and getting his consent to proceed upriver to the Indian villages of Molongotuba and Simao. In the end I mentioned that the Representative of the Forestry Development Institute in Manaus was aware that I intended to collect on the river as far as Simao. With this, his manner changed, for he had been an employee of this organisation and knew the Representative from time past. But he was adamant about leaving our cameras, although I pointed out that any photos of Indians who looked healthy and happy could do no harm to F.U.N.A.I.

Guilherme, a young man from Ponta Alegre, acted as our guide and we left the settlement and travelled upstream, the river narrowing as we passed with forest and *igapó* each side. We reached Molongotuba where we met the *tushaua* and his two nieces. They were short, sturdy and nice-looking girls, though one had an opaque eye. We took all three on an outing further upriver, between forest, *molongo* and grassland, to Simao. Here we were introduced to another *tushaua*, Manoel, who, unlike the others, spoke Portuguese. The Indian villages were very interesting and the houses of *babaçu* palms — *Orbignya phalerata*, were well ventilated and spotlessly clean. *Tushaua* Manoel took us to a spacious hut where Christopher and I sat on either side of him whilst half the village — some naked others half-clothed — sat in a semicircle facing us.

We conversed with these delightful people, *tushaua* Manoel translating for the tribe. They appeared to be very independent of the outside world, and their quiet courtesy was most refreshing. We returned to Ponta Alegre in the dark, a journey made difficult by the *molongo*, though we had a large moon to help us.

On our return, Christopher and Manoel were invited by the *tushaua*, Franca, to hang their hammocks in the nearby Indian village. I slept in my boat. Early in the morning, the kindly Guilherme brought me plants to add to my collection. Later the same day I found a bromeliad, *Neoregelia leviana*, a very beautiful specimen with five plants forming a candelabra.

I have neglected writing my diary in favour of collecting, or trying to do so, for the *igapó* of which I had great hopes yielded nothing but one catasetum and a few streptocalyx. But the principal reason for not writing was due to the ordeal we went through after leaving Ponta Alegre. We were literally shipwrecked in the Bay of Sapucaia. We were on our way downriver and, as the day had been squally from the start, we decided to find a place to camp earlier than usual. We found an ideal hut — abandoned — though it was scarcely a hut for all the walls were missing. However, we moored the boat on the sandy beach, and then Christopher and I set out in the small canoe to search an *igapó* for a strange bird, the hoatzin, which I had seen there earlier. These brown, pheasant-like birds, are poor fliers and spend most of the day in bushes close to the water. Here the hoatzin is known by the Indians as *ticuan*, an onomatopoeic word. The *igapó* was a beautiful place but with a profusion of dense bushes. We had reached a very complicated part and, fearing that we should get lost, I suggested returning. On nearing the shelter we heard Manoel calling frantically to hurry, as a tempest was threatening. We had scarcely got aboard before a fiece wind struck the boat and shelter. We were hurriedly strengthening the mooring fore and aft and stowing possessions, when a series of large waves broke over the stern. We unloaded everything, throwing things to the shore in a frenzy, and somehow we got our possessions undercover just before the wooden planks in the bottom of the boat began to float away. My boat and its motor had sunk. The rain teemed down, but we worked to salvage the craft. Manoel's experience proved a godsend, for he knew how to refloat. With Christopher's help, he cut a strong fork from a tree and forced it under the prow, while standing neck deep in the river. So, together, they raised the boat and, being a lightweight, I went aboard and baled out. Eventually we beat the waves and emptied the boat completely just as the light faded.

All was drenched, but nothing lost. I looked at Christopher whose hair hung streaming over his face, and burst into laughter, as he did when he looked at me — a couple of drowned rats! Manoel seemed puzzled by our strange outburst and odd sense of humour.

Christopher and I spent the night under the shelter of the hut's frail roof, while Manoel slept in the boat as his hammock was drenched. I slept scarcely a wink, not because of the sounds of the forest, but because I shivered without a blanket, having lent it to Christopher who, in turn, had lent his to Manoel. We left early in the morning after a hurried breakfast.

'A strong wind is driving against us as we dip and toss across the vast lakes. We left the lakes of Andirá soon after midday and entered the narrow channel once more. The *paraná* is next and we will head upstream but we have a few hours to go before reaching Barreirinha. Now Manoel cannot be restrained from rushing ahead, though normally on the journey his pace has been slow...

I have picked up my pen again after a terrible storm. We came through the mouth of the Andirá into foul weather. A dreadful wind was blowing, but we went with it until the sky became too threatening, and there were peals of thunder, so, fearing to repeat our ordeal in the Bay of Sapucaia, we moored to a fallen tree and sat the storm out. We left, only to meet another tempest with heavy rain. Just at the peak of the storm, I caught sight of a magnificent catasetum in flower high on the trunk of a large tree. Before it lay a great barrier of floating grass. Heroically, Christopher volunteered to get it, paddled off in the

Margaret Mee
August, 1981

Catasetum macrocarpum L. C. Rich.
Amazonas.

Catasetum macrocarpum *(male)*.

Margaret Mee
July. 1981

Catasetum macrocarpum
L. C. Rich. (fem. form)
Amazonas

Catasetum macrocarpum *(female)*.

canoe and, trying to avoid the impenetrable grass, found a way through to land. He stepped out of the canoe on to what seemed to be firm ground, but promptly sank waist deep into the black mud of the river-bed. He returned, crestfallen and tortured by mosquitoes and ants. So Manoel, who was familiar with these grass 'islands', took the canoe and, with the paddle, fought his way through until he reached the tree. He was just able to reach the orchid, detaching it with the blade. It is a beautiful *Catasetum macrocarpum*. An absolutely gorgeous plant, and I must paint it soon...'

When we arrrived in Barreirinha we moored, as before, in the little port beside the mission where a drama took place. Christopher was harangued by a drunk, a great burly *caboclo* who, for some reason still unknown to me, manufactured an argument with Christopher, insisting that all food, when eaten, passed through the heart. Christopher had scarcely time to warn me about him before the man strode over to me and Manoel, where I was taking a photograph of an orchid. The drunk demanded the flower. I explained that this was not possible, whereupon he offered bananas in exchange. Using all the tact I could muster, I turned down the offer firmly. He flew into a rage and, brandishing his large *tercado* (bush knife), advanced, shouting that I must move my boat, that I was a *contrabandista* (smuggler). As he advanced, knife raised on high, heroic Manoel, who scarcely reached to his waist, ran at him and pushed him in the stomach, shouting at him to clear off. A small crowd had gathered and I seized one of the Indian girls, telling her to run quickly to fetch the priest, an Italian, and a large and vigorous man. He came at the double, seized the drunk and led him off. The incident over we sighed with relief. I realised that every village had one black sheep.

We waited in the port by the Malaria Service hut for I was running short of money and needed to find someone, a trader perhaps, who would accept a Rio bank cheque. I also hoped a boat would pass from which we could beg a tow either to Itacoatiara or Manaus. Whilst waiting I tried to draw, but dozens of *caboclos* gathered and it was impossible to work with any concentration, so I had to stop. Then, of course, they drifted away!

'We are heading for Manaus on a river boat, the *General Osorio*. The passage was arranged for me yesterday. The plants are well packcd and the canoe stowed aboard and we should arrive tomorrow morning. On this journey the boat is following the main Amazon river and not going through the Paraná do Ramos. This means we are keeping to the north bank, passing the rivers Urucará and Urubú, on the way to Itacoatiara. It has been a short journey beset with problems, but I have some interesting plants and my new hip has behaved marvellously.'

Early the following year Margaret returned to Amazonia to meet three friends from Britain. When she arrived at their hotel, the Lord in Manaus city centre, she was greeted with two pieces of good news. Newspapers had just reported that she had been awarded the Honorary Citizenship of the City of Rio de Janeiro, and the local State Government, as a gesture of gratitude to Margaret for her activities, was offering her and her friends a box at the grand reopening of the Teatro Amazonas — the magnificent Manaus opera house.

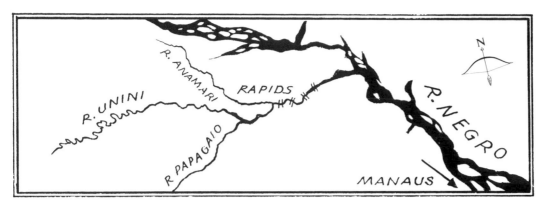

16th January, 1975

My three companions, Sally Westminster, Michael Szell, an outstanding designer and decorator, and David Vickery, a distinguished architect, had come to Brazil to see the Amazon and I wanted to take them to the River Unini, a tributary of the lower Negro. It was a river I had passed several times on my previous journeys and been told was a rich area for plant hunters. Michael especially hoped for inspiration from the tropical flora and to find orchids for his collection.

Our journey began with a memorable event. The Teatro Amazonas, built at enormous cost during the height of the Amazon 'rubber boom', had been neglected for years. As part of a plan to bring prosperity and development to the Amazon, the Government and a private foundation had spent over a year restoring the theatre. When some years earlier I had browsed there, the lovely wrought-iron balustrades were shabby, the original cane chairs dusty though attractive, and the backstage was badly in need of ventilation.

President Ernesto Geisel of Brazil, together with an ex-President, ministers and Amazonas State officals were gathered in Manaus for the inauguration of the restoration work. Having packed only small travelling cases for our Amazon journey, all four of us felt totally unprepared for the occasion as we set out for the theatre, only five minutes away from the hotel. On reaching the Praça Sao Sebastiao we found a large crowd waiting in front of the opera house. It had all happened. The exterior had been beautifully painted in white and grey, the interior possessed new balustrades, the paintings and chandeliers had been cleaned and repaired and behind the scenes everything had been modernised and improved. In the auditorium red plush seats substituted the humble cane chairs whose disappearance I regretted along with that of the wrought-iron banisters on the stairs.

Feeling very conspicuous among so many exquisitely dressed Brazilians, we were led to our box, one of the best in the theatre. The programme was mostly Brazilian music from the Rio Symphony Orchestra and, among other pieces, we heard 'The Amazon Forest' by Villa Lobos. Then came the Rio ballet — the second act of 'Swan Lake'. Such a night had not been enjoyed in Manaus since the days of the 'Rubber Barons.' After the performance we were invited to the official reception and were introduced to the President.

We were still talking about the performance when, next day, we went down to Roadway, a jetty in the port where our boat, the *Jaraguá*, was moored. Here we met Dr. Clodivel, whose Ministry was responsible for the boat and who had kindly put it at our disposal. He had generously thought of everything for our comfort and convenience. The crew were under his orders, but I had found a guide, Paulo, an Indian both in appearance and character, who had the reputation of being an excellent man in the forest.

The *Jaraguá* was spacious and almost luxurious by my modest standards, but it was a pleasant change to have a cook to prepare meals, to be free of the problem of purchasing fuel and of the constant baling out. Although there were bunks in this well-equipped craft, I soon decided to fix my well tried hammock on deck where I could breath the perfume of the jungle and pure air of the river. Without further preparation we moved out from the port and upstream on the Negro heading first to a popular beauty spot.

The Teatro Amazonas — the Manaus opera house, built during the nineteenth century 'rubber boom.'

A mormodes orchid from near Urucará.

A tillandsia bromeliad from the River Unini.

The Jaraguá — the river boat lent by the Ministry.

After about three hours we arrived at the mouth of the River Taruma. When Richard Spruce journeyed through the Amazon, he was fascinated by the abundance and variety of the vegetation surrounding what he described as 'the loftiest fall known on the Rio Negro.' The Taruma plunges thirty to forty feet into a ravine which, in high water, is filled from the Negro. Spruce gave a scenic description of the magnificent towering trees and the rocks over which the clear waters of the river cascaded. Today, much of the surrounding woodland had been senselessly destroyed and the giant trees, which could have lived for centuries, have disappeared, giving the scene little more than a mundane aspect.

We stayed that night near the shore and were all up early, eager to reach the Unini. As soon as the sun lifted the mists from the river, we were sailing upstream again. The

Margaret and Sally Westminster search the igapó.

Aechmea tillandsioides, *a bromeliad, Taruma, River Negro.*

Paolo collecting an orchid.

air was fresh and cool, ideal for paddling up the inlets and streams to look for the wonders which we expected to see, and we were not disappointed, for, in a patch of sunlight perched a large toucan with red and black plumage and an ivory-coloured neck and bill. Alarmed, he called his mate, and together they sat protesting at us, the unwelcome creatures intruding on their territory.

We reached the mouth of the River Unini half an hour after passing Old Airao, once a Portuguese settlement on the southern bank of the Negro. The only remnants of the abandoned town are three eighteenth century buildings, now in ruins. As we passed by, one of the crew told me that, in November, when the waters are at a low level, manatees or sea cows, the mermaids of legend, are hunted when they come there to breed. In these shallows the manatee becomes a large defenceless animal. The female bears one calf every other year, but the ruthless hunters butcher adults and calves indiscriminately, though the species is nearing extinction and is on an international 'protection' list. The loss of this mammal along the Amazon could have serious repercussions, for it lives on aquatic vegetation and is responsible for keeping the rivers clean and clear. Happily a number of these creatures are being studied by my friends at I.N.P.A., and hopefully this may help to protect them in the future.

After about twenty miles the easy flowing Unini is broken by a *cachóeira*. It was early morning when we called on Raimundo, known as 'Keeper of the Rapids', to pilot us past the great underwater rock which extends for some miles. It took us an hour and a half to pass an impressive series of waterfalls, and even with our experienced pilot the *Jaraguá* struck rock, fortunately without damage to the hull. The water level was unusually high for January, which made it easier to pass the falls, but the channel was most devious and the river had to be crossed from side to side more than once, each time weaving through the rocks. Old and wizened though he was, Raimundo navigated with ease, admitting, however, that his sight was beginning to fail him.

We landed in a very dark forest where many of the towering trees seemed as skilfully ribbed as Gothic columns. From the branches of one hung coils of heavy rope-like lianas, and in the midst of them a snake of about seven feet dangled from the canopy, silver-green in colour and almost imperceptible against the background of sinuous vines. Above the serpent circled two parrots uttering angry outraged cries, obviously defending their young against the marauder. Unheeding the drama being enacted beside him, a woodpecker tapped loudly on dead wood, searching for insects. The place was a paradise, and I found a beautiful catasetum which I was busily detaching when a cloud of angry wasps emerged from a fallen tree. We fled.

On the sixth day of our journey we were still on the Unini, passing our days pleasantly in the forest and the warm dark waters of the river. We eventually reached the inlet of a small stream, the Papagaio, really more of an *igarapé*, and when we went ashore to do some collecting there was scarcely any terra firma. However, we managed to wade through the large areas of swamp and, as we struggled along the marshy scrubland, we were rewarded by finding and even stroking a sloth which was hugging the base of a small tree, sound asleep. Paulo, trying to be helpful, removed the struggling animal so that he could be photographed at closer quarters, and the poor creature fell into the water. Lifting him out of the mud of the *igapó*, Paulo then tried to put him up a tree, but the incredibly slow-moving sloth sat with his bottom in the stream, clinging to a branch, his little head drooping and a sad smile on his face. I stroked his shaggy great coat — full of green algae and insect life — and left him to his dreams.

On returning to the *Jaraguá*, we found the crew had decided the *igarapé* was too narrow for the boat to proceed, so it was moored in a creek while Paulo paddled us along the *igarapé* where I was able to find a number of small orchids and enormous clumps of bromeliads, mainly *Aechmea setigera* and *Aechmea tocantina*, both species armed with terrible thorns and almost impossible to collect. As I had already painted them I decided to leave them. Plants were not profilic on the Papagaio, though parrots of all kinds were, and during the dawn chorus toucans, *japims* and hosts of other birds could be distinguished. Nights were no more silent than the days, for frogs provided orchestral music when it was dark.

Flowers of a norantia, Marcgraviaceae family sketched on the River Unini.

As we left the Papagaio, rose-pink river dolphins were playing in the broad expanse of the Unini. They were leaping and diving, full of *joie de vivre*, and the big males were shooting sparkling fountains of water into the air. Sally and Michael, full of enthusiasm at the sight, dived into the river, whilst I hesitated, having recent memories of being chased by a dolphin into the bushes of an *igapó* when I was in a small canoe. A dolphin will overturn a canoe either in playful mood or in anger at a trespasser in his territorial waters.

From this sunlit area we glided in the canoe into a strange, dead world where the forests were disintegrating. The surviving trees stood stark and dried out, some black where fire had charred their limbs, others spindly, white and rotten. Many orchids still clung to the crumbling branches, with catasetums and galeandras in flower, but it was hazardous to reach the highest plants. Paulo took a long crook and prodded the dead wood to loosen the roots but, more than once, not only did the plant fall but a bough full of sawdust came crashing down, some falling beside the canoe and narrowly missing us.

According to the local people this forest had been water-logged for two years, instead of the usual six months each year and, as a result, they could not keep their cattle, having nowhere to graze them. The trees of the *várzea*, which they seasonally cultivated, having adapted to a pattern over countless years, were rotting as a result of these changed conditions. People blamed a *furo da terra* (literally 'hole in the earth') for the catastrophe, and I could only interpret this as being some kind of earthworks

for a dam. I had seen a great deal of such rotting forest on this journey and concluded that it was not only burning which was wreaking widespread destruction but, most likely, interference with the river systems.

On 26th January we started our homeward way, sheltering at times from frequent rainstorms and stopping to scan the forest for plants or to swim in the black waters, often in company with large grey *piranha*. Thus the days passed idyllically until we reached Manaus with its noise, bustle and pollution, and it was sad to part from the wonderful companions of a short but memorable journey.

Before returning to Rio, Margaret made a short excursion to Urucará, two days downriver, where she had friends. Already she was planning her next journey, and in Manaus she arranged to have her boat painted in preparation.

On 1st January, 1976, Margaret Mee, then sixty-six years old, was honoured in Britain with the M.B.E. — Member of the British Empire, for services to botany in Brazil. Her work was also recognised in Brazil, where she was given Government support to continue her travels, with the objective of producing a limited folio edition of a book entitled Flowers of the Amazon.

A maxillaria orchid from the Taruma river.

A three-toed sloth.

Catasetum barbatum *(Orchidaceae).*

224

Catasetum barbatum
Lindl.
Amazonas, Rio Unini

Margaret Mee
1976

JOURNEY ELEVEN: 1977
The Sad Fate of the Blue Qualea

Paintings for Flowers of the Amazon *absorbed much of Margaret's time. Then, in September 1977, she was invited with Greville to Brasilia, the boldly designed Brazilian capital completed in the 1960s. Here President Geisel opened a major exhibition commemorating Brazilian Independence, and the lavish catalogue for the event included much of Margaret's work, which was being widely acclaimed at the time. After crowded receptions in the Itamarity building and the Presidential Planalto Palace, Greville had to return to the studio in Rio. But Margaret, who was preparing to travel along three rivers, all new to her, left directly by air for Manaus. Over the years she had kept in touch with Rita from St. Paul's and they agreed to meet on the Amazon again and explore the Rivers Cauhy and Nhamundá. But first, Margaret was to make a brief trip to the Jaú and Jufari rivers.*

6th September, 1977

A bitterly cold wind had been blowing in Brasilia, sweeping across the unprotected plains, so it was quite a shock to step out of the Boeing jet in Manaus to a temperature of ninety degrees. I had been promised a room in the students' quarters of I.N.P.A. and as I travelled there by bus I saw just how far the city had expanded. The Institute had once stood in virgin forest; now, with the exception of those within the grounds themselves, all the surrounding trees had gone.

'I am planning my journey in the solitude of Apartment 3. There are problems over my equipment, as the 'stores' deny that I left any of my possessions there, and I shall have to hire a boat for the journey as mine has mysteriously disappeared from its place in the port. Desperate and upset I made enquiries of all possible sources of information but only gleaned that the boat went down in a tempest in May. But then it was seen again in the port only last month and recognised by holes I had drilled in the roof supports to hold my hammock. In July it was seen once more, but in spite of all this information I have been unable to trace it. I have been unlucky with my boats to which I become attached, having braved many difficulties with them as well as enjoying the freedom which they give me.

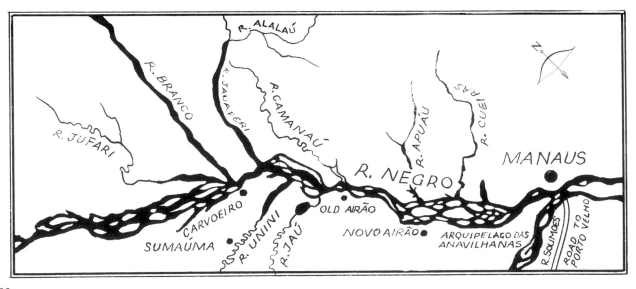

I have had to interrupt my writing as a band of *macaco do cheiro* has just invaded the trees, and I have been feeding them with bananas. They are black around the eyes, with a black smudge over the nose and their limbs are yellow-gold. They are playful, fascinating little creatures.

The animals and birds in this forest enclave are quite varied — *pacas*, lizards, toucans, *mutums* — and a tiny *tamanduá* (anteater) is being raised here. Last night I fed two large spectacled owls with raw meat. They landed on my shoulders and arms, which was rather painful as they have powerful claws. They are magnificent birds. '

When he heard of my difficulties, the Director of I.N.P.A. kindly offered the use of a small boat, the *Pium*, and arranged for a crew of three to help. As the boat would not be available for three or four days, I had time to make an excursion to the other side of the Solimoes to the new road, the BR319, leading to Porto Velho over four hundred miles up the Madeira. This road was to be part of the great route across western Amazonia and south along the Brazilian frontier with Bolivia. My companion was Reinaldo, a Brazilian who travelled with me on my journey to Urucará, and he arrived with a small Volkswagen car to collect me at half past five in the morning. It had rained heavily during the night and the morning was cool. We crossed the river by ferry and drove about eighty miles to Igarapé das Lajes, where Reinaldo said there was a unique rock-formation. The I.N.P.A. scientists were trying to get the area established as a special reserve.

The new road was a disaster, at least as far as the point known as 'KM.130', both for destruction of the forests as well as for the resulting erosion, and many stretches of the dirt highway were flanked on either side by sheer precipices of eroding ground. But in spite of this, areas of beautiful forest remained, and where it had been ruthlessly destroyed, *embaúbas*, always the first to claim cleared ground, were valiantly trying to protect the young growth.

We arrived at the River Preto, an *igarapé* which must once have been a lovely river, but instead was surrounded by mounds of earth and roadworks. Like most of the *igarapés* we passed on the route, it was choked by spoil from cutting the road across its course. The land could not be drained as nature intended, and great pools of stagnant water were collecting in which the trees rotted and collapsed. Thousands of trees must have perished in this way, to which the tragic appearance of the scenery bore witness.

At the Igarapé das Lajes I found that the rocks, which only a few months earlier must have been splendidly adorned with plants, were now a mess as a result of the road building. However, I found a few flowers. A lovely white-flowered orchid — a sobralia, which I had last seen in the Gurupi, some catasetums, and a gesneriad. Next to this beauty lay the few pathetic endeavours of some settlers who had come up from the south. They had set fire to the forest and sprayed defoliant on some areas which had resulted in the complete destruction of the vegetation. The net gain from this family's cultivation was one *mamao* tree, a few pineapples and some goats which were helping to wreck the forest, still being hacked away when we arrived.

As I looked around I could not help wondering if the I.N.P.A. attempt to preserve the area had not come too late — a case of 'closing the door after the horse has bolted', for it seemed doubtful that there would be anything left worthy of saving if such indiscriminate devastation continued.

Beside the rocks I entered a natural grotto of amazing design, and beautiful caves which seemed to have been used by hunters as night shelters, for fires had blackened the walls. Light filtered between the leafy canopies of the trees in the remaining old forest, falling on swamp plants around a small lake, whilst a short distance away a

Sketch of a tree with adventitious roots from the trunk indicating the annual rise of the river.

The sketch for
Philodendron arcuatum.

black-water river flowed through some *caatinga* teeming with plants. Many were in flower — *Acacallis cyanea* the 'blue' orchid, delicately perfumed *Scuticaria steelii*, and the lovely *Philodendron arcuatum*, a climber whose white spathes were pink spotted and stems covered with what looked like the russet fur of a forest animal.

I walked until I was exhausted, wading through streams and then, with soaking canvas shoes, ploughing onwards through black, swampy ground. But I was delighted with the results of my journey, for I had material for many paintings. The trek over, I sank down in the comfort of the little car which Reinaldo had parked on the edge of the woods. A storm was brewing and I watched fascinated, noticing strange black clouds which seemed to dangle from the sky like streamers. When they reached the ground a violent storm broke and rain fell in torrents. We started the return journey in the downpour which made driving on the slippery mud road very difficult.

We had been travelling for barely half an hour when Reinaldo saw in the rear view mirror a bus bearing down on us, the driver obviously blinded by the sheets of rain. To avoid it, Reinaldo went too close to the edge and skidded, slithering sideways into a deep ditch, by then transformed into a raging river. We were stuck; and the rain continued. The water was well over my knees when Reinaldo helped me to the road. There was nothing for it but to wait for help, and eventually we were eased from the ditch by a young soldier, who had seen our plight from his truck, and passengers from a bus which the fellow commandeered. We arrived in Manaus long after dark.

'At last arrangements have been finalised for my journey to the rivers Jaú and Jufari on the Negro, and we leave tomorrow. I have the small boat, the *Pium*, for the next month. Adalto is pilot, Paulo, the cook and Pedro my *mateiro*. All seem well used to the river and I feel I am in good hands.

We left at eleven this morning having had a tedious time arranging and stowing the cargo. The clutch or gear change failed as we left, but was quickly repaired, though there were still more delays, as we needed bottled *guaraná* and ice for the crew. They also asked me to buy bullets for them, but I told them that I had my own defences and that their guns are their responsibility.

We are now well up the Negro heading towards the maze of islands called the Arquipelago das Anavilhanas. It is said to be the largest fluvial archipelago in the world and in most parts it is forested and swampy. Here the river is ten miles wide, and on the western side it is divided from the main course by a long, narrow island making the boundary of a channel, the Paraná Anavilhanas. This is the route followed by many of the boats. I have never had the chance to dally here as most of my pilots have wanted to hurry through — they say there is a lot of leprosy in the area. But the banks of my beloved river are almost unrecognisable — fire after fire on the horizon. Only two years have passed since

Philodendron arcuatum (Araceae).

Margaret Mee

Philodendron arcuatum Krause ex descr.
Near Manaus, Am. Oct. 1977

Strophocactus
wittii
Cavilanhas, Amazonas

Margaret Mee
February, 1978

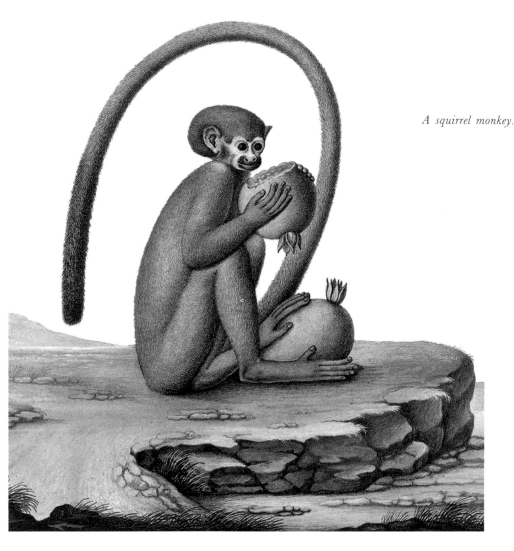

A squirrel monkey.

A pygmy (silky) anteater.

I was last here. Now, there is not a big tree to be seen on the banks. No birds. The remnants of the forests are poor and thin. The rapidity of this destruction is appalling!

   We have moored at the mouth of the River Cueiras, also a devastated area, beside three small huts where half a dozen Indian children are playing. Their father is out, but I am waiting in the shade until he returns in the hopes that I can hire a canoe from him at a reasonable cost — there are still some honest people along these rivers. It is too late to continue and the crew have gone fishing hoping, no doubt, to catch a *tucunaré* for their supper. This is a lovely spot to pass the night, in spite of the burned trees which stand in front of the huts. Birds are reappearing at last and pink dolphins have surfaced close to the boat.'

We left soon after dawn and continued upriver in the *paraná* where, at mid-morning, I asked the crew to pull into the bank so I could search the dry *igapó*. Since my first visit to the Negro I had been looking for the unusual *Strophocactus (Selenicereus) wittii*, about which very little is known. The plant was first collected around Manaus at the beginning of the century, and its flowers are rarely, if ever, seen. Here I was fortunate and after some hard walking through dry, tangled wood I found one plant, its deep crimson leaves flattened closely to the trunk of a rotting tree. Pedro climbed to get it and after searching we found more plants, though most of them were dying. They were without flowers, but on one I found a new fruit with the leaves, so I thought the flowering season must have passed some months earlier.

Strophocactus (Selenicereus) wittii *(Cactaceae).*

Sobralia margaretae Pabst
Rio Urupadi, Amazonas
1974

Margaret Mee

A great potoo, or urutau. *'During the day they remain motionless on dry or decaying trees; their camouflage is marvellous.'*

We left the Paraná Anavilhanas and, towing the canoe I had hired, continued upriver to reach the Jufari which enters on the right in a confusion of waterways just beyond the mouth of the River Branco.

'Wildlife is becoming more plentiful and interesting — flights of parrots, large black ducks, solitary kingfishers with vivid plumage skim the water hunting fish, *tucanos* fly from the trees as we pass, unmistakable in their bobbing flight. At dusk many *bacurau* (nightjars), were darting low over the river. *Guaribas* showed very early in the morning, the eerie sound carrying across the forest like a wind. They seemed very close.'

The next day we set out early in the morning, having been delayed by the fuel operations, etc. I passed a wonderfully peaceful night, only awaking temporarily to hear the notes of a nocturnal bird, the great potoo, which has a beautiful and melancholy cry. We are close to the Branco now; at midday we passed the mouth of the River Jauaperi and then, an hour later in the Paraná do Cuperi, I saw the exposed and drying root structures of giant trees ready to fall. They finally collapse when the banks are eroded further. A happier sight was a flock of *anu* (birds related to cuckoos), flying low and weaving in and out of the vegetation, their indigo plumage glancing in the sun. The beautiful *Bombax munguba*, the local kapok tree, is in fruit now, its great scarlet pods hanging from the boughs.

We crossed the river near the mouth of the Branco late in the afternoon when a short storm left the river steaming. We had to search for the mouth of the Jufari as it is one tremendous lake which seems to merge into the Negro, already very wide and without apparent boundaries. I was breathless — the scene was primeval, not a habitation in sight, nothing but an enormous area of water surrounded by distant *igapó*. Herons and toucans perched in the stunted trees and four black ducks on the river seemed scarcely aware of us before they flew low into the *igapó* where all was gold and green in the evening sun. The river was low, and groups of small delicate palms stood in the water lapping against beaches of pure white sand.

It was a dream world and I felt that I must be the first person to go there. However, the crew did not share my enthusiasm for this glorious place and shuddering slightly proclaimed it '*Muito deserto*' (very deserted).

Plantwise the river has proved disappointing. The forest is walled by *molongo* and low, sterile *igapó*, quite impossible to penetrate without cutting a way through, which would take hours. So, after spending one night on the river, surrounded by storms and battered by waves and strong winds, I decided to limit the journey to just a few hours upriver. Eventually we arrived at a small settlement with a little church where a *festa* seemed to be in progress. To my surprise the old *delegado* (mayor) from Carvoeiro on the River Negro was presiding; a strange old man whom I remembered having met much earlier when *en route* for Pico da Neblina. He was unfriendly and unhelpful then, and the *caboclos* in this village took the cue from him and, with hostile looks, refused to sell me baskets for my plants.

'After some deliberation and discussion here I have decided to go back to the River Jaú as it is on our route downriver and people here say that to get to it is not difficult. We can cross the Negro where it is not so wide, though there is

Sobralia margaretae (Orchidaceae).

The sketches for Heterostemon mimosoides, *a legume, from the Cueiras river.*

some opposition from the members of the crew, who claim they have never travelled on the south bank of the river and can visualise problems. They say we shall have to cross at a point where there are no isles and the south bank is hardly visible, and we must aim for a point not far from the settlement called 'Old Airao'. '

We left the Jufari and turned downstream through the Paraná Carica which connects with the River Branco; it is heavily yellow water with plenty of mosquitoes. I did some collecting — at least Pedro did, climbing trees which seemed impossibly high, to get epiphytes. On one tree which had been ripped out of the forest and lay in the water *Oncidium ceboletta* grew, and though completely saturated it was still managing to flower. I was also able to draw a tree with fan-like adventitious roots which indicated the tremendous annual rise in the water level.

We had a delay for yet more repairs and a stop to buy *pirarucu* at a *Baiano* settler's hut. He was a trader who kept a small 'bar' — a meeting place where river gossip was exchanged — a little to the west of the mouth of the Branco. As I sat drawing my newly found oncidium, hordes of *pium* attacked me; there seemed to be a plague of them there. Since my last journey to this area destruction had been widespread, and the *macaco prego* (capuchin monkey) which I saw in the forest then have doubtless left the region or died out. The only plant which I wished to collect, an interesting aroid, was the home of wasps and in my attempt to get it wasps poured out of the nest and I fled.

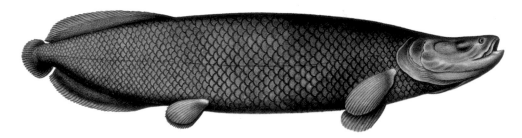

A pirarucu, *one of the largest freshwater fish.*

The heterostemon bud.

234

Oncidium lanceanum *(Orchidaceae).*

Margaret Mee
July 1985

Oncidium sp.
Amazonas

A storm was brewing as we reached the River Negro. Brilliant white clouds, piled high and masked by black spread across the horizon. Then, quite suddenly, torrential rain without any wind broke over the glassy river. Evening added mystery to the forests, as flights of *araras* and parrots in pairs crossed the darkening river on their way to roost. The moon, red through the heavy sky, rose behind an arabesque of trees, more like a setting sun. Towards dawn a tempest swept over the forests with a terrific wind and pelting rain, and though the crew rushed to pull down the storm blinds I was drenched in my hammock.

We reached 'Old Airao' and its three derelict houses, though a line of washing showed that one was in use again — as a meteorological station we discovered. One of the crew who did not trust my directions, landed to make enquiries as to our whereabouts. The man in the old house explained that we were less than three miles from the river mouth.

A caboclo's *riverside home.*

That night we moored the *Pium* outside the first habitation on the River Jaú as the owner was a relative of Pedro. Only the wife, Dona Francisca, was there and next morning I had breakfast with her. She was angry because a 'safari' arranged by a tourist company from Sao Paulo had recently been up the Jaú, hunting birds and mammals of the forest. According to her, some of the local *caboclos* collaborated with the hunters, catching birds in nets, especially the friendly *socos* (bitterns), and releasing them for the visitors to shoot. Often, she said, the *caboclos* caught animals and birds in cages, taking them back to sell in Rio or Sao Paulo. These safaris, said Dona Francisca, were a menace to the riverine dwellers who depended on controlled fishing and hunting for their food, which consequently was becoming scarce. The family was warm and welcoming but they were worried by outsiders coming into the region, and especially by people who knew nothing of the Amazon and were destroying it for a measly handful of food. The river people, she suggested, especially those living beside the rapids, would be in a position to act as voluntary forest guards and would willingly take on the task.

I decided to explore the surrounding forest and we took the *Pium* upriver as far as the first rapids, where only a canoe could proceed as the boat was too large and the water too low. We continued a short distance, no more than half an hour, beyond the rocks, for the journey was unrewarding and depressing. I pushed my way into the forest where, beyond a façade of live trees, I was appalled by what I saw — an area of death. There was not a spot of green to be seen. The trees were sick with bark peeling and rolling off the trunks. I waded up to my knees through piles of dead leaves and felt contaminated by them, and I avoided touching anything with my hands. A strange chemical smell hung in the still air. Unlike other parts of the forest, where the river rose and covered the banks, where new shoots and fresh green leaves were bursting, in that place there was not a sign of regeneration. I felt certain that some diabolical defoliant had been sprayed.

To counteract this experience I decided to retrace my steps and land in an unspoilt part of the forest, where for a moment I stood admiring a beautiful tree with a fluted trunk of enormous size. The air was sweet and scented by plants. Insects abounded and I even forgave them their irritating bites. Suddenly my reverie was interrupted by rude voices and coarse shouts from a boat moored on the opposite bank, though by forest regulations it should not have been there. '*Sai d'aqui! Esta invadando nosso terreno!*' (Clear off! You are trespassing on our land!). A group of toughs was cutting down trees behind the shelter of their boat. My pilot revved up the *Pium's* motor and Pedro and I embarked, sailing towards the clandestine craft. The thieves left in great haste. 'That gave them a shock', my crew laughed, 'they think we are inspectors from I.B.D.F.' (Forestry Development Institute, also responsible for National Parks).

From the River Jaú we headed once more into the Negro and I asked the crew to sail back across the river and slightly downstream to the Paraná do Camanaú. We edged into the mouth of the Camanaú river where, seven years earlier, I had talked with an old *caboclo* about the Atroari-Waimiri Indians who had killed a priest and his team nearby. The Indian land is about seventy miles away on another river, but each year they make their way to the Camanaú to fish and hunt turtle.

'Even here the sound of the chainsaw is not far away and I have just heard a giant tree crashing down. The beautiful *paraná* is being devastated by charcoal burners.'

With Rita to the River Nhamundá, November 1977

Rita, companion of my first journey to Pará in 1956, was waiting for me in Manaus, and we embarked in the port on the *Coronel Sergio*, one of the regular river boats sailing between Manaus and the river port of Urucará. I had been there two years earlier and stayed with two missionaries, Phyllis and Clinton, who told me about other rivers with interesting plants. Rita, recently widowed, had always hoped to make another journey with me, but her husband had always deterred her from travelling, being anxious for her safety in Amazonia.

We chose the *Coronel Sergio* principally because it did not have a noisy radio. Furthermore, it was clean and above all had a pleasant, very likeable 'comandante'.

The two day journey was uneventful. We called at Itacoatiara, and then entered the Paraná do Silves connecting the main river with the River Urucará. In Urucará we stayed in a house which stood amongst dark, old mango trees. They were in fruit and attracted hundreds of noisy parrots. At night the garden was perfumed by the star-like flowers of a cactus, as big as a small tree. It may not have been a native of the region, perhaps introduced at some time as a garden decoration. When morning came the flowers closed, never to open again, having been pollinated during the night by bats or night moths.

'There was a terrific storm last night, but I slept deeply, recovering from the effects of a prophylactic against malaria, and so heard nothing of it.

We are now on a short journey along a small local river, the Taraquá, where all is fresh and green.'

As we journeyed silently up the little river the most wonderful birds appeared — *japim,*

A sunbittern.

japu, socós, egrets, and the exquisite *pavaozinho do pará* (sunbittern). In a shallow part our boatman spotted a *poraque* (electric eel) which watched us with curiosity from a hollow between tree roots in the river bed. We were told that these eels have a unique way of killing by electrocution, using their own 'batteries' of specially modified muscles. They can kill cattle which stray into the river by coiling around one of the animal's legs and giving a shock which stuns the animal so that it falls into the water and drowns.

In the *igapó, cuia de macaco* (monkey cup) of the Lecythidaceae family was blooming and humming-birds abounded. Amongst them I saw one which was metallic blue from beak to tail. I was pursued by wasps when I landed, but fortunately had my head veil with me and thus escaped their stings. We turned to another small river, the Tabori, and found it to be a heavenly spot. The trees on the banks were laden with orchids, including a brilliant yellow mormodes and *Catasetum gnomus*.

But the beauty was not to last. From a clearing beside the river we encountered a road being made to connect Castanhal, a tiny settlement, to Marajá, an even smaller settlement. The road had been cut through the most spectacular forest that I had ever seen. Enormous trees were being felled, many of which must have existed when the naturalist explorers, among them Martius, Spruce and Bates, were finding their way through the Amazon. The road was being built by the local mayor, I was told, who had property in Marajá, and it was rumoured that it would facilitate the moving of seven giant red cedar trees of the Meliaceae family, of which there had been nine, each worth a fortune. The wood, which was used for furniture, was so much in demand that the species had been completely cleared from many places. By contrast, on our return journey to Urucará, we crossed a small lake surrounded by luxuriant forest. It was teaming with life, and on the *buriti* palms which stood deep in water grew vines and epiphytes. *Nymphaea rudgeana* opened their white flowers in the sun, and myriads of dragonflies skimmed the surface of the lake.

Nymphaea rudgeana *(Nymphaeaceae).*

Margaret Mee
August 1978

Nymphea rudgeana G.E.W.Meyer
Urucará, Lower Amazon

In 1962, when in the Mato Grosso, I had seen three trees of a vochysia, the 'Blue Qualea' *(Qualea ingens)*, in the gallery forest bordering three different rivers. The spectacle of these wonderful trees with massed gentian-blue flowers had remained with me, and I was always looking for one I could paint. At last I believed I had a chance, as the tree had been reported by Adolpho Ducke on the verges of the River Cauhy, a stream draining into the River Nhamundá, about twenty-four hours downriver. The Nhamundá river flows into lakes and *paranás* on the north bank of the Amazon, almost opposite the river port of Parintins which I knew. Rita and I agreed we would take the next *gaiola* leaving in that direction, and as this was a good month I anticipated that we should find the trees in flower.

Aboard the crowded boat there was scarcely a space left to hang our hammocks, and even when they were hung it was impossible to get to them, and I had to ask the captain to intervene. He was helpful, and after a certain amount of rearrangement, we found suitable places. But sleep was impossible, and the toilet door was barricaded by a group of men gambling with cards, while underneath Rita's hammock an old country woman was enveloped in a cloud of smoke from her *cigarro da palha* (literally 'straw cigarette'). Animals, children and enormous bundles lay everywhere. Suddenly I awakened from a doze to see flames rising towards Rita as the old woman kindled her hand-rolled cigarette with wrapping paper. I roused Rita and shouted to the smoker to put out the flames, which she did, only to repeat the performance throughout the night, keeping us in a continual state of panic.

It was four in the morning, cool and damp from rain, when we disembarked in Parintins. We were exhausted and bewildered, but amazed to see one or two Volkswagen taxis at the port. We bundled into one and asked the driver to take us to the nearest hotel, which he was at pains to assure us was the only one in town. It was an appalling place, and we were shown to a miserable room. When we enquired about a bathroom we were told the kitchen sink could be used for washing and that there were two showers 'just round the corner'. These turned out to be cupboards, black from lack of light and dirt in which hordes of cockroaches were scurrying. We decided not to wash that night. Tomorrow we would scour the town for another hotel. So we hung our hammocks on the hooks provided and endeavoured to sleep until dawn.

The day began more cheerfully when a short distance out of town we found the pleasant little Hotel Joia where we breakfasted. Next we called at the town hall where we met the agreeable mayor who kindly provided an official to accompany us to the port to help us hire a good boat for the journey to the Nhamundá. We would have to cross the Amazon, here about three miles wide at the main channel, but with a watery border extending over twenty miles of lakes and low land which flooded in high water.

At half past nine in the morning, we left in the *Izabel Mariá*, a small cabin boat owned by two brothers, Joao and José. The cabin was spacious enough for our hammocks. José hung his hammock beside the motor, ready for any eventuality, and I was very encouraged for the boat was also spotlessly clean and newly painted. We also had a small, well-made canoe which was put on the deck.

'We are now sailing across the Amazon towards a channel which Joao says will take us into Lago Faro, the lake at the mouth of the Nhamundá. This is watery maze with forest on every side. We are making good time and Rita is thrilled to be travelling again.

Last night was very disturbed, boats coming and going to the settlements of Nhamundá or Faro. But the forests cannot be far distant, for we heard the *guaribas* roaring.

Margaret had read the account of the 'Blue Qualea' by Adolpho Ducke who explored this part of the Amazon for plants. The eastern side of Lake Faro was sandy, partly dry, part swampy and crossed by little streams of 'black water.' Along the banks of one of these streams — the Cauhy, the botanist found a gallery forest. A line of trees followed the watercourse where dense vegetation flourished. Adolpho Ducke said this forest was notable for two species of very rare trees of great beauty, both of the Vochysiaceae family. One of the trees was a qualea, possibly Qualea ingens, or alternatively a new species, with a magnificent single petal of strong blue. These trees were found, he said, only in the forests of the Cauhy and he had seen only a few examples.

These photographs were taken by Shelley Swigert, a friend of Margaret Mee, in the Mato Grosso near Cuiabá soon after Margaret's visit in 1962.

241

Collecting on Lake Faro.

The two brothers are very pleasant and good-natured, though rather stubborn at times. It was difficult to persuade them to put the canoe in tow, though when I insisted, explaining it was essential for plant collecting, they saw reason, and now the dugout is riding the waves behind us.

Tomorrow we should reach the Cauhy. The landscape we are passing is wonderful — sandy beaches on the margins of the river, and beyond forested plateaux, hills and wooded plains. This lower Amazon has a completely different aspect when compared with the Solimoes. In this part, too, habitations have disappeared and the country seems unpopulated.

We have now reached the great lake, Lago Faro, and have just made our first stop to collect at one of the white beaches. The winds have bent the trees into twisted, contorted forms and the sweet scented *Galeandra devoniana* clings to the fibrous trunks of *jará* palms. *Aechmea tocantina* is clustered on the hardwood trees. Its thorns are formidable.

There is little destruction on this most beautiful lakeside, though unhappily some signs of it are appearing. Behind gleaming, sandy beaches lie wide gullies, tree filled and dark . . ., these depressions must become lakes when the waters rise. Beyond the lakes and *paranás* the land slopes to high, forested hills. As we pass along the banks the ipé, full of yellow blossoms, have been gorgeous, and

'A land of lakes and paranás.'

242

The Izabel Mariá *and the sandy beach where Margaret nearly stepped on a small nightjar.*

in one area the canopy was red with flowers of *Symphonia globulifera*. This towering tree is a Guttiferae, the same family as the clusias. The birds are numerous and varied. '

Moving slowly up the river we searched in vain for the mouth of the Cauhy, enquiring of one or two solitary fishermen who were unable to give any information concerning its whereabouts. Then the narrow mouth of the Nhamundá bordered by an attractive *igapó* appeared, a complex mass of islands where the stunted trees were almost obscured by masses of epiphytes in their branches; red was the dominant colour, and I found bromeliads with scarlet leaves and inflorescences, *Aechmea huebneri*, a marvellous treat, and black-green clusters of orchids, schomburgkia, and large-leafed anthuriums. As the River Cauhy was proving to be so elusive I decided to first explore the Nhamundá, a promising and fascinating river.

'The landscape is changing to dark forest with many *jauarí* palms, immense, emergent trees, whose ribbed trunks tower like Gothic columns, and below them the fern-like leaves of spreading macrolobium, a legume dipping over the river.

Spume is appearing on the water which means we are nearing rapids, so we are sailing cautiously as the river is shallow here. We are now following in the wake of a boat, the *Fernando*, which is probably heading for the camp of a mining

'*We travelled comfortably on the* Izabel Mariá.'

'*This beach was a veritable cemetery.*'

243

A curassow, one of the caboclo's *favourite game birds.*

company exploring for bauxite, from which aluminium is extracted.

It is evident, too, that *garimpeiros* are about who, with their usual lack of respect for nature, are eroding riverbanks by felling trees and causing the consequent silting up of the river bed. It is like the early goldrush, with regard for nothing. The crew have said that many men come from the drought stricken north-east of Brazil to work in mineral companies, and that devastation has followed in their wake.'

The small canoe Margaret and Rita used on one of their collecting trips.

Yesterday we reached the beginning of the rapids of this river. We could get no further, and even there we struck rock, fortunately without any damage to the *Izabel Mariá*. Perhaps it was just as well that we were forced to return downstream, for on our way we had seen camps of the mining company and the men around them. They seemed to be clandestine *garimpeiros*, and pretty villainous types, so when the crew suggested we should stop at an attractive beach for the night, about fifteen minutes away from the last camp, I firmly vetoed the suggestion.

At another camp we noticed at least ten of these *garimpeiros*, under a blue plastic tent half hidden by the trees, who glowered in a very hostile manner. Long white tubes connected to a pump in the river disappeared into the undergrowth of the forest. On a platform constructed on the bank sat an Indian lad, obviously a watchman. We moored far from the gang and slept soundly, though, taking no chances, I had my gun ready beside me in my hammock.

The silence of night was broken only by nocturnal birds, owls and the potoo, with a chorus of frogs singing from deepest bass to highest treble. At about two the *guaribas* set up a deafening roar on the other side of the river. It is a sound I shall never tire of, one of the most thrilling to be heard in the forests of the Amazon. 'Ju-tapú!', cried a bird in harsh tones, and the toucans, *curicas* and other parrots joined in the swelling dawn chorus.

Early next day we moored by a sandy promontory, and as soon as I landed I nearly stepped upon a small nightjar sitting on the sand among a few dry leaves. She was hardly visible against this background, her mottled feathers and beak whiskers in perfect harmony with her surroundings. I called to Rita to come and look at her and, startled, the bird flew up uncovering two eggs mottled the same colour as her feathers. She sat on a branch a few yards away from us, but soon overcame her fear and returned to her nest. After seeing this lovely creature it was a shock when we discovered that this beach was a veritable cemetery of wildlife: skulls of *jacaré*, turtle shells, bones of *capybara* and other large animals, black wings, complete with feathers, of *jacu*, *mutum* and other Galliformes — the game birds. Around the beach we found hunting lookouts, rough constructions of branches about six feet from the ground or built in the low canopies of the trees.

As we sailed downriver after a night of heavy rain, having slept in wet hammocks and now wearing saturated clothes, we were hailed from the far bank by a gang of men armed with rifles. When they insisted on us crossing the river to meet them we became very wary, but quickly discovered that they only wanted information. They were employed by a mining company to keep intruders from its claim, and the men were going up the river to hunt for illegal *garimpeiros*. Rather maliciously we replied that we had seen a boat far down the river where it had broken down. It was, we said, being paddled by two men. On hearing this news the gang demanded that we should pick them up and take them to the camp near the rapids. I refused and we left them hastily lest they should take the law into their own hands.

Hunters had occupied the beach where we had hoped to bathe and dry our hammocks and clothes. Moving on we discovered that all the sandy spots which we considered proved to be covered with bones of hunted animals. But at last we found a wonderful natural *campina* on leached soil where four rough-hewn crosses stood in the sand. They marked graves, presumably of a family. There were no bones or wings of hunted animals there, so perhaps the hunters had some respect for the dead, an incongruous thought, as they certainly had no respect for the living. Or maybe they feared that spirits still lingered there.

We moored beside the trunk of a fallen tree on which grew orchids, including a catasetum, the first I had seen in this area. I climbed into the canoe and edged my

A wasps' nest, of light paper-like material.

way under the arch formed by the toppled trunks. Standing up in the dugout — a rather precarious balancing act at the best of times — I tried to detach the plant with my bush knife. The movement disturbed a small wasps' nest nearby and without warning the creatures attacked. I felt a sharp pain in the neck, and then another on my bare wrist. Stunned I fell into the canoe moaning *'Caba!'* The stings were agonising and from then on I understood why the *caboclos* are so terrified of *cabas*. But not so Joao and José, for when my pain had subsided slightly and I was prepared to try again to get the catasetum, they intervened. Despite my protestations and even though they got close to the angry wasps, they very carefully and cautiously detached the orchid without getting one sting.

Not all collecting was so hazardous and one day proved excellent, for I collected a wonderful bromeliad which I had seen from afar. It was *Aechmea huebneri*, a crown of coral plumes on a palm tree. The climax came, however, when I sighted another bromeliad, *Aechmea polyantha*, in the fork of a large tree. I had found this new species some years

'Packed for the homeward journey.'

Aechmea huebneri *(Bromeliaceae).*

246

Aechmea huebneri Harms
Amazonas, Rio Nhamunda   *December 1977*   Margaret Mee

A jacaré.

previously, and to the best of my knowledge it had not been found again. In my enthusiasm I drew until the light faded at which point we agreed unanimously to make for a promontory of a remote white beach. It appeared to be an ideal place to pass the night, except that it was not remote enough to have escaped the awful litter of hunters. A dead *jacaré* lay on the sand, it had been slashed in half, probably too young and small for profit.

In the days that followed we saw evidence of how the riverine dwellers seemed to assist the clandestine hunting gangs, for outside more than one hut *jacaré* skins were hanging to dry in the sun, and on the ground nearby we always saw a bloody mess of flesh and entrails which, I was told, would be used as bait to attract *onças* and ocelots. On occasion we heard that we had been mistaken for inspectors of the I.B.D.F., and the hunters had thrown illicit skins into the forest in fear of being caught red-handed.

From the slaughter of the forest animals to the murder of mankind is not a long step and, with considerable emotion, Joao and José told us a grim story concerning the death of their father, late owner of the *Izabel Mariá*.

The old man had been carrying valuable cargo up a river not far from where we were. He had moored for the night and had settled in his hammock when five bandits invaded the boat and killed him and his cook with hatchets. Leaving the bodies in the river, the bandits made off with the boat to a deserted *igarapé* where they moored and repainted the hull. By coincidence, a friend of the dead man happened to pass the boat when it was 'in port' and noticed the name appearing through the thin paint. The police were informed and four of the bandits were caught, though they spent only a short time in jail before being released.

Perhaps as a result of this horrible story I passed a rather uneasy night, awakening from fitful sleep to hear a shot ringing through the forest at no great distance, and on looking out from the depths of my hammock, saw a fire burning on the shore. Hunters of course!

11th November

'We began another search for the River Cauhy and the 'Blue Qualea' today, but to no avail. Adolpho Ducke will be turning in his grave.'

After many enquiries along the river we returned to the settlement of Nhamundá and just as a forlorn, last hope I asked the owner of the only shop, from which I purchased some stores, if he knew the Cauhy. The shopkeeper who had been a former mayor of the town, called a friend, Pedro, who seemed to know the name and offered to accompany us to the *cabeceiras* (headwaters) of the Cauhy, though assuring us most firmly that no river of that name existed. The idea of headwaters without a river seemed as unlikely as a 'grin without a cat'! However, Pedro arranged to meet us at the mooring where we waited more than two hours for him to appear. Eventually we proceeded to retrace our steps with him, this time calling at Faro on the opposite shore. There Pedro led us to 'Big Bar' and introduced us to the cream of Faro society. There was a nice old gentleman who, it turned out, had met Ducke, but without having any idea who the great man was. The botanist had lived in the neighbourhood for a year or so, going into the forests for days on end — 'a very kind and modest man', the gentleman said.

I treated them all to beer, hired the only car and embarked with Rita, Joao, José and Pedro. The car broke down frequently but eventually we reached an abandoned airstrip outside the village. From there we proceeded on foot along a rough track leading to a devastated area with a sprinkling of *bacaba* palms remaining in a hollow. Once these palms had marked the course of the Cauhy, Pedro told us. Burning was continuing and pungent smoke lay over the scene. This was clearly the headwaters of an extinct river, perhaps the Cauhy. A shallow swamp was all that marked its former bed — little wonder that no one remembered its existence.

Pedro, who was hopelessly drunk, having had too many beers at 'Big Bar', laughed so much when he learned that I was looking for a special tree, that he fell down in a helpless heap. As Joao and José would not help the inebriated fellow, I had to assist him whilst he burbled incessantly that trees meant nothing to him, he could well do without them. We then visited another *cabeceira*, first using a canoe and then walking through thick swampy mud. Another devastated place and still no sign of the 'Blue Qualea'.

Dispirited, we trooped back to 'Big Bar' where I told the old gentleman the sad story and conclusion of our journey. His eyes filled with tears when I told him that Adolpho Ducke's discovery had been ruthlessly destroyed. *'Que vergonha para nos!'* he kept repeating (Shame on us... Shame).

Margaret returned to Rio and Rita left for Santa Catarina, in the south of Brazil, where she still lives. They continue to correspond and are always planning to make another journey. In 1979 Margaret was honoured by the Brazilian Government with the Order of Cruzeiro do Sul. She completed the paintings for the new folio book Flowers of the Amazon *which was launched in Brazil in 1980. In the same year, a small exhibition of her work was held at the British Museum (Natural History) in South Kensington. Greville and Margaret attended the opening reception, an event which was recorded with a photograph in* The Times.

Another year passed with more paintings and a short journey to the east of Brazil to help illustrate another book. But all the time Margaret was concerned that her work on Amazon flora should be kept up to date.

The forest bordering the Paraná Anavilhanas.

JOURNEY TWELVE: 1982

The Cactus of the Flooded Forest

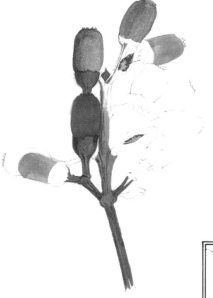

The folio, Flowers of the Amazon, *and preparing her diaries for this book fully occupied Margaret's time until early 1982. Then in April and May she made a short journey to the Arquipelago das Anavilhanas in the River Negro. Apart from a love of the Negro, other reasons prompted her visit. The islands had just been designated a Biological Reserve and placed under the protection of forest guards. This was particularly encouraging because Anavilhanas was one place where Margaret knew she could find the unusual strophocactus. Also she had friends who could help with the search, and very fortunately one of them, Gilberto Castro from Rio, maintained a small* sitio *on the bank of the river. Gilberto, an enthusiastic 'outdoorsman' preserved his land in its natural state. He offered Margaret the hospitality of a small, rustic house, his boat and assistance from the* caseiro, *Paulo Saldanha and his wife Mariá.*

Margaret arrived in Manaus after another long Brazilian Airforce flight with many stops.

A sketch for the parasitic plant of the Loranthaceae family from the Furo de Castanha, a channel in the Arquipelago das Anavilhanas.

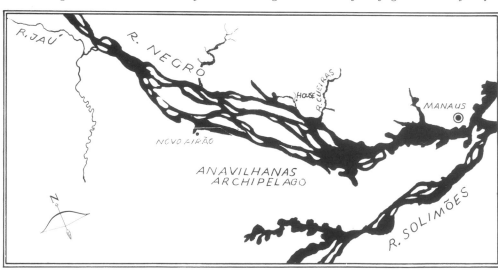

Psittacanthus cinctus *(Loranthaceae).*

Margaret Mee

Loranthaceae
Rio Negro, Amazonas
May. 1982

14th April, 1982

Paulo, short, greying and perhaps rather uncertain of who to expect, was waiting to take us to the boat moored in the Igarapé Sao Raimundo, a riverside suburb of Manaus. I was travelling with Sue Loram, a slim, young British lady who had worked at the National Institute of Amazon Research, I.N.P.A., and been involved with a scientific project concerning the forest.

We made our way in pouring rain to the market, splashing through muddy pools in which the port abounded, to purchase supplies for the journey. We had planned to leave Manaus in the cool of the early morning, but eventually left in the burning sun; then only to be delayed still further by a stop for fuel at the *flutuante* moored on the river. Paulo had brought with him not only his wife and grandchild, but another family with three children so, with Sue and me in addition, the little boat was crowded. Unfortunately there was a dearth of shade aboard and the firstcomers had claimed it until they eventually moved to the bows to cook their *merenda*. But the sun had done its damage, and I was burned to a frazzle. Enormous red patches covered my face and feet. How I suffered! For my large straw hat was of no avail against the tropical sun and reflection from the river after a long break from travelling.

But the worst of my suffering was not physical, for the first few hours were more than painful to one who has known and loved the river and its glorious forest for many years. The transformation was a visual shock, for all the trees of any size had disappeared, sacrificed by *fazendeiros* to that ghoulish spirit, the charcoal burning factory.

Another five hours brought us to the outskirts of the archipelago. We kept close to the side of the long island of Anavilhanas, filled with ancient trees, many crowned with massive philodendrons, their air roots forming curtains. Arabesques of bromeliads were ranged against the sky and gesneriads hung on branches beside the scarlet leaves of phyllocacti. As daylight began to fade, bands of parrots crossed the river to their roosting places and *bacurau* skimmed over the water's surface hunting and, while flying, taking toll of myriads of insects.

We lounged on the roof of the boat, watching the sun disappear behind the forests and gilding the complete horizon. Long after the burning disc had gone from view its glowing embers hung in the night clouds. Sunsets over the River Negro surpass all others for beauty.

After another three hours, Paulo eased the motor and turned towards the bank. We landed in complete darkness and, barefoot, stumbled up a grassy slope to the house, its roof a silhouette against the stars. Paulo unlocked the door and arranged some candles and an oil light. We had luxury. Two rooms, painted simply, mosquito net screens at open windows, a small kitchen and clean shower. But even with such luxury, I chose to hang my hammock on a covered patio facing the darkened river; the night sounds were wonderful. Paulo, whose home was not far away along one of the forested channels, left us and went his way having kindly offered to stay as a guard. I believe he was under the impression that we were nervous, foreign tourists.

At break of day a light mist hung over the river, masking the forests of Anavilhanas, and I hurried out to explore the surroundings of the little house. The garden was an 'orchard' of *assaí* and *buriti* palms, *caju* (cashew) and *cupuaçu* trees. The land upstream was bounded by a broad *igarapé* where already birds and insects were busy. A lofty tree supported by *sapopemas* was hung with a colony of *japu* nests, beautifully woven and purse shaped. I soon discovered that the *buriti* palms sheltered hordes of parrots who were accustomed to roost there, leaving again at dawn for the islands.

Our breakfast was simple, just some cracker biscuits, cheese, honey and tea. Then Paulo arrived from his house and took us in the boat through the archipelago. It covers the full width of the river, about fifteen miles, and extends to more than sixty miles upstream with, according to some estimates, over five hundred islands. We were sailing amongst them, and trees that were gaunt and sculpted by nature stood in the water. Grass and floating plants formed a barricade between us and the forest, which was deeply flooded. Not a scrap of dry land could be seen as the dark water was rising quickly, and was already more than twenty feet higher than when I had stopped there on my way to the Jufari in 1977 in the dry season. Without local experience it would be too easy to be lost in this place if one ventured far from the *paraná*, but Paulo took us skilfully from one channel to the next, at times almost doubling back on our tracks. It was midday when we arrived at three white wooden buildings on rafts marking the entrance to the Biological Reserve.

We landed from the boat, very eager to enter the new reserve. The guards questioned us, and only when they were satisfied that Sue had worked with I.N.P.A. and a World Wildlife Fund forest project, and that I was a botanical artist were we allowed to enter and were even invited to stay for some days. Paulo and the hardworking Mariá left us there and said they would go to a comparatively new village, Novo Airao, where they could buy fuel for the boat. The village was some hours distant on the southern bank of the Negro but they planned to return that night.

One of the guards, a kindly man called Raimundo, let us borrow a canoe and Sue and I paddled into the swamp forest along waterways overshadowed by trees standing in water. In a silent world I found endless subjects for my sketch book, but even as I worked the sky darkened with ominous rumblings of thunder heralding a storm. Knowing that the little canoe would never survive a sudden downpour and wind, we left this enchanted area in great haste, Sue paddling her hardest. We had had visions of being swamped whilst struggling to take shelter in the *igapó*. Fortunately, Raimundo had thought of our possible predicament, and at the first signs of a tempest he had taken to his outboard powered canoe and sped towards us. We quickly scrambled across to the larger canoe and, towing ours, returned to the reserve's rafts. We landed just as the first big drops of rain fell and within minutes were riding out a tremendous *banzeiro*.

Needless to say Paulo and Mariá did not reappear that night and we felt they would have stopped to find shelter. While waiting for their arrival, Raimundo took Sue and me to explore the archipelago, so again I was able to do some hurried sketches, all the time looking out for the strophocactus. On the outskirts of the reserve was a 'stream' which was 'owned' by a *caboclo* who lived in a small hut. He gave me permission to collect there and offered to guide the canoe through the tangled trees of the Furo de Castanha, a complex canal dividing into many channels. He knew his way like the back of his hand and seemed to understand what I was looking for.

We searched for some hours without success among a group of old trees, many hollow and riddled with termites. Here we found a toucan's nest, and from a hole in one of the trunks emerged a toucan's head, curious to see who was invading his territory. Then not liking the appearance of the crowd he flew away rapidly, displaying brilliant plumage.

Raimundo was convinced that the *caboclo* would return to raid the nest, and later sell the young birds. Unhappily he could do nothing to prevent this, he said, as the Furo was outside the limits of the reserve.

We also heard how turtles were being destroyed along with fish and countless other aquatic species. For every day, apart from one Sunday, there would be dynamite explosions somewhere along the river. The fishermen throw dynamite in a stream and everything is killed or stunned. I heard them at work and after the blast there was dead silence, not a bird's note, but just an awed hush as though nature's heart had stopped

A schomburgkia orchid.

beating. The guard pointed to a lifeless young *jacaré* floating on its back in the still water of the *igapó*, just one of the victims.

Paulo and Mariá arrived from Novo Airao and related with gusto how, in the dark hours of the previous night, the boat had been entangled in a tremendous grass island at the height of the storm. They had found shelter and waited, but now it was time to return to Gilberto's small house.

'Today I rose early, awakened by the cries of parrots and *tucanos*. I painted all the morning a superb specimen, one of the true parasitic plants which flourish on the bushes and trees of the *igapó*. The flowers, which are brilliant yellow and orange attract hosts of humming-birds, and are still in bloom when the blue and cerise fruit ripen.'

Gilberto's house overlooks the River Negro.

Paulo and Mariá in the Arquipelago das Anavilhanas.

Margaret during her seventh visit to the River Negro.

A macrolobium tree in the flooded forest of Anavilhanas.

After a lunch of *piranha* caught by Paulo that morning, Sue and I passed into the *igapó* beside Gilberto's house, where I attempted to collect a bromeliad, *Streptocalyx longifolius*, but at the lightest touch of my bush knife hordes of furious ants swarmed out. As the flower was very fresh I decided to wait until the next day. While I was thus deliberating I was being observed from the tree above by a powerful *pica-pau* (woodpecker), a handsome black and white striped bird with a large red crest.

> 'I have neglected writing up my diary as every night I have collapsed into my hammock, completely exhausted by an appalling cough allergy. Today we went out in the boat with Paulo, Mariá and grandchild to Lago Surubim, a lake which Paulo said was well stocked with fish.'

We left early with two canoes in tow. It proved to be all that Paulo claimed, and for one and a half hours we sailed without passing one habitation — just forest and *igapó*. The lake was isolated from the river by barriers of grass, forming little islands, the hunting grounds of wild ducks, and before we landed long black necks reared from the green, and a flight took to their wings. Paulo moored the boat and untied the canoes and pushed one to me. Sue climbed in, then Paulo, but in seconds the water lapped over the side so he scrambled out again. Sue and I then paddled off on our own and Paulo and family went together in the other canoe to fish. Dipping along beside the shore and up shady waterways I was able to observe the magnificent plants surrounding the lake.

On the outer fringe of forest there was a strange area where dried out shells of trees, riddle by ants and weathered by the beating winds and rains, mingled with young trees bearing luxuriant foliage, many in flower. Epiphytes clustered in their branches — philodendrons with large dark leaves, spiny bromeliads, *Aechmea setigera*, the very aggressive *Aechmea tocantina*, armed with black thorns, and giant clumps of schomburgkia orchids.

During the days which followed the heat was intense and for respite we sought the cool shade of the *igarapé* near the house, and from there went to the lake. We were not alone in seeking the shade of the great trees which bordered the water, for as soon as we arrived a band of about fifty monkeys were leaping from tree to tree, a line of sturdy chestnut-coloured animals with long prehensile tails. As they sped by they uttered shrill whistles.

Buriti *palms beside the River Negro.*

Whilst observing the monkeys' antics we were being watched closely by a *bico-de-brasa* (nun bird), magnificent with her orange beak and dark green plumes flecked with white. Another onlooker, a large grey hawk tucked in a cranny of an enormous tree, stared unblinkingly at us, the strange intruders disturbing the tranquillity. Tree creepers flitted silently from tree to tree, flattening themselves with tails spread against the branches in their search for insects. Myriads of tiny bats emerged from tree roots and disappeared as suddenly as they had come. I watched spellbound by the beauty and Sue, who needed a rest from work, treasured every moment.

'The River Negro is rising at an alarming rate, and since the rains it has crept up the banks, and many more of the bushes and small trees now stand under water. Each year the natural rise is about twenty-eight feet, with its height in June. The canoe must be moved from its mooring or we shall awaken one morning to find it out of reach in the middle of the river. It is not easy to go collecting now in the rain, as we could be swamped in the canoe, but there is plenty of work to be done and plenty to see from the window which faces the river. Black-plumed ibis, with their yellow sickle bills, are in the wet places by the water. Rare red-fan parrots with red and blue ruffles, dark green bodies and wearing spectacular white capes, appear in the *assaí* palm tree and, of course, a sunbittern is fishing as usual!'

At last the rain ceased and there were just occasional showers. The day of departure was to be Sunday and we informed Paulo of this, but as every day is the same to him we arranged to go and fetch him when the time came. Meanwhile we decided to make the most of our time and went to the *igapó*. As soon as we arrived on the still water we heard sounds high in the trees and turned to see a band of jet black monkeys. No sooner had they departed, than there was a loud splash from a green iguana which, dropping from a branch, began swimming across the open water. At first it seemed to be a snake by the extraordinary length and serpentine movements of its tail. Our canoe was moored to a small leafless tree in the middle of the water, which to our surprise the iguana climbed with incredible agility. And thus I was able to observe him at close quarters. Rapidly I sketched this beautiful reptile and made notes before he decided to continue on his course, swimming to shore and disappearing into the shades of the *igapó*. He was an intense green, the body markings and tail rings were dark grey, graduating to white. His ears had a fine membrane like mother-of-pearl. From the crown of his head and all the way down his spine were saw-like projections of a darker

Margaret sketching on the patio of Gilberto Castro's 'house.'

A sketch of the bromeliad Streptocalyx longifolius *from the River Negro.*

green. A ruffle hung elegantly from his lower jaw, and the immensely long tail merged from green to rust brown. The delicate hands and feet were long and bony.

'The storms of the last two days have brought up the water level to such an extent that the ants which prevented me from collecting the bromeliad *Streptocalyx longifolius* have left their refuge, as the flower was all but submerged. It was easy to secure.'

After excursions to different parts of the archipelago, I began to consider that we must continue to search the *igapó* as the sparse botanical information suggested this was the place to find the strophocactus I sought. As I sat on the patio, painting recently collected plants, Sue, who had been paddling the canoe in the nearby *igarapé*, came back greatly excited at having found leaves of this very plant. So I abandoned my work and together we paddled to the spot where the strophocactus was growing. Sue pointed to the plant about eight feet above us and we forced our way through a tangle of flooded bushes. The forest closed perfectly behind us and we were out of sight from the open water. If we tipped over, we would never be found. But how wonderful! Not only did I see a long strand of scarlet leaves growing flat against the tree trunk, but two large flower buds were just within Sue's reach! The stalks of the flowers were very

Strophocactus wittii (Cactaceae).

Margaret Mee

Strophocactus wittii
Rio Negro, Amazonas

The tree in the igarapé *with the rare strophocactus.*

long, about twelve inches, and the sepals reddish green; the petals were white, not red as I had been led to believe.

Above the plant in the fork of the tree grew a large red-veined philodendron, a very distinctive landmark. Every day after this discovery we visited the *igarapé*, watching the flowers and waiting for them to open.

Hopeful that the heavy rain the previous night could have encouraged the flowers to open, we again made for the *igarapé*, but the buds were unchanged. As we were leaving, two dark shapes loomed in the densest part of the *igapó*, monkeys with thick, bushy tails and dark brown fur. They were sakis, but on sensing intruders they left their feast of *inga* (bean-fruits of a legume), and disappeared rapidly into the depths of the forest.

We made an early start in the canoe after a frugal breakfast of porridge without milk (our supplies were getting low) and paddled straight for the tree on which the cactus grew. One flower seemed to be opening and with much hesitation and in fear and trembling, I decided to take it, lest it should close forever during the heat of the day for, being a white flower, I imagined that it would be pollinated at night by moths or bats. Sue reached the flowers and with a knife cut at the base of the stalk, so the plant was undamaged on the tree. In spite of her intense care the flower fell into the canoe and was slightly damaged, for it was no easy task to detach it. Holding the precious bloom in my hand I examined it carefully. The twelve inch stem was very robust and fleshy and the white silken petals of the large flower seemed to have a hidden light in

Trees of the várzea, *the annually flooded land, with a flowering bromeliad.*

the centre giving it a yellow glow. The arrangement of the stamens was most intricate.

I felt like death the next morning when I woke, but improved rapidly during the day — perhaps the cure would be a visit to the *igarapé* where the cactus grew. We paddled slowly and found the plant was unchanged except for the remaining bud. The flower was half open with its delicate petals carefully entwined. Seeing it like that, I guessed the truth. The flower had opened and closed overnight. The one Sue had taken so carefully the day before had also spent its one brief night of glorious show. Flowering was over, and all I could do was to think of searching again in another year.

In the evening, as I watched the magnificent sky, the sunbittern came fishing, uttering soft, plaintive cries and snapping up tiddlers at a great speed. She was the daintiest and most delicate of creatures. As the light faded the parrots came home to roost in the *buriti* palms beside the house with their usual noisy flurry, bickering and arguing until darkness silenced them.

'Tomorrow is the sad day of departure from the glorious River Negro and I shall be back in the world of turmoil, pollution and politics. When shall I be able to return? At the moment the sun is sinking, sending a pink glow over the sky and reflected gold in black water. Rapidly it is changing to a glowing brilliance against the shapes of birds of darkness; *bacurau* flit and skim above the river surface. All the birds are silent, but there will be a late comer, I feel — the sunbittern has just appeared to do some late night fishing.'

We paddled to Paulo's hut to tell him that we wished to leave and he soon was round with Mariá and the grandchild, who has *tosse quariba* (whooping cough). It was nine in the morning, and a glorious sunny day with a ripple of wind. We proceeded calmly

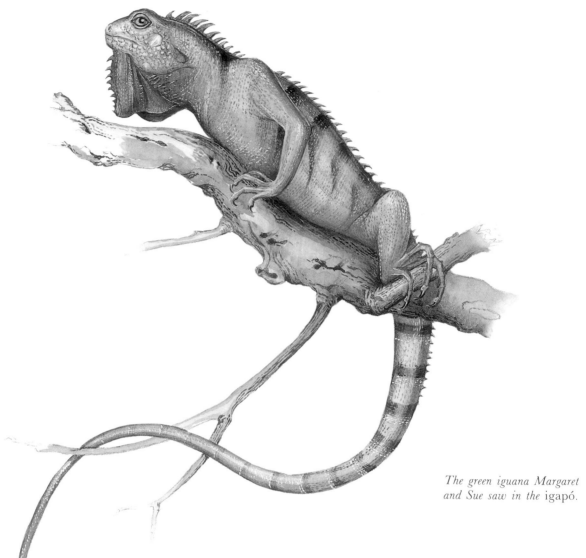

The green iguana Margaret and Sue saw in the igapó.

until half past two, when we ran into a *banzeiro* and choppy water. So Paulo took refuge at the mouth of a small river, the Tupi, as he was making little headway with great difficulty, and we moored by the sandy beach. I explored this lovely spot with interest, for there was fascinating vegetation. Meanwhile, Paulo and Mariá had cooked themselves a large fish meal and were sleeping deeply, but I felt that we were losing too much time and should press on, so I awakened the sleepers and we set off for the last stretch of our journey. The big waves had died down leaving the water slightly choppy.

Suddenly there was panic aboard and the steering went haywire, the chain having snapped in two. We were heading straight for a large tree, the spreading canopy of which was half immersed. Branches cracked and crashed and we were well tangled in twigs and foliage. Paulo managed to stop the motor just before we hit an immense trunk, and with superhuman force pushed the hull clear and moored the boat to the tree. I had visions of spending the night in the tree tops, for the light was fading rapidly and the steering might prove impossible to repair. However, Paulo and Mariá worked on, sometimes under water, until the craft was again 'riverworthy'.

Night had surrounded us and we sailed along a watery, shining path dappled by the full moon towards the distant lights of Manaus.

Margaret returned to Rio with sketches of the closed cactus flower, adding them to her growing collection which included the plant as she had seen it earlier. Sue Loram also returned to Rio and a new career. She kept a close friendship with Margaret, who was already planning another journey.

262

Heterostemon mimosoides (*Leguminosae*).

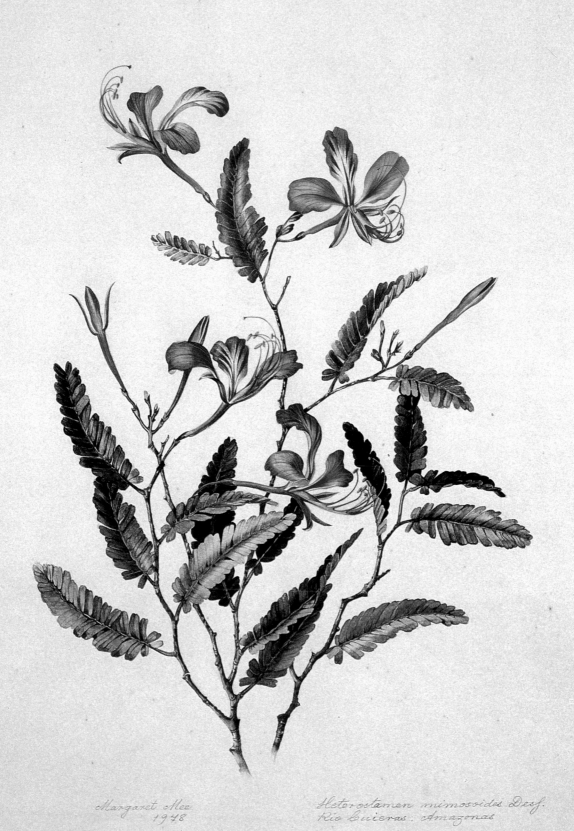

Margaret Mee
1978

Heterostamen mimosoides Desf.
Rio Cuieras. Amazonas

JOURNEYS THIRTEEN & FOURTEEN: 1984
A 'Storm' on the River Trombetas

Early in 1984 Margaret appeared twice on Brazilian television drawing an audience of millions. Her theme concerned threatened Amazonia and the importance of vanishing species. The response was immediate and she was invited by the Rector of the Federal University of Rio to stay at a medical field station at Oriximiná near the mouth of the River Trombetas. Margaret accepted. This was fresh ground for her, and demanding because the Trombetas, a major north bank tributary of the lower Amazon, had become the centre of a massive mining operation. Many Brazilians, anxious for the future of the rainforest, were concerned by the huge scale of the project, which was already drawing a stream of people into the region.

In order to reach the immensely valuable sixteen foot thick layer of bauxite, thousands of trees were being cleared and twenty-three feet of overlaying soil removed. Afterwards, the red gash in the forest was to be replanted. Only a few miles to the north of the mine the Government had secured 1,500 square miles as a Biological Reserve.

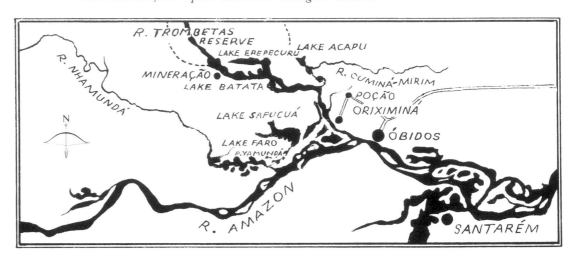

9th June, 1984

At five I left with fifteen other souls aboard a Brazilian built Bandeirante plane of the Brazilian Airforce. We were bound for Amazonia, flying north along the Araguaia river, when we changed direction slightly over a large port, Conceiçao do Araguaia, and headed towards the Xingu. After the spectacular beauty of the 'Planalto' of central Brazil, where range upon range of folded mountains are cut by streams and narrow valleys, the vista of the landscape beyond Conceiçao was a visual shock as the cloud cleared above miles of devastated land. Over 100,000 people were settled there, lumbering, raising cattle and farming. The forests were totally destroyed and never had I seen such an expanse of man-made desert. I was only thankful when the clouds returned to hide the grim scene.

Our first stop was at Santarém on the southern bank of the Amazon where it is joined by the clear 'blue' water of the Tapajós. Then the flight followed the Amazon upriver for almost a hundred miles to Oriximiná. The little town of fairly recent construction is set away from the main Amazon beyond a broad expanse of lakes and land which is under water for some months each year.

The University field station, called 'José Verissimo', was at the edge of town. I was given a room in a pleasant bungalow standing in its own grounds where mature native trees provided shade and fruit in season. A large *caju* provided a home for a red and blue macaw, one-eyed since a fledgling when he had been captured to be sold in the streets. The field station was used mainly by medical students and doctors who worked

River boats at Oriximiná.

264

'A group of three huts built of posts and straw.'

for some months at a time in the local hospital, journeying to the surrounding villages giving medical treatment and advice to the inhabitants. It was on these expeditions that I was invited to accompany them.

The port provided moorings for many and varied boats, mainly used for carrying cargo or for fishing. On the first journey I left at the crack of dawn to embark on the *Sacurí*, a battered craft well loaded with passengers, doctors and their medical equipment so that the water came well above the non-existent Plimsoll line.

The boat chugged heavily across Lago Jacupá, the nearest lake to the port, and we sailed for two hours westward past distant forest until we reached Sacurí, a village scattered through swamp land bordering a large open lake, Lago Sapucuá, connected by more lakes and *paranás* with the Nhamundá some sixty miles away. We moored in view of the tiny church and a group of three huts built of posts and straw around which *bacaba* palm leaves lay drying in the sun, to be used later for repairs to roofs and walls. Whilst the medical personnel were working and giving injections to the villagers in a large open barn, I went for a trip in the *Sacurí* with a veterinary surgeon and two students. I was pleased to see that we towed a canoe.

The team's duties led them to many huts where hospitable owners invariably offered coffee, oranges and even cooked fish. Sometimes we used the canoe to visit isolated places on the small streams and I was disturbed to find that people and houses were spread everywhere through the forest, much of it cleared. The day progressed well until the last visit when, having moored the canoe beside the steep bank in a well-wooded part of a stream, we scrambled up rickety steps leading to a wattle cabin. There a horrifying, macabre scene came to view — a *caboclo* was cutting up a bull's head on a rough wooden table. The animal had been very tame and friendly, he said, but had grown too fat. That had sealed his fate, and his bloody head, almost stripped of flesh, lay there with one dark eye looking at me from its socket with a reproachful gaze.

Sickened by the place, I was thankful when we returned to the canoe. We rejoined the river by tracing devious channels, and in one shady copse, massed on the mossy

The orchid Ionopsis
utricularioides *from the*
igapó *of the river Cuminá.*

*A galeandra orchid from
Lake Caipuru.*

trees, gleamed the delicate white flowers of a rare orchid, *Zygosepalum labiosum*, of
which I eagerly collected a plant or two. Still gliding silently we passed unnoticed by
a handsome iguana fully three feet long, green, black and grey, gracefully draped over
the thick foliage in the canopy of a tree. Nearby three of his companions basked on
branches in the dappled sunlight. Startled by the canoe, one fell with a loud splash
into the water and the others rustled hastily through the leaves.

There were many such journeys to the lakes around Oriximiná. On the banks of
Lago Acapu, in the village of Conori, I was trailed by a group of curious children and
was able to sketch a group of palms. Then followed a voyage on the mayor's boat,
embarking in the small hours of the morning. The return next night led through forest-
shadowed waterways under a full moon, where kapok trees (*Bombax munguba*) appeared
to be one mass of white flowers, but in reality were the crowded roosting places of
white herons.

Still with the medical team I travelled overland along the new road, the PA 439,
north of the Amazon to the village of Poçao on the way to Óbidos, an old town at the
narrowest point of the lower river. The journey was a bitter disappointment, as I had
read the descriptions of the countryside by nineteenth century travellers, among them
Henry Bates who wrote that the hills and lowlands there were covered with forest.

Zygosepalum labiosum (*Orchidaceae*).

Zygosepalum labiosum
"L. C. Rich." *Garay.*   Margaret Mee

Para

'A blackened sea of giant skeletons.'

22nd June, 1984

'I will write while I am still in a state of visual shock on the 'road'. Road it is not, but a track so dangerous and eroded that it defies imagination, and the landscape (what is left of it), is a sad stretch of *capoeira*, and where once virgin forest existed, there is now a blackened sea of giant skeletons. *Embaúbas* are stuggling to regenerate the almost exterminated jungle. In spite of the destruction and fencing in of the land I have found a survivor, a marvellous vine, *Memora schomburgkii*; then as the driver sped along the awful track I saw a flash of brilliant orange, then another at which I stopped and found a glorious orange bignone, a trumpet vine. I had to sketch it in an old notebook immediately I arrived in Poçao as it was already starting to wilt.'

Poverty and sickness in the village were very evident — children with large stomachs and thin limbs, dull eyes and yellow skins. The village 'nurses' told me that worms were the main affliction but that malaria was prevalent too.

My excursions around Oriximiná continued, but all the while I was waiting for permission to visit the Trombetas Reserve several days upriver beyond the mining camp of Mineraçao, a Brazilian-Canadian project. The permission seemed endlessly delayed by the regular internal bureaucracy. Whilst still awaiting news I was invited to visit the nearby Lago Caipuru, on what turned out to be a noisy, crowded boat with a load of over-excited infants and rowdy parents of all shapes and sizes, who ate too much and certainly drank too much and then danced it off on the white sands and in the river. On the picnic 'grill', above the embers of a driftwood fire, were not only the usual fish, but three large *tracajas* roasting on their backs. The wretched creatures had been cooked alive. I was so disgusted at this cruelty that when offered *tucunaré* I refused it as it was served with the gruesome roast.

Another journey, this time to the River Cuminá-Mirim, had been arranged through the kind help of Dr. Oswaldo at the field station. The boat had been hired specially and I had high hopes for the excursion as it was to a new area and close to hills bordering the north side of the Amazon. The boat, the *Santana*, was berthed at the far end of the port, and the friendly doctors and students, forming a small procession,

Memora schomburgkii *(Bignoniaceae)*.

Memora schombergia "De Candolle"
Meirs

Oriscimina, Pará

Margaret Mee
June, 1984

carried my baggage and a basket of provisions down to the river. We were to set out at ten, rather a strange hour, I considered, to set sail, and I was even more suspicious when an unsavoury youth sitting on a wall overlooking the mooring, told me that the *Santana* was a passenger boat and that he and six others were to embark that night. I could see their hammocks had already been hung on the deck and was most annoyed, not only by the fellow's insolent manner but because I had hired the boat exclusively for my work and had no intention of carrying other passengers. When he told me that he and his fellow *garimpeiros* were all bound for the *garimpo* at the first falls, I really saw red, and even thought of cancelling my trip.

At this threat, the 'comandante', who had just arrived from a bar in the port, became conciliatory and promised that I should be the only passenger, and the six hammocks were removed. However, when I stepped aboard he was far from pleasant, and quite furious that I had not bought meat amongst the provisions which I had handed over to him. I almost turned back, but the attraction of the Cuminá-Mirim was strong for I believed that I should find new plants. So I decided to brave it out, and bidding farewell to my somewhat anxious friends I hung my own hammock. The young man with whom I had spoken was one of a band of desperadoes, like many gold collectors, and I was most disturbed that he was a colleague of the 'comandante', and somehow became an 'assistant' and fellow passenger. But the night passed uneventfully as we proceeded up the long narrow lakes in the lower Trombetas and into the River Paru do Oeste, sometimes called Cuminá. The tranquillity of the dawn calmed me and I watched from the depths of my hammock as the forested landscape slid by. The moon still hung in the sky above golden streaks of cloud, heralding a magnificent dawn.

The sun rose behind the arabesque of forest and black fringes of *jauarí* palms. My frugal breakfast consisted of a cup of tea as all the supplies were with the 'comandante', and even more annoying was the canoe — or absence of one. I had not noticed in the dark, but in spite of my hire arrangements stipulating a canoe they had not put one in tow.

We had been maintaining a good speed all through the night and the boy announced that we were nearing some rapids. The Cachóeira do Verao (summer fall) spanned the complete width of the river and was at first hidden from my view by a forested island which appeared to divide the river into two arms. The lofty north bank was composed of many strata of rock, in varied colours, and crowned by palms and hardwood trees. A narrow *igapó* masked hanging ferns and plants growing between the cracks of the stratified stone, and on the margin of the river giant trees stood as sentinels before a castle wall. These were some of the oldest rocks in Amazonia, and I was eager to see more of the raging falls at closer quarters, so I disembarked and made my way through bushes and over rough ground.

The 'comandante' and his companion were walking ahead when I heard another voice and was suddenly aware that I was near the *garimpo*. Under a blue tarpaulin suspended on poles sat a motley collection of *garimpeiros*, all unhealthy looking *caboclos*, surrounded by saucepans, hammocks and a mass of jumbled equipment. In the water a simple dredge dangled long white tubes. An aluminium speed boat and outboard motor were nearby. The 'comandante' introduced me to the 'Boss' as a plant collector from the medical post of Oriximiná. The 'Boss' was an elderly white-haired man, short, with a belt holding up his paunch, a red skin, bristly chin and brushcut hair. I must have appeared cold and unfriendly to this sinister looking crowd which was destroying such a beautiful spot, and the 'Boss' responded with a hard, antagonistic stare. The other *garimpeiros* glowered at me, sensing my enmity, possibly suspicious that I was a 'spy' for another gold-seeking company.

A garimpeiro *at Oriximiná.*

This encounter was not what I was there for, and I turned to the 'comandante' and suggested we should continue so I could collect in the *igapó* instead of wasting my time, which was short enough. After a lengthy whispered conversation between the 'Boss' and the 'comandante', we left the *garimpo*. The youth who had travelled in the *Santana* joined his fellow *garimpeiros*.

Plant hunting along the river banks is well nigh impossible in a big and clumsy boat, and to enter the *igapó* in *Santana* was out of the question. I was even more upset by the lack of a canoe, as we passed fascinating plants without a hope of getting near enough to identify them. I decided that at the first opportunity I would borrow a canoe and collect alone. My chance came when the *Santana* was moored at the 'port' of a hut belonging to a friend of the 'comandante'. We remained there for the rest of the day. A *cabocla* who came from the hut with a little boy, paddling her canoe, spoke to me in a friendly way and arranged to take me into the nearest *igapó*.

She was a pleasant, communicative woman, and from her I learned that the Cuminá-Mirim river was still some distance away, and I was unlikely to reach it. We paddled among trees and bushes recently devastated by fire, though their wounds had begun to heal, and I found plants which had escaped the conflagration. There were orchids in plenty, the prize of them being *Ionopsis utricularioides*, with a mass of fragile violet flowers. The bromeliads were more of a problem and I was hacking away at the roots of one with my bush knife when the unsecured canoe slipped forward landing me, legs in the air, in the bilge. My hat flew off and was rescued by the boy. With a struggle I managed to extricate myself without injury.

The 'comandante' did not reappear on the boat and seemed to be enjoying a holiday with his friends. Consequently my food was completely neglected and I lived on a packet of biscuits and a few tangerines, once only receiving a plate of thin soup, and hot water for my tea which I had to demand. Famished, I lay in my hammock and heard the crew eating noisily, late and long into the night, but no offer of a plate for me! At daybreak, there was loud drunken singing as visiting *garimpeiros* raced away in their speed boat towards Oriximiná. The *Santana* then headed downstream quickly, and though I still had a full day of 'hire' to go we reached Oriximiná early. I paid the rapacious boatman the full amount, and he lost no time in getting rid of me, giving

The garimpo, *the place being worked by the goldworkers.*

271

Couropita
Rio Yamunda, Pará

Margaret Mee

my baggage to a loitering vagabond type. Back at the bungalow my friends were surprised by my early return and concerned by the way I had been treated.

But in spite of the frustrations of that journey I still wanted to see the Trombetas Reserve, for which I needed permission to enter. The letter of authority I was expecting had not arrived, so telling everyone I would return in two months, I took the first Airforce flight back to Rio.

8th September, 1984. Return to Oriximiná

Two months had passed which I had devoted to painting the plants found in Trombetas, and I was flying north with the Brazilian Airforce.

When the clouds cleared after Santarém in its rich, warm surroundings, I was able to enjoy the 'eternal forests' of the Amazon again. In Oriximiná the University field station had been repainted and looked spick and span, but the absence of the faces I had known on my last visit gave the place a slight feeling of sadness, for few of those friends remained and there were many newcomers.

I was thankful to learn that the *garimpo* of Cuminá had closed, having yielded no gold, though I gathered that the very destructive one I had seen on the Nhamundá river was still functioning, and that many wild animals were being killed there for their skins. Also the local news was that Cachoéira on the Trombetas was swarming with *garimpeiros* who were fast destroying the beautiful surrounds of the falls.

My permission to visit the Trombetas Reserve had been granted, but the letter had still to arrive. So with the encouraging news I felt there was time for short excursions. On one to Lago Caipuru, I found many epiphytes growing in the trees fringing the forest. With help from Joao, a young dentist, and Dido, a boatman, I collected *Streptocalyx poeppigii*, a bromeliad with a flame-like infloresence. It was protected by a multitude of thorns and was difficult to detach from its host, a monkey cup tree. Further afield, in old forest, the smoky purple flowers of erisma trees, Vochysiaceae, sheltered orchids, and in the branches grew a dainty galeandra, whilst *Schomburgkia crispa* encircled a huge trunk with a wreath of golden-brown flowers. Joao acted as main collector until he cut his foot on the sharp wood of a dry tree when Dido took over. But he tired quickly and after a snack I suggested that we should return. As we left the stillness of the *igapó* a black sky was lowering over the landscape, and we were just too late to escape the storm.

Rain poured into the open canoe until everyone and everything was soaked and dripping. Then a strong wind whipped the shallow lake into foaming waves which made our progress hazardous. We made little headway against the lashing wind and as we were without a baling tin the boat began to fill with water. But we kept going and eventually, exhausted, we landed in the darkness like three drowned rats. Joao and I hurried through the torrential rain to the welcome shelter of the University bungalow.

My next excursion was more rewarding. A visiting botanist, Klaus Kubitski, invited me to accompany him and his assistant, Lais Sonkin, on a journey west along the Paraná Yamundá to Lago Faro where he planned to collect specimens from trees in flower. I accepted this kind invitation with alacrity for the lake had a great appeal since my journey to find the 'Blue Qualea' in 1977. Joao the dentist was also to accompany the expedition.

The hired boat was a trifle inadequate, as we discovered on our way, for there was no lighting at all and the gas stove of two burners did not always function. Nevertheless, every moment of the journey was fascinating. The Paraná Yamundá is not to be recommended for spectacular Amazon scenery, and cattle are mainly responsible for the somewhat shabby landscape. Small, uninviting huts of farmers

Phryganocydia corymbosa *(Bignoniaceae).*

Detail sketch of a
couroupita, cannonball tree,
from the Paraná Yamundá.

A tortoise from the forest.

Couroupita guianensis,
the cannonball tree.

The orchid Galeandra
devoniana from Lake
Sapucuá.

sprinkle the river banks. Trees are almost confined to a dozen or so species: couroupita
— cannonball tree, sapucaia — a lecythid whose seeds can be eaten, ficus of the
Moraceae family and *jauarí* palms being preponderant.

In spite of the rather sterile surroundings I collected a lovely white bignone, the
trumpet vine *Phryganocydia corymbosa*, which I sketched on board, working far into the
night. In this area, which once must have been rich in many species of Amazon plants
and trees, there was little to be found. Lais, the assistant botanist, and I wandered over
pathless fields and there sighted clusia flowers on a large bush, but the bush was owned
by a snake and we decided not to dispute his territorial rights.

On reaching the end of the *paraná* the scenery began to improve — more trees and
in greater variety lined the banks, and the botanist became more animated and halted
the boat many times to gather specimens. Eventually we reached Faro, one of the
oldest towns of the region, a quiet, peaceful settlement, sleepy apart from the very

Symphonia globulifera *(Guttiferae)*.

Margaret Mee
October 1985

Symphonia globolifera
Rio Yamundá, Pará

vocal and lively children who mobbed Klaus, insisting he was a priest. 'Padre' they called after him as we walked along.

We wandered past the church and through the village, searching for somewhere to buy a meal. Faro is one of the most charming towns I have visited in Amazonia and Pará. Near to the church we found an unpretentious café where the owner managed to arrange a very satisfying table of *farofa* (manioc flour), rice, eggs and chicken. The villagers were unassuming and friendly, as Lias and I discovered when we swam in the little 'port', the only way we could take a bath.

We set off early in the morning as the days were sunny and warm, and soon reached a beautiful shore where Klaus avidly collected tree flowers and Lais pressed them. Landing from time to time on the laterite rocks of the shore I was entranced by the vegetation. A swamp plant which I had found and painted many years ago in Içana had a close relative growing here in profusion — rapatea. The lovely aroid *Urospatha sagittifolia*, with its curious spathe which spirals and a mottled stem, flourished in the marshy land. The most spectacular of all the trees was a tall guttiferae (*Symphonia globulifera*), with a trunk clear of branches up to the crown. Seeking light, the flowers grew in brilliant scarlet-cerise clusters above the spreading branches. I remembered having seen one or two groups of these impressive trees as I sailed up the Nhamundá. That time they had been far out of reach, but here I found a tree which had been felled and lay on the ground, so I gathered some of the rare flowers.

I could have spent many days on this enchanted lake with its wealth of plants;

A rich forest of trees filled with lianas.

nevertheless as the journey proceeded new delights appeared. The forested slopes gave way to low trees on dazzlingly white sand, and there were small inland lakes of clear dark water in the depths of which very ornamental algae flourished, firmly attached to twigs on the sandy bed. They were to be avoided, I was told, when swimming, as they give an allergy known locally as *caushi*.

Klaus and Lais took the canoe and paddled far up one of the lakes, often crouching down to avoid the mass of low branches, whilst I remained on the boat sketching the sculptural forms of dried trees resting on the hot sand. Hearing loud shouts, I looked up from my sketch book to see a strange sight. The canoe was approaching with Lais paddling rapidly and beside her swam Klaus, a white linen hat on his head, dark

A clearing is opened in the forest.

glasses and fully clothed. The canoe had capsized far away from the shore and both had fallen into the lake but Lais, apprehensive of *caushi* and snakes, had scrambled in again whilst Klaus heroically swam alongside.

Too soon the excursion came to an end. It had been stimulating and enjoyable and greatly relieved the tension and frustration of my postponed visit to the Trombetas Reserve.

The main objective of my visit to Oriximiná had been a journey to the reserve and the enormous Lake Erepecuru. The Forestry Development Institute (National Parks) had built a field station cabin on a raft moored in the lake and I hoped to stay and work there for some days. My permit was ready but alas the reserve's boat was out of action due to lack of funds, and I had to devise other means of transport.

Luis Carlos, the director of the University field station had informed me on my return to Oriximiná that a passenger boat, the *Elo*, would be leaving at nine at night for Mineraçao, the mining company port on the Trombetas and the nearest stop for

Palms at Oriximiná.

Margaret Mee
1946

Urospatha sagittifolia
Amazonas   (Rudksch) Schott.

Lake Batata 'now a red-brown lake of sludge.'

the reserve. From there I was assured that another boat, the *Perola do Nhamundá*, run by the Port Authority, would take me upriver and land me on the raft. It was already six, so I packed hastily, realising that there would be no time to purchase supplies before leaving. Joao the dentist, who was to drive me, got caught up at the last minute with fifty pregnant women for advice about their teeth, so another medical assistant drove me down to the port.

Kindly Luis Carlos had already hung my hammock before I arrived and saw me installed in the boat, which by then was full to overflowing. After five hours the *Elo* reached Mineraçao and, bemused with sleep, I disembarked. Before leaving I had time to observe the destruction of the Amazon forests. It came as a shock, having been told in Oriximiná of the care that had been taken not to damage the ecology and to plant trees for those that had been felled.

Lago Batata, once a richly forested lake beside the river, was now a red-brown lake of sludge, the residue from bauxite mining.

'Great trees, species extinct in many areas, are being exterminated, and this 'dead sea' extends for seven miles down a valley of considerable width. Where this mud has drained into the earth it has destroyed the humus with a coating of noxious substance, suffocating all life. Dead and bleached trees stand by the thousand warning of what is to come when the seeping tide envelopes other areas. Not only the trees, but with them animals and other plants have perished. It is a valley of death.'

I was to see more of this destruction a few days later, when passing a padlocked and chained gate I saw what no journalist had been allowed to see and report, a place where the transformation of the large Lago Batata was complete. It had become solid red mud. The natural barrier between this lake and the river threatened to collapse with the weight of the slurry. Formerly, Lago Batata was teeming with life — fish, turtles and aquatic birds — but this deadly residue had killed all life in and around the lake and was seeping further afield as evinced by yellowing leaves and rotting branches.

At eight the *Perola do Nhamundá's* captain arrived and almost immediately we left the port and turned upstream where, in little more than an hour, we entered Lake Erepecuru through a broad channel. Then within sight of the raft the lovely *Perola* developed propeller trouble, and the reserve's forest guards' canoe had to be sent to pick me up.

The Biological Reserve of the River Trombetas is a protected region reaching north to ranges of hills. The cabin constructed on the raft consisted of a main room used for living, cooking and dining, and partitioned off from it a small shower room and a dormitory where I was able to hang my hammock. The raft was moored close to the forest, so I had a splendid view of the trees and birds.

Urospatha sagittifolia (Araceae).

In the igapó *of the Trombetas Reserve.*

Under the wise guidance of Alberto Guerreiro, three guards lived there — young, vigorous men who were authorised to challenge and search any craft arriving inside the reserve. They were kind and friendly and treated me with great consideration, taking me over the lake in the canoe with its noisy outboard motor — hence its name, *Perereca*. I sat and sketched for hours, though unfortunately my permit to stay and work in the reserve contained the usual clause that no plants were to be removed. And as that precluded scientific painting I had to content myself with general drawings made from some distance, and I knew they were suitable only for showing the habitat. It was an exacting task, seated in the canoe under a burning sun, but so satisfying that I longed to do more than my limited time allowed.

The forests of the Trombetas Reserve had been little disturbed. Nature flourished in and around Lake Erepecuru. Turtles and various aquatic creatures thrived unmolested.

‘Although it is already September, the level of the lake has scarcely fallen, and trees stand deep in the water, strangely weathered shapes, many heavily laden with bromeliads in flower, orchids and the scarlet leafed phyllocactus.’

Seated in the canoe I had the unique opportunity to sketch a colony of *japims'* hanging nests in a small acacia tree, in their midst a white bell-shaped wasps' nest, such as are frequently found in the proximity of these purse-shaped dwellings.

The birds were very vocal and scolded so loudly and in such varied tones — they are great imitators — that the toucans joined in with their cries, also defending their territory against the invaders. The cacaphony grew so loud that we left the spot. With the fading light, black ducks flew low above the lake moving into arrow head formation as they rose. I was told that the *onças* are increasing in numbers in the reserve and that howler monkeys and other primates are more numerous now that hunters have been expelled from these forests. Life is returning to its former state.

Margaret returned to Rio delighted by the seclusion of the reserve which was so close to an intrusive project. But she was outspoken about the bauxite mining and the destruction of Lago Batata. Rio newspapers reported her opinions and a mining company spokesman was called to deny that the facility had polluted more than a small body of water, saying that only mud and not chemicals were discharged into the lake. The argument was never fully resolved, and no official Government comment followed.

By early the following year, when Margaret was nearing seventy-five, she realised that her untreated hip was to prevent further journeying. It too needed replacement surgery. Meanwhile, another major exhibition had been arranged, this time at the Missouri Botanical Garden. Her work was again acclaimed in the United States and she used the chance to tell reporters of her fears for the Amazon's forests.

Japim *and wasps' nests.*

Couroupita species (Lecythidaceae).

Margaret Mee
September, 1984

Phryganocydia corymbosa (Vent.) Bur.
Rio Yamunda, Pará

JOURNEY FIFTEEN: 1988
The Moonflower

By the beginning of 1987 Margaret was back in Brazil. Her other hip had been treated in Britain and she was at home with Greville, planning another journey. An ambition she had held for a long time was to paint the flower of the night-flowering strophocactus, one of the most unusual plants she had seen. Known by specialists as a selenicereus — or 'mooncereus', after Selene the Greek personification of the moon as a goddess, the cactus had never been studied in the wild.

The plant was named at the end of the last century by a German botanist when he was sent a specimen by Mr. N.H. Witt, a collector in Manaus at the time of the 'rubber boom'. For European professional and amateur cultivators in those days the night-flowering plant from the Amazon forests was a novelty, but from Margaret's point of view the plant was a special challenge. Its natural history was a mystery, and paintings of night-flowering cacti are rare. Only two pictures have become famous and both were made from cultivated plants. The celebrated Belgian flower painter, Pierre-Joseph Redouté, painted the 'Queen of the Night' cactus for Marie Antoinette — 'before the assembled Court' — according to a story dating from the time. And the other, 'The Night Blowing Cereus', appears in Robert Thornton's nineteenth century classic folio The Temple of Flora.

From experience Margaret knew where to look for Strophocactus wittii, *and she could estimate the flowering season to within a matter of weeks. But specialists she approached for help were far from confident that the flower could be found at the right moment. As Margaret had realised on her journey to the Anavilhanas Archipelago in 1982, the plant does not flower every year and when it does, it opens once, for just one night.*

My search for the strophocactus continued, for my boatman in Tapurucuará had thrown the prickly leaves away in 1964, when unloading the canoe. I had found the plant growing on a *pau-d'arco* close to the water's surface in the *igapó*. Since then I had collected it three times on journeys along the River Negro and tributaries of that river, but never with flowers.

May, 1988

Still in search of this wonderful cactus Sue Loram and I met Sally Westminster in Rio airport. Sally had arrived on the direct overnight flight from London and we had reserved seats on the first Varig flight to Manaus. Even by the big jet it was four hours later before we stepped out into the Amazon heat. Manaus had expanded in the five years since my last visit so that the outskirts of the town were unrecognisable, and where once beautiful forest surrounded the city, the land had been cleared and was covered with houses and factories.

For the first night we stayed in a small hotel in the old part of the town close to the port and shops. We were met by Gilberto Castro who had been in Manaus preparing his boat and purchasing supplies, for we intended to travel up the River Negro to his little house where we would stay for some weeks searching the surrounding *igapó* for the elusive strophocactus flowers. We were driven in the hotel van to the port of Igarapé Sao Raimundo where we were joined by cameraman Brian Sewell and Tony Morrison. The boatman Paulo and his wife Mariá were waiting to load the boat there.

Paulo started up the fifty year old diesel motor and by mid-morning we were heading slowly up the Negro, passing the Varig tourist hotel which was already being enlarged. The river was calm and for two hours we kept to the middle where the banks could only be seen as lines on the distant horizon. As the new high buildings of Manaus gradually slipped from sight behind us I sighed with relief — at last I was away from the pollution and disturbance. But these thoughts were short lived for as we drew closer to the right bank, I saw that the forests had gone. Large areas of land

On the River Negro; Paulo and Mariá by the fifty year old motor.

had been devastated by *fazendeiros* and charcoal burners, whose huts appeared at frequent intervals complete with ugly corrugated or plastic roofs. By mid-afternoon a stiff wind was blowing and the sky darkened. As we approached the Arquipelago das Anavilhanas waves built up and the boat lurched, making Sally's hammock swing so violently that it almost touched the roof. Rain swept across the water and for an hour we had to motor on with the canvas side-screens lowered. This part of the river can be dangerous. At dusk the wind dropped and we entered Paraná Anavilhanas, where on the left bank magnificent forests lined the river. Huge trees were draped with philodendrons, bromeliads clung to the branches and an occasional orchid glowed against the green curtain.

Gilberto's boat in the Paraná Anavilhanas.

The dark water of the River Negro.

We continued through the darkness watching the moon rise, dappling the still surface of the *paraná*. Lights gleamed on the right bank from the huts of *caboclos*, though otherwise we were alone. Ten hours after leaving Manaus the motor was shut off and in perfect silence the boat slid to the bank in front of the hut where we had stayed in 1982. Little had changed thanks to Gilberto's care, though many more trees were now growing there. The *buritis*, home of the parrots, stood dark against the clear sky and we formed a procession carrying stores up the grassy bank. Paulo and Mariá left for their home, promising fish for the morning.

A catasetum orchid.

The search

From the door we looked across a broad channel lined with unbroken forest, and beyond lay the *paraná* and *igapó*. The river was far up the grassy slope approaching high water season, though in the next two months it would rise another seven feet. Breakfast was beautifully prepared by Sue who has the misfortune of being an excellent cook. Fruit, eggs and fresh bread had been brought from Manaus and we had fish caught by Paulo. We were excited and optimistic as we planned the search.

Some weeks before we had set out from Rio, Paulo had been instructed to scout around for the cactus on his fishing excursions. After three or four miles by motor canoe up the *paraná* we entered the *igapó*. Islands of grass lay across the still water from which grey, weathered trunks stood like skeletons, water up to their boughs.

I was disappointed when Paulo pointed out his first find, which was a *Phyllocactus arapari* whose red leaves he had mistaken for those of the strophocactus. Undaunted, he piloted the boat to the base of a robust tree where, on a forked branch, clung the scarlet leaves of *Strophocactus wittii* pressed against the trunk like transfers. But the plant was without flower buds, perhaps because it was on the outer fringe of the *igapó*, unsheltered from the strong sunlight.

We were not far from the *igarapé* where Sue had found the plant in 1982, but the vegetation had changed and the plant had disappeared. So our search began in another *igapó*, using the large boat to take with us food and a canoe so that we could spend a full day away from home. In this *igapó* skeletons of trees stood in the open river, beyond which a barrier of smaller trees and bushes, half immersed, sheltered the high forest. Big trees stood deep in the water like columns of a sunken temple. The closely packed canopies, hanging lower over the water dimmed even the midday sunlight.

We entered the *igapó* in the small canoe which tipped unsteadily as we forced our way through the thorny, tough bushes, then we slid silently between the trees. To my great excitement, on a large tree, hung a strand of fading leaves of the cactus with three large buds. It hung loose, just above the water, held by a liana. In a tempest it must have fallen and the next wind would blow it into the stream, so I decided to take it to plant in an *igapó* nearer to home, where I could observe it developing. Higher in the tree, amidst many leaves there were other flower buds of the cactus which would doubtless produce seed to germinate in the *igapó*.

Notes in Margaret's diary record the changes along the river.

Further afield as we scanned from the deck of the large boat, in an open part of the *igapó*, a group of brilliantly coloured cactus leaves came to view on a large tree. Anxious to get closer I scrambled to the roof, using Gilberto's shoulder as a welcome step, and examined each bud in turn. As it was getting dark and it would take two hours to reach the house I decided to return next day.

The morning began with a cloudy sky which soon turned to steady rain and I spent some hours sketching and writing my diary. But by mid-morning the rain had stopped and Sue and I went to search another *igarapé*. The water was high among the branches of the lower trees and only birds and insects were about. We paddled slowly, searching first one side of the channel and then the other. When we came to a fallen tree which blocked the way we turned back retracing our path to the river. The peace was disturbed when suddenly a flock of tiny green parrots chattering noisily descended to

Sue Loram cleans fish for supper.

a flowering tree. A large blue morpho butterfly flapped lazily along the forest edge, its wings so dazzling on the upper side that as it flew by the colour seemed to wink at us. The naturalist Henry Bates said that these morphos with a wingspan of seven inches can be seen at a distance of a quarter of a mile. Perhaps this may be their downfall as so many of their gorgeous wings are used in making trinkets for tourists in the cities. Again we were disappointed not to find a cactus, and I had to conclude that the plant was not common or was restricted to certain trees or places.

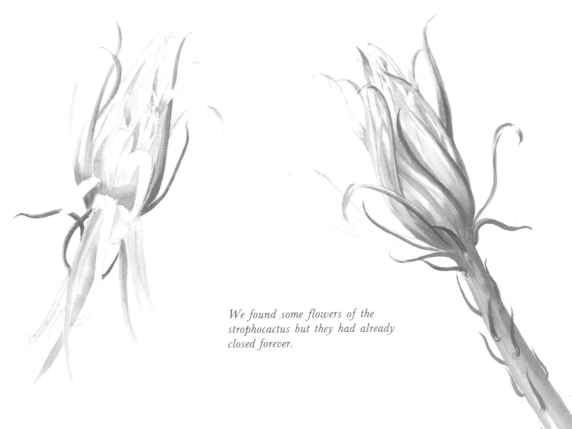

We found some flowers of the strophocactus but they had already closed forever.

286

Buds of the cactus on a part of the plant which had fallen from the tree.

Crimson coloured cactus leaves 'pressed like transfers against the trunk'.

A dry tree in the igapó, River Negro, sketched during the search for the strophocactus. The tree is covered with epiphytes, including an anthurium (Araceae). The dried leaves of some species have an aroma similar to vanilla, and in a tea-like infusion are used as an aphrodisiac.

After a simple lunch we set out in Gilberto's boat crossing a small *paraná* to the *igapó* where we found the buds. On the way we stopped only once, when we sighted more reddish cactus leaves, but they were of a phyllocactus, so we continued. We arrived at the *igapó* at four in the afternoon. The two buds which had been tightly folded the previous day had burst, their twisted petals now loosely closing the flowers, just as I had seen with Sue on my journey six years before. Another flower was drooping and two more were ready to open, surely it had to be that night. We decided to stay, and while Gilberto helped me to the roof Sue and Sally took a dip in the dark water.

The plant was obviously healthy, its leaves flattened to the trunk were green turning to crimson and some were completely changed. From the vantage point I observed that there were many epiphytes on the tree including a gesneriad which partly masked the cactus. From the midst of the foliage a tiny lizard, green with crimson markings was watching me. He was beautifully camouflaged and blended perfectly with the cactus leaves. I kept still, the warmth of the low afternoon sun on my back until, his suspicion satisfied, the sleek creature scuttled along one leaf and cleverly dropped to another.

One of the weather sculpted trunks of a dead tree in the igapó, *River Negro, sketched during the search for the strophocactus. Margaret is fascinated by the shapes and spaces formed in these curious trunks: 'My days at Camberwell taught me that'.*

The trunk was a wonderful home with all the roots of the epiphytes packed with tiny plant remains forming a humus for a complete garden of species. Ants busily foraged and a host of other insects, beetles among them, scurried about. The lizard no longer bothered by my presence simply darted from one good feast to another.

Sue and Sally scrambled aboard just as the sun was setting. It sent a golden shimmer across the water. lighting the forest a pale yellow green. The birds were quieter and slowly, one by one, frogs joined in a resounding chorus. We prepared for our vigil. Gilberto produced some torches and we ate the last of our dry biscuits from Manaus with coffee brewed by Mariá. Within the hour the sky was black and only the brightest stars showed through a layer of thin cloud covering the silent forest. We took turns to keep watch on the buds using a torch beam briefly, so we would not disturb the opening. Once in the confusion of the dark a torch slipped over the side of the boat and we watched its powerful beam slowly dim as it fell through the deep, tea-coloured water.

The forest, brilliant in the setting sun.

The flowering

We had been waiting almost two hours and the buds had not changed. The flooded forest was quiet apart from the frogs and an occasional grunting or whistling call from a night prowling animal — all the inhabitants can swim or climb.

As I stood there with the dim outline of the forest all around I was spellbound. Then the first petal began to move and then another as the flower burst into life. It was opening so quickly. A chair was passed to the roof, and Sally found the rest of my sketching materials whilst Sue stood beside me with a small portable battery light.

Sue Loram holds battery powered fluorescent lights as Margaret sketches the opening cactus flower.

Sketches of the cactus — the Amazon Moonflower —
opening and closed.
Strophocactus (Selenicereus) wittii.

Brian and Tony prepared to record the event. The flower was nearly open but the strong photographic lights seemed to slow down the opening, so I begged that the light be dimmed, and we continued with only a faint illumination and the light of the full moon rising over the darkened rim of forest.

In the early stages an extraordinary sweet perfume wafted from the flower, and we were all transfixed by the beauty of the delicate and unexpectedly large bloom, fully open in an hour.

The petals or perianth leaves were long and slightly wider than the outer ones we had seen on the closed flowers. Open at last it was a curious flower and totally different to any I had painted before. Also it was a challenge as I was balanced precariously on the six foot wide top of the boat and anxious that the slightest movement would cause us to tip. Luckily the night was still and without a breath of wind, so I could work easily. As I sketched I hoped for the pollinator to arrive, which specialists deduce from the structure of the flower should be either a large moth or a bat, and possibly quite specific to this species. Very few accounts have been made about pollination in the wild for night-flowering cacti, so we were hoping for a discovery. But no large insect came by and the only nocturnal visitors we saw were dozens of small flies which gathered on the stamens. The strong perfume faded after two hours though it was still possible to detect it by bending close to the flower.

Seated on the roof of the boat, Margaret sketches the background and colour for the final painting. The flowers are closed and beginning to wilt.

The Amazon Moonflower, Strophocactus (Selenicereus) wittii.

Selenecereus wittii
Rio Negro Amazonas

Margaret Mee
May 1988

Margaret in the igapó.

Leaving the igapó *at dawn.*

The moon climbed higher disappearing occasionally behind cloud though for most of the night giving a bright clear view of the *igapó* dotted with the pale grey trunks of the weather sculpted trees. Our vigil was long and I conclude that our intrusion had deterred the pollinator, upsetting the delicate balance between the plant and the animal which has taken tens of millions of years to evolve. As the Moonflower began to change again, the effect of intrusion multiplied across all the species in the length and breadth of Amazonia was too much to contemplate. With the dawn the flower closed and we watched fascinated and humbled by the experience.

To complete the painting I needed more sketches for the background and as everyone needed a rest we decided to return to Gilberto's house for breakfast, intending to visit the tree again later in the day. But getting out of the *igapó* was more difficult than expected, for floating grass had badly clogged the propeller and partly closed the channel we had made when we came in. The grass around the propeller had to be cleared and holding his breath Gilberto plunged beneath the boat to cut it away. A second dive was needed before we were clear to move, then Paulo and Mariá using the canoe, took a rope and fastened it to one of the skeleton trees as an anchor. We heaved and the boat slid from the forest stern first. After repeating the procedure several times we reached an open channel where Paulo started the motor and headed for home.

We chugged slowly past wonderful, undisturbed forest, its canopy glistening with dew. A light mist lay in patches above the warm river. Birds from their roosting places were flying over the islands. A *tucano* appeared, in dipping flight above the trees. An elegant heron was fishing. Another day had dawned across Amazonia.

By the time we reached the *paraná* near Gilberto's house, the river traffic was already moving. A heavily laden *gaiola* was heading upriver to Novo Airao and beyond. Another, larger boat came downstream with a flat barge carrying wood lashed

Weather sculpted trunks and fields of grass in the igapó.

alongside. We passed families in canoes and saw their huts surrounded by cleared land, the great trees destroyed and the open ground hardened. Where the earth was not brown it was tinged with green by *capim tiririca,* a straggling, sharp grass-like relative of sedge which is one of the few species to thrive in these places. Then long before we reached Gilberto's protected forest we heard the sharp whine of a chainsaw as another settler carved out a home; it seemed that the entire riverside was busy with people and their work.

Our intrusion on the life of the Moonflower was minor in comparison with what I have seen happening along the Amazon waterways, for the forest has changed considerably and the lovely plants I have painted along the Negro have disappeared. I can remember my excitement on my first journey there, when I moored my boat to a swartzia tree, full of perfumed white flowers, among the great trees on the banks. The changes have been disastrous, and the destruction and burning of the forests arouse fears for the future of our planet.

Beside the River Negro, May 1988, Margaret's seventy-ninth birthday and fifteenth Amazon journey. Sue Loram with champagne and a cake of the Amazon fruit cupuaçu.

Fully open, two hours after dusk, the Amazon Moonflower Strophocactus (Selenicereus) wittii.

After the great achievement of finding and sketching the night-flowering cactus, the journey downriver was not entirely uneventful, as travelling at night in bad weather Paulo missed colliding with an oncoming, unlighted boat by a hair's breadth.

Back in Rio, Margaret transformed her sketches into the painting on page 293, the first of its kind. No conclusions about the flowering and natural history of the cactus were made after the journey, though Margaret noted how all the buds she found were at the same stage of development, and opened within a few days of each other. Also, remarkably, all the plants found during the search were approximately ten feet above the water level, which means that by June/July, when the river is at its greatest height, the water would be less than three feet from the plants, possibly suggesting a connection between the flowering season and the rise of the river.

But the life of the cactus will have to wait for another year or even longer before specialists can unravel its secrets. Meanwhile Margaret's painting and sketches chronicle an exceptional flowering and we must be thankful for her courage and determination to seek out such wonders. For in a wilderness inundated by thirty feet of water every year, and throughout Amazonia, other treasures must surely await discovery.

'The glorious River Negro. When shall I be able to return?'

297

bixa — urucu

caatinga forest

canopy, Amazon forest

cashew — caju, fruit and nut

bromeliads, epiphytes

Glossary

Apuí. Local name for various species of clusia which begin their life as epiphtyes (q.v.) on trees and eventually send roots to the soil, enveloping the trunk and branches. These plants take nutrients from the ground and eventually the supporting tree dies, hence the name strangler is often used.

Assaí. Palms of the genus (q.v.) Euterpe, producing fruit used for food and wood for Indian houses.

Babaçu. A large palm, *Orbignya speciosa*, of great economic value, particularly for the oil from its fruit. It is cultivated in many parts of north-eastern Brazil.

Bacabá. A tall palm, *Oenocarpus bacaba*, yielding a valuable edible fruit.

Barzinho. A little bar or drinking place.

Bignone. An informal name for plants of the Bignoniaceae family. Bignonia is a North American genus but is used here by Margaret for bignone.

Bixa. Informal name for *Bixa orellana*, a small tree with seeds which can be pulped to yield the red colour *urucu* (known as *achiote* in parts of Amazonia). Also used medicinally.

Black water rivers. Such rivers (including the Negro) usually rise and flow across the hard, very ancient rocks of Amazonia, from which little sediment has been left to be carried. Humus colours the water like tea.

Bombax munguba. Incorrectly used as a species name, it is the popular name for two separate species of the Bombacaceae family. Both are large trees.

Bromeliad. General name for members of the Bromeliaceae family of plants including the pineapple.

Buriti. A major palm of Amazonia, *Mauritia flexuosa*, with many uses.

Caatinga. In Amazonia, a distinctive forest growing usually on white sand lacking nutrients. Many plants found in the *caatinga* grow only in these places.

cecropia — embaúba

cerrado

liana

igarapé

strangler — apuí

Caboclo. A word derived from the Indian language meaning 'out of the white' and referring to a person of mixed Indian/Portuguese descent.

Cachaça. A strong spirit distilled from fermented sugar cane, often incorrectly called Brazilian rum.

Cachóeira. A place where the river course descends steeply, as rapids or low falls.

Campina. A type of *caatinga* (q.v.).

Caseiro. Used in Brazil for a man and wife working as caretakers of property.

Cerrado. A tropical American vegetation typical of strongly seasonal climate zones. Derived from the Brazilian Portuguese, meaning 'closed fields', the *cerrado* contains stunted trees often with thick corky bark, evergreen leaves and ranged in open grassland.

Cipó. A general name for climbing or twining plants.

Embaúba. (In other parts of Amazonia called cecropia.) A tree of the Cecropiaceae family related to figs and nettles. These trees are typically found in previously cleared places, appearing in the first of the new growth.

Epiphytes. Plants which grow on a support, such as another plant, without any direct contact with the soil. Their roots develop to take up water in such conditions, often from the humus which collects between the plant and the support.

Farinha. Generally meaning a flour prepared from grated tuberous roots of mandioca, a small shrubby tree, *Manihot utilissima*.

Farofa. A simple dish prepared with *farinha* and melted butter or oil, mixed with grated vegetables or hard-boiled eggs.

Garimpeiro. A gold and gem washer, usually working along the river on his own account.

Garimpo. In the diaries used for a place where gold was being washed.

Genus. A group of animals or plants with common structural characteristics. In naming, the genus name is placed first and followed by the species name.

Gongora maculata. An orchid, now called *Gongora quinquenervis*.

Igapó. A forest flooded naturally by the rising water.

paraná

River Solimoes — River Negro

várzea

garimpeiro

Igarapé. A natural canal like a creek which is usually filled with water in the high-water season and may be completely dry when the river is low.

Ingá. A name given to various members of the Leguminosae family.

Jará. A small palm, *Leopoldinia pulchra,* usually of black water rivers. Also the leaves used for thatching.

Jauarí. A palm, *Astrocaryum jauari,* of which parts are used to make mats, sieves, *tipitis* (q.v.), hammocks. The fruit yields an edible oil.

Lecythid. Informal name for plants of the Lecythidaceae family.

Liana. Large rope-like woody climbers which hang freely, sometimes for 150 feet or more, from trees rather than twining round trunks.

Maloca. Usually the name for a large Indian house occupied by several related families. Other names for such houses may be used in different parts of Amazonia.

Manioc. See *farinha.*

Mucuim. (Sometimes *mucuinho.*) A minute six-legged early stage or larva in the life history of a small tick (related to spiders). Often met in clusters on low vegetation, they produce highly irritating patches on the skin.

Paraná. A channel taking part of the normal flow of the river.

Patauá. A large palm of the humid forest, it yields a purple fruit rich with oil. The leaves are used for thatching.

Pau d'arco (also *ipé*). A medium-to-large tree, *Tabebuia serratifolia,* of the Bignoniaceae family with striking yellow flowers.

Paxiúba. A medium-size palm, *Socratea exorrhiza,* with a tall narrow trunk supported by roots spreading cone-shaped at the base.

Piaçaba. A palm, *Leopoldinia piassaba,* which yields a dark brown fibre with many commercial uses.

Piranha. A fish of the characin family, Characidiae, several species, and not all are carnivorous. Other local names, pirana, paku, piraya.

Pium. The small, blood sucking flies of the Simuliidae family. They produce severely irritating swellings.

Podostemon. The informal name for a plant of the family Podostemonaceae. The plants often live submerged and flower when the water level seasonally falls.

Red cedar. Member of the Meliaceae family, this is a good timber tree with wood resembling but not related to cedars.

Sapé. A giant weedy grass, *Imperata brasiliensis.*

Seringá. Usually the Brazilian rubber tree, *Hevea brasiliensis,* related to spurges. (Also used for the latex the tree yields.) *Seringal* is a place where the trees are found (in Amazonia they grow scattered in the forest). *Seringueiro* is a rubber tapper, the worker who collects the latex.

Sitio. Normally applied to a piece of land and a house, which may be used like a small farm.

Strychnos. Usually a vine of the genus Strychnos with about a dozen species which produce a component for the arrow and blow gun dart poison curare.

Sumaúma. One of the giant trees of the forest, *Ceiba pentandra,* with enormous buttress roots (see page 76). Often called the silk cotton or 'kapok tree'.

Tanga. In Amazonia a simple pudendal covering of strings with tiny beads or seeds used by women of some Indian tribes.

Tipiti. An extensible basket-work container used to express the poisonous sap from *mandioca.*

Tracajá. A river turtle, genus Emys, highly prized for its meat and eggs. Very much endangered in most of Amazonia.

Várzea. Land on either side of a river with turbid, muddy white water which is flooded in the high-water season. Nutrient rich silt is deposited there and when the water recedes the ground is planted and crops raised before the next flood.

Xoto. A large basket supported on the shoulders by a band passed around the forehead.

Acknowledgements

My thanks and gratitude to the many people who have in various ways helped me:

Sir George Taylor, former Director of the Royal Botanic Gardens, Kew; The Hon. Aylmer Tryon, The Tryon Gallery; The late Dr. Guido Pabst; Dr. Emidio Vaz de Oliveira, Varig, Manaus; Dr. Artur Cesar Ferreira Reis, National Research Council; Dr. Luiz Emgydio de Mello, National Museum, Rio; Dr. Lyman Smith, The Smithsonian Institution; Dr. Simon Mayo, Royal Botanic Gardens, Kew; Dr. Raymond Harley, Royal Botanic Gardens, Kew; Dr. William Rodrigues and Dr. Marlene de Freitas, both of I.N.P.A; Dr. Alcides and Dr. Beulah Coe Teixeira, Instituto Botanica, Sao Paulo; The late Dr. Moyses Kulhmann; Dr. Ilio Molinari, Federal University, Rio; The National Geographic Society; The late Dr. Leonard Carmichael; Minister Said Farhat and National Travel Agency; The Guggenheim Foundation, U.S.A; Sister Elza Ramos and Padre Antonio Goes, Salesiana Missions of Rio Negro; Dr. Heitor Dourado; Dr. Carlos Alberto Xavier, Rio Botanical Garden; Mr. Jo Barnett and Mr. Denis Clare, both of the British Council; Sir John Pilcher; Sally, Duchess of Westminster; Maria Adriana de Pagter Brouwer; Mary Aune; Sue Loram; Christopher Abel-Smith; Gilberto Ricardo Moraes e Castro; Brian Sewell; The late Harald Schulz; The late Paulo Cardoso; Cdr. Carlos Malm; Dr. Kubitsky; Lais Sonkin; David Lorimer; George Clarke, H.M. Consul, Manaus; Ian MacPhail, International Fund for Animal Welfare; Dr. David Hunt, Royal Botanic Gardens, Kew; Dr. Wilhelm Barthlott, Botanisches Institut, Der Universitat, Bonn; Dr. Leia Scheiner, Universidad Nacional, Mexico; Bruce Nelson; Soft Landing, Assesoria do Empresas Ltda.

My special gratitude to the many Indians, pilots, guides and helpers.

My thanks also to Força Aerea Brasileira for landing me there, even though I had to get up at three in the morning.

Further Reading

Early Travel and Natural History: Henry Walter Bates, *The Naturalist on the River Amazons*, first published in two volumes in 1861, reprinted by the University of California Press; Richard Spruce, *Notes of a Botanist on the Amazon and Andes,* edited by Alfred Russel Wallace, Macmillan and Co., Limited, 1908; Alfred Russel Wallace, *A Narrative of Travels on the Amazon and Rio Negro,* first published in 1853, Ward Lock, Bowden and Co., 1892; William Lewis Herndon and Lardner Gibbon, *Exploration of the Valley of the Amazon,* published 1853/1854 in two volumes; James Orton, *The Andes and the Amazon,* Harper and Brothers, Publishers, New York, 1876. **The History:** John Hemming, *Red Gold, The Conquest of the Brazilian Indians,* Macmillan 1978; *Amazon Frontier, Defeat of the Brazilian Indians,* Macmillan, 1987; Robin Furneaux, *The Amazon, The Story of a Great River,* Hamish Hamilton, 1969. **Travel:** H.M. Tomlinson, *The Sea and the Jungle,* Duckworth, 1912; *Lizzie, A Victorian Lady's Amazon Adventure* (from letters) compiled by Tony Morrison, Ann Brown and Anne Rose, BBC, 1985. **Natural History, Ecology, and Future of the Forest:** Jean Dorst, *South America, a Natural History,* Random House, 1967; Anthony Smith, *Mato Grosso,* Michael Joseph, 1971; Tom Sterling, *The Amazon* (second edition), Time Life Books, 1982; Betty J. Meggars, *Amazonia, Man and Culture in a Counterfeit Paradise,* Aldine-Atherton Inc., 1971; Ghillean T. Prance and Thomas E. Lovejoy, *Amazonia,* Pergamon Press in collaboration with I.U.C.N., 1985; Roger D. Stone, *Dreams of Amazonia,* Viking Penguin, Inc., 1985, Penguin Travel Library, 1986; Margaret Mee, *Flowers of the Brazilian Forests,* The Tryon Gallery, London, 1968; *Flowers of the Amazon,* Distribuidora Record, Rio de Janeiro, 1980; *Margaret Mee's Amazon,* illustrated catalogue of paintings, text by Simon Mayo, Royal Botanic Gardens, Kew, 1988.

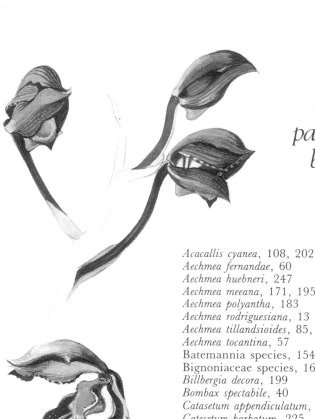

Index to coloured paintings and sketches by Margaret Mee

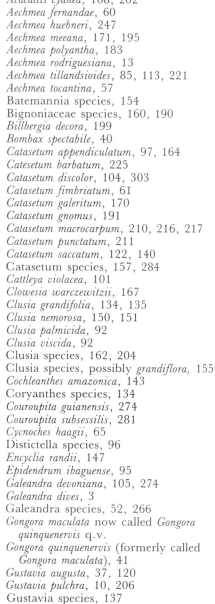

References to unidentified or undescribed species in this listing indicate that the species illustrated or described have not been identified or described at publication.

Catasetum discolor.